ACCOUNTING MANUAL & COMPUTERISED

Gill & Macmillan

Gill & Macmillan
Hume Avenue
Park West
Dublin 12
www.gillmacmillan.ie

© Ursula Mooney 2014

978 07171 5949 9

Print origination by Carole Lynch
Printed by GraphyCems, Spain

A CIP catalogue record is available for this book
from the British Library

CONTENTS

1 Introduction

This book is designed to cover the modules of Level 5 validated by QQI:
- Accounting Manual and Computerised 5N1348
- Bookkeeping Manual and Computerised 5N1354 (the setting up of stock and product codes are part of the student resources).

It also covers the modules of Level 6:
- Bookkeeping Manual and Computerised 6N4865, except for:
  - Learning Outcomes 2 and 3 – Analysis of Reports
  - Learning Outcome 5 – Recurring Journals and foreign currency.
- Computerised Accounts 6N3911, except for:
  - Part of Learning Outcomes 2 and 3 – Set up foreign currencies and recurring transactions
  - Learning Outcomes 9 to 12 – Management Reporting.

The book clearly explains the process of accounting, using practical assignments from the source documents to the preparation of a Profit and Loss account and Balance Sheet with end-of-year adjustments to the accounts. This is demonstrated manually, in *TASBooks* and in *Sage 50* Accounts.

Part 1 explains the concept of double-entry, preparation of manual accounts, bank reconciliation and VAT. This part also explains the main accounting concepts and the importance of an audit. The tasks are demonstrated using a practical example with detailed explanations and a solution to each task.

Part 2 explains the Profit and Loss account and Balance Sheet, together with end-of-year adjustments to final accounts. The tasks are demonstrated using examples with detailed explanations and solutions. This part also demonstrates ratio analysis of a business.

Part 3 introduces forecasts and budgets, listing their types and purposes. It demonstrates the preparation of a cash budget and forecasted Profit and Loss account and Balance Sheet.

Part 4 introduces computerised accounts, with advantages and disadvantages. It also lists the various accounts packages currently available. It covers the importance of data accuracy and anti-virus software.

Part 5 starts with the installation of *TASBooks*. It explains the use of the main ledgers in *TASBooks*, using the same practical example as in Part 1, Manual Accounting. This section also demonstrates the creation of final accounts with end-of-year adjustments and explains VAT reporting, bank reconciliation and entering opening balances.

Part 6 starts with the installation of *Sage 50* Accounts. It explains the use of the main modules in *Sage 50* Accounts, using the same practical example as in Part 1, Manual Accounting. This section also demonstrates the creation of final accounts with end-of-year adjustments and explains VAT reporting, bank reconciliation and entering opening balances.

Student Resources are available on www.gillmacmillan.ie. They contain set-up files for both *TASBooks* and *Sage 50* Accounts. They also contain source documents for the three different businesses that are used as examples in this book. In the case of the business Daly's Pharmacy Ltd, this also includes the *TASBooks* configuration and the setting up of a Chart of Accounts (COA) using *Sage 50* Accounts.

There are practical assignments and questions at the end of the sections to give students a clear understanding of the tasks demonstrated throughout this book.

Part 1

Manual Accounting

1.1 Principles of Accounting

Learning outcomes (Accounting Manual and Computerised 5N1348): 1, 2, 3 and 4
Learning outcomes (Bookkeeping Manual and Computerised 5N1354): 1 (part)

Accounting is the mechanism that provides us with reliable financial information. This financial information is used by managers, employees, shareholders, potential purchasers, customers, suppliers and financial institutions. Accounting is an information system that identifies, collects, describes, records and processes data and then communicates it as financial information. The accounting system will vary from one business to another, depending on its nature and size, the volume of transactions and the demands made by its management, but the system's components and the method of processing the information are essentially the same in all accounting systems.

In order to be able to provide such financial information for users, each business must keep an accurate record of its activities on a day-to-day basis. Bookkeeping is defined as the recording of financial transactions of a business in daybooks and ledgers – collectively known as the books of prime entry.

Accounting can be defined as using these daybooks and ledgers and the preparation of a Profit and Loss account, Balance Sheet and cash flow statements.

Double-entry principle

The term 'double-entry' infers that every business transaction has a dual aspect – a debit and a credit. The dual-aspect rule arises from the recognition that every time a transaction takes place, there must always be a two-sided effect within the business. The method of recording these dual transactions is through the ledger accounts. Ledger accounts are normally known as T-accounts; the terms *debit* and *credit* apply to the left and right sides respectively and are used repeatedly in the recording of entries.

The bookkeeping process

Most businesses have such a large number of transactions each year that it would be very difficult to record them directly into the accounts. This problem is resolved by using the bookkeeping system that includes daybooks and ledgers, i.e. the books of prime entry. The recording process uses them in the following steps:

1. Analyse each transaction in terms of its effect on the accounts.
2. Enter the transaction information into a daybook.
3. Transfer the daybook information to the ledger, where a double-entry takes place.
4. Balance each ledger account.
5. Summarise the balances of the ledgers in a Trial Balance.

Before examining the books of prime entry in depth, keep in mind that the actual sequence of events begins with a source document, such as a sales invoice, a cheque received, a purchase invoice or a cheque written, which is analysed before being recorded in the books of prime entry.

Daybooks

The daybooks are used to compile lists of similar transactions. They are totalled periodically (usually at the end of the month) and these totals form the basis of entries into the ledgers (the T-accounts). In this way, a business such as a retailer with thousands of transactions can effectively handle its workload. A business can have daybooks for any type of transaction; the most common are:

- **Sales daybook (including returns):** a list of credit sales and returns, with date, invoice number, customer name and amount of sale
- **Purchases daybook (including returns):** a list of credit purchases and returns, with date, invoice number, supplier name and amount of purchase
- **Cash book:** a list of cash receipts (with date, lodgement slip number, 'received from' and amount received) and a list of cheque payments (with date, cheque number, payee and amount)
- **Petty cash book:** a list of small cash payments and receipt transfers from the bank current account.

Accounting terms and definitions

Before considering the double-entry system, some explanation is needed of the main accounting terms.

- **Debtor:** a company or individual who owes money or its equivalent. A trade debtor is a person or business that buys goods on credit and makes payment for such goods at a later date.
- **Creditor:** a company or individual to whom money or its equivalent is owed. The term specifies a party who has delivered goods or services on credit and is owed money by one or more debtors.

To put it simply, the debtor–creditor relationship is complementary to the customer–supplier relationship.

- **Asset**: something of value that a business owns, benefits from or has use of in generating income. Examples are: machinery, property, vehicles, stock of goods, cash and debtors.
- **Liability**: an obligation that a business has to others, arising from past transactions or events. Examples are: creditors, bank overdrafts and loans.
- **Expense**: an item of day-to-day expenditure that a business incurs in order to function. A business incurs expenses through its operations in order to earn income. Examples are: rent paid, wages, insurance and telephone charges.
- **Income**: an amount of money or its equivalent received during a period of time, in exchange for goods or services. Examples are: sales income, rental income and investment income.
- **Profit**: the excess of income over expenses during a period of time.
- **Loss**: the excess of expenses over income during a period of time.
- **Capital**: the money or equivalent invested in a business by its owner or owners. It is the practice to think of the owner as being separate from the business. The capital account records what the owner has contributed to the business out of his/her private resources in order to start the business and keep it going. In other words, it shows what the business 'owes' the owner. In accounting, it is always the records of the business that are presented and therefore capital is treated as a liability. It is part of the 'owner's equity' of the business.
- **Dividend**: a share of the profits from a company, either paid or payable to its shareholders as cash.
- **Shareholder:** a person, company, or other institution that owns at least one share in a company's capital. A company is a separate legal entity, distinct from its owners, who are known as members or shareholders. A shareholder may also be referred to as a stockholder. They have a direct or indirect interest in the activities of the business. The shareholders of a limited company have limited liability, meaning that they cannot be required to contribute more capital than the value of their shares. There are two main types of shareholders: preference and ordinary shareholders.
  - **Preference** shareholders always receive their dividends first, assuming that a dividend is declared by the company. This dividend is fixed as a percentage of the nominal value of the preference share capital. Preference shareholders are ranked higher than ordinary shareholders in the event of company liquidation.

    As with ordinary shares, preference shares represent ownership in a company, although they do not enjoy any of the voting rights of ordinary shareholders. The main benefit to owning preference shares is that the investor has a greater claim on the company's assets than ordinary shareholders.
  - **Ordinary** shareholders are the owners of any shares that are not preference shares and do not have any predetermined dividend amounts. An ordinary shareholder has capital ownership in a company

and is entitled to a vote in matters put before shareholders in proportion to their percentage ownership in the company.

Ordinary shareholders are entitled to receive dividends, if any are available after dividends on preference shareholders are paid. They are also entitled to their share of the residual economic value of the company should the business unwind; however, they are last in line after secured creditors and preference shareholders for receiving business proceeds. As such, ordinary shareholders are considered unsecured creditors.

Accounting standards and principles

Generally Accepted Accounting Principles – GAAP

Generally Accepted Accounting Principles (GAAP) are a common set of accounting principles, standards and procedures that companies use to compile their financial statements. GAAP are a combination of authoritative standards (set by policy boards) and simply the commonly accepted ways of recording and reporting accounting information.

GAAP are imposed on companies so that investors have a minimum level of consistency in the financial statements they use when analysing companies for investment purposes. Companies are expected to follow GAAP rules when reporting their financial data through financial statements. If a financial statement is not prepared using GAAP principles, it may not give a true and fair view of the state of affairs of the business.

That said, keep in mind that GAAP is only a set of standards. There is plenty of room within GAAP for accountants to distort figures. So, even when a company uses GAAP, a reader needs to scrutinise its financial statements.

(Adapted from: www.investopedia.com/terms/g/gaap.asp)

International Financial Reporting Standards (IFRS)

International Financial Reporting Standards (IFRS) are designed as a common global language for business affairs so that company accounts are understandable and comparable across international boundaries. They are a consequence of growing international shareholding and trade and are particularly important for companies that have dealings in several countries. They are progressively replacing the many different national accounting standards. The rules are to be followed by accountants to maintain books of accounts which are comparable, understandable, reliable and relevant as per the users, internal or external.

IFRS began as an attempt to harmonise accounting across the European Union but the value of harmonisation quickly made the concept attractive around the world. They are sometimes still called by the original name of International Accounting Standards (IAS). IAS were issued between 1973 and

2001 by the Board of the International Accounting Standards Committee (IASC). On 1 April 2001, the new International Accounting Standards Board (IASB) took over from the IASC the responsibility for setting International Accounting Standards. During its first meeting the new board adopted existing IAS and Standing Interpretations Committee standards (SICs). The IASB has continued to develop standards, calling the new standards International Financial Reporting Standards (IFRS).

(Adapted from: http://uk.ask.com/wiki/International_Financial_Reporting_Standards?qsrc=3044)

The importance of accounting standards

If accounting is the language of business, accounting standards are its grammar. Properly developed and implemented, they can encourage business expansion and help regulate the economic system. High-quality accounting standards can facilitate the flow of information from businesses to a range of different users. These include investors, banks, creditors, revenue commissioners, regulators, employees and the general public. The availability of accounts prepared in accordance with recognised accounting standards encourages trade by promoting confidence in business.

However, financial statements are inherently limited in nature. They provide a snapshot of financial position, performance and cash flows of a company as at the reporting date. They are a function of the estimates and judgements of directors and of the choices made under accounting standards.

Accounting standards are themselves not without controversy. Both the financial crises and recent developments in international accounting standards have drawn attention to the content of accounting standards, the process by which they are developed and the role accounting standards have played in the economic system. For example, both the G20 leaders and the Report of the Financial Crisis Advisory Group have called for the development of a single set of high-quality global accounting standards to facilitate transparency and stability in the global economic system (IASB, 2009a; 2010a).

Section 149(1, 2) of the *Companies Act 1963* requires that company directors present to their shareholders financial statements which give a 'true and fair view' of the company's financial position and profit or loss. What constitutes a 'true and fair view' is not defined by legislation in Ireland or internationally. Rather 'a true and fair view' is a concept which originates in the nineteenth century and has subsequently been refined by case law. This case law has established that if company directors comply with accounting standards in preparing the financial statements, this is very strong evidence that the financial statements give 'a true and fair view'. In other words, accounting standards define best practice in accounting.

Financial statements presenting a true and fair view are prepared applying GAAP (in Ireland – either UK and Irish GAAP or IFRS) whilst audits are carried out having regard to independently established auditing standards – in Ireland, International Auditing Standards as published by the Auditing Practices Board (APB).

(Adapted from: www.oireachtas.ie/parliament/media/housesoftheoireachtas/ libraryresearch/spotlights/accounting_standards.pdf)

Accounting concepts

We can make three observations concerning accounting entries:

1. Accounting measures transactions in money.
2. Agreement is reached among people as to the monetary value of a transaction.
3. There is consistency in the preparation of financial statements, e.g. in layout, the yearly time interval and the methods of dealing with transactions.

These are obvious characteristics, but accounting does not tell us everything about the business. If a business makes a healthy profit, do we assume it is healthy and will be in existence in the future?

Basic accounting concepts – SSAP 2

Historically, the starting point for accountants has been the four 'fundamental accounting concepts' listed in the Statement of Standard Accounting Practice (SSAP) 2 'Disclosure of Accounting Policies'. This was superseded from December 2000 by the International Financial Reporting Standards (IFRS) 18. This applies to all accounts within its scope for accounting periods ending on or after 22 June 2001.

SSAP 2 was issued in November 1971 and its objective was to ensure the disclosure in accounts of clear explanations of accounting policies adopted for the purpose of giving a true and fair view. There was no statement of how accounting policies were to be defined but the four accounting concepts were introduced. These concepts were regarded as expedient and working assumptions, having general acceptance at the time the standard was issued.

Under SSAP 2 there were 'broad basic assumptions' underlying the periodic financial accounts of businesses. The four main assumptions are explained in the following sections.

1. Prudence concept

This requires that revenue and profits were not anticipated, but recognised by inclusion in the Profit and Loss account only when realised in the form either of cash or of other assets, the ultimate realisation of which could be assessed with reasonable certainty. Provision is made for all known liabilities (expenses and losses), whether the amount of these is known with certainty or is a 'best estimate' in light of the information.

The prudence concept injects a note of caution where estimates are required in uncertain situations. Managers generally tend to be over-optimistic when making predictions about future sales or cost overruns. For example, slow-moving stock may suggest obsolescence, a fact that a manager may be reluctant to accept, and similarly, a customer with an overdue debt may have to be considered a write-off. Where loss is probable, prudence requires that these losses be accounted for immediately. If in doubt, overstate losses and understate profits.

2. Consistency concept

This requires that accounting treatments be applied consistently within accounts, and from one period to the next. Users of financial statements need to be able to compare businesses based on performance and financial position. They must also be able to compare a business's performance over a number of periods. For example, if a business depreciated its equipment using the 'straight-line' method in the first year, then it should continue with the same method in subsequent years. Where there is a change in the accounting method, the effect of this change has to be calculated and recorded, for example, if it gives a more accurate picture of the state of the business. This concept provides confidence to users of accounting statements when comparing present and previous sets of accounts.

3. Going-concern concept

This requires that the business will continue in 'operational existence' for the foreseeable future and that the value of its assets is appropriately accounted for in the accounts. If the business is being wound up, then the assets need to be valued at their market value.

4. Accruals (matching) concept

This requires that revenue and costs be accrued, i.e. recognised as they were earned or incurred, not as money is received or paid, and matched with one another in so far as their relationship can be established or justifiably assumed. They are to be dealt with in the Profit and Loss account of the period to which they relate.

The intent here is to have revenues and profits of a period matched with the associated expenses incurred in earning them. As we will see later, cash received in a period could be for payment of goods sold in the previous period or even for services to be performed in a future period. Later, we will distinguish between the accruals basis and the cash basis of accounting, a distinction greatly assisted by the matching concept. For now, we can say that when a business has provided a service or sold goods in a period and is not paid until the next period, then the business must accrue the amount for that sale. Similarly, if a business has paid for goods or a service in advance, the business must recognise that one asset, cash, has been translated into another asset, prepayment.

Further accounting concepts

In addition to the four concepts listed above, there are a number of other concepts that are accepted as general accounting practice.

- **Materiality:** An error in the accounts may or may not have a significant impact on the financial statements. What constitutes 'significant' is determined by how 'material' that error is. As long as the financial statements give a true and fair view, an immaterial error need not be accounted for. Where errors are deemed to be material, they must be corrected.

    Judgement on an accountant's part is often required to decide on what is material. For example, a €1,000 error in the cash account of a multinational company may be immaterial, unlike a small business where such an error would materially affect the reported position.
- **Entity concept:** A business is a separate entity and exists distinct from its owners. Whether it is a profit or a non-profit making business, only the financial matters relating to that entity can be included in the accounts and not those of the owners and others. Establishing the dividing line between private dealings and the transactions of the business is imperative for the accountant.
- **Dual aspect:** This is the basis for the bookkeeping equation, where there are two aspects to accounting for financial information. This means that wherever there is a debit in the accounts, there is a corresponding credit.
- **Monetary measurement:** Only those transactions and events that can be measured in monetary terms can be recorded in the accounts. Without this monetary measurement unit, we could not make any meaningful comparisons of value.
- **Historical cost:** The historical cost concept values transactions at their original cost and is recorded in the books as such. Although events such as inflation may affect costs, subsequent changes in prices or value are usually ignored.
- **Realisation:** This concept allows a business to realise a transaction when a value can be placed on it and when we are certain that the resources will be transferred. This means that if there is a sale in August, but the business does not get paid until October, we can recognise the sale in August, as long as we are reasonably certain of payment.

    The rules or concepts listed are the foundation of accounting. The most important are stipulated in SSAP 2, as issued by the IASB. Although many have been superseded by International Financial Reporting Standards (IFRS), some are still in force.

Accounting policies of FRS 18

FRS 18 deals primarily with the selection, application and disclosure of accounting policies. Its objective is to ensure that for all material items:

- an entity adopts the accounting policies most appropriate to its particular circumstances for the purpose of giving a true and fair view
- an entity should prepare its financial statement on a going-concern basis, unless the entity is being liquidated or has ceased trading, or the directors either intend to liquidate the entity or to cease trading, or have no realistic alternative but to do so
- the accounting policies adopted are reviewed regularly to ensure that they remain appropriate, and are changed when a new policy becomes more appropriate to the entity's particular circumstances
- sufficient information is disclosed in the financial statements to enable users to understand the accounting policies adopted and how they have been implemented.

The FRS supersedes the SSAP 2 'Disclosure of accounting policies', which was published in 1971. Although in many respects SSAP 2 was still broadly satisfactory, the framework within which it discussed accounting policies was out of step with modern accounting. The FRS updates that framework to make it consistent with the IASB's Statement of Principles for Financial Reporting.

(Adapted from: www.frc.org.uk/Our-Work/Codes-Standards/Accounting-and-Reporting-Policy/Standards-in-Issue/FRS-18-Accounting-Policies.aspx)

The FRS came into force for accounting periods ending on or after 22 June 2001. It summarises the qualitative characteristics of financial statements and requires that the characteristics of relevance, reliability, comparability and understandability pertain to all statements in order to have confidence in them.

Control of accounting systems

It is the responsibility of the owner of the business to safeguard its assets and to maintain the integrity of the financial data. This is a great challenge facing the accounting profession, focusing as it does on the issue of adequate controls in accounting systems. In a business, there are internal and external control systems in place and internally created control systems are tested by an independent external source – the auditor.

Internal control environment

The threats to a business are significant and broad. The main threats are from dishonest and/or incompetent employees, human error and poor management practices. Internal control management consists of the methods and measures maintained in a business to safeguard all assets from theft/ unauthorised use and enhance the accuracy and reliability of its accounting records by reducing the risk of errors and irregularities.

To achieve these control mechanisms, the business must follow a number of internal control principles. Specific control mechanisms may vary from one business to another, but the following principles apply to most business environments.

* **Establishment of responsibility:** This calls for assignment of responsibility to specific employees. Control is most effective when only one person is responsible for a given task.
* **Segregation of duties:** Related activities such as ordering, receiving and paying for goods, run the risk of abuse if completed by the same person. For example, goods might be ordered from friends who give kickbacks, or payments might be approved for fictitious invoices. Also, sales-related activities should be assigned to different persons. Another example of segregation of duties is to ensure that the bookkeeper of an asset does not have access to that asset; equally, the person in charge of an asset should not maintain or have access to the accounting records for that asset. Similarly, an employee in charge of cash is not likely to make personal use of it if another employee is responsible for the accounting of that cash.
* **Document procedures:** Procedures should be established for all documentation. First, documents should be pre-numbered and all documents accounted for. Source documents such as invoices should be promptly forwarded to the person responsible for the accounting to help timely and accurate recording of transactions.
* **Physical controls:** Physical controls, such as safes and secure warehouses, should be in place to safeguard the assets of the business. Computer security is particularly challenging. All computer facilities should have password controls and backup systems, and there are natural dangers to secure against, such as blackouts and obsolete technology. Due to human-made threats, such as hacking, viruses and data manipulation, access should be restricted by an ever-challenging password system.
* **Independent internal verification:** This involves the review, comparison and reconciliation of information by internal employees acting independently. This can be in the form of verification by an employee, on a periodic basis, of information supplied by another department. A large business will almost certainly have its own internal auditing system, where regular verification constitutes a significant part of the work. Any discrepancies or exceptions should be reported to the senior management, who are capable of corrective action.

External control environment

An external audit is carried out by outsiders, who investigate the accounting system and transactions of a business and then ensure that the financial statements have been prepared in accordance with accounting principles. These auditors should be expert and independent so that investors, lenders and the Revenue Commissioners can rely on their report. External control relies on effective internal control procedures being in place and on the ability of management to enforce those controls.

The external auditor, who is appointed by the owner of the business or, in the case of a company, at the AGM on behalf of its shareholders, reports on the accounts of the business. The auditor states, in his/her opinion, whether the accounts and records fairly and accurately reflect the activities of the business in the period under review. This also includes the state of its assets and liabilities at the end of that period. The auditor effectively acts as a check on management.

Role of the auditor

The **internal auditor** is often employed in medium-to-large companies to install and maintain internal controls. It is impossible for senior management in large companies to exercise direct control and supervision of operations. An internal auditor is able to bridge the gap in controls and, in a sense, provide an independent check on the accounting records and other operations of the company.

While the scope of the internal auditor is defined by management, maximum benefit is obtained if the auditor's duties extend beyond mere checking for accuracy of records. They should cover all aspects of financial and non-financial matters. In order to do this, the auditor must be completely independent from executive responsibility and allowed to investigate any area of the company's activities. This independence is underlined if the internal auditor reports directly to the board or a committee made up of board members and senior-management personnel.

The **external auditor** is an outside person, not employed within the business, who investigates the accounting systems and transactions of the business. The external audit is conducted by independent reviewers whose objective is to express an opinion on whether the financial statements give a true and fair view of the business's affairs at the end of the period under review and of its profit and loss for that same period. It also includes an opinion on whether the accounts have been properly prepared in accordance with relevant legislation and applicable accounting standards. The focus of the external auditor's attention includes not only financial statements, but also notes, reconciliations and estimates associated with the statements.

The external auditor will report to the shareholders of a company and must state whether:

- the auditor has had access to all records and information considered necessary
- the Balance Sheet and Profit and Loss account are in agreement with the accounts in the ledgers
- the accounts give a true and fair view of the state of the company's affairs

- the Balance Sheet and Profit and Loss account comply with the legal requirements contained in the various companies acts
- proper books of account have been kept.

The primary function of an auditor, whether internal or external, is not to detect fraud and error, but rather to obtain sufficient, appropriate audit evidence to form an opinion on the financial statements. However, the auditor is bound to exercise due care in the conduct of the audit. Auditors should be conscious that the possibility of fraud and errors may occur, which may result in a significant misstatement of the accounts. They should therefore plan and perform their work accordingly. As long as the audit provides a reasonable expectation of detecting material fraud or error, then the auditor is not liable for failing to detect it.

Advantages and disadvantages of an audit

There are inherent *advantages* in having accounts audited. These include:

- An auditor may well discover material fraud or errors during the audit, even though such a discovery is not the primary objective of the audit.
- The in-depth examination of the business may enable the auditor to give constructive advice to management on improving the efficiency of the business.
- Applications to banks and other parties for finance and for dealing with potential purchasers may be enhanced by providing audited accounts.

Disadvantages include:

- Audits can be costly as they involve the services of a professional.
- Disruption of the work of employees is unavoidable as the audit requires management and employees to spend time providing information to the auditor.

Review questions

1. Identify the appropriate accounting concept suggested by each of the following statements (SSAP 2 Disclosure of Accounting Policies):
   a. '…the profit and loss account and balance sheet assume no intention or necessity to liquidate…'
   b. '…accounting treatment of like items within each accounting period and from one period to another…'
   c. '…revenue and profits in the Profit and Loss account are matched with associated costs and expenses…'
2. State which accounting rule is referred to in each of the following:
   a. telephone expenses incurred in one period and paid for in another period

b. a demand by the owner of the business to include every detailed transaction in the preparation of the financial statements

c. a valuation of three litres of petrol in a motor vehicle at the end of the accounting period

d. a proposed change in the method of depreciation

e. a fixed asset that could be sold for more than its cost price.

3. State whether each of the following statements are true or false:

   a. Accounting is based on a theoretical framework.

   b. Accountants can adopt different rules to suit different businesses.

   c. The owner's personal property should be part of the accounts of his/her business.

4. The checking of, and reporting on, accounts is termed:

   a. Financial accounting

   b. Management accounting

   c. Auditing

   d. Financial management.

5. Name three main financial statements.

6. Name three internal threats to a business's resources.

7. List three functions of the internal auditor.

8. List three functions of the external auditor.

9. What is meant by Generally Accepted Accounting Principles (GAAP)?

10. Name and briefly explain the four fundamental accounting concepts as defined by SSAP 2.

1.2 Value-Added Tax (VAT)

Learning outcomes (Accounting Manual and Computerised 5N1348): 9 (part)
Learning outcomes (Bookkeeping Manual and Computerised 5N1354): 1 (part)

Value-added tax (VAT) is a tax on consumer spending. It is collected by VAT-registered traders on their sales of goods and services within the State to their customers. Each such trader in the chain of supply from manufacturer through to retailer charges VAT on his/her sales and is entitled to deduct from this amount the VAT paid on purchases. The effect of offsetting VAT on purchases against VAT on sales is to impose the tax on the added value at each stage of production – hence 'value-added' tax. The final consumer, who is not registered for VAT, absorbs VAT as part of the purchase price.

VAT rates

The standard rate of VAT is 23%. There are reduced rates of 13.5% and 9% and a zero rate.

In Ireland, the 23% rate mainly applies to goods, such as:

* certain beverages – alcohol, soft drinks, bottled waters, cigarettes
* transport fuels – petrol, auto diesel, motor oil, liquid petroleum gas
* vehicles – cars, lorries, car accessories, tyres, motorcycles, pleasure boats, mobile homes
* consumer goods – adult clothing, adult footwear, jewellery, cosmetics, pottery and glassware, sports goods, stationery, toys, bicycles, CDs/DVDs, computers, electrical equipment, carpets and floor coverings, furniture, soft furnishings, household goods
* hiring/leasing/rental of equipment, vehicles, household goods, DVDs/videos
* certain services – accountancy, advertising, haulage, telecommunications, professional services (e.g. legal), toll roads
* confectionery – sweets, chocolates, ice cream, crisps, peanuts.

Examples of zero-rated goods include:

* most food
* children's clothes and shoes

- books
- oral medicines.

Examples of items at the 9% reduced rate include:

- tourist accommodation
- commercially provided meals, e.g. in hotels, restaurants
- cinema admissions
- hairdressing
- newspapers.

Examples of items at the 13.5% reduced rate include:

- electricity, gas, home-heating oil, fuel for domestic use, e.g. coal, turf, peat briquettes
- new houses and the construction sector
- locally-supplied, labour-intensive services, e.g. car repair and maintenance, small repair services
- certain agricultural and horticultural services.

VAT registration

To register for VAT, a Form TR1 must be completed if the trader is an individual or partnership, or a Form TR2 if the trader owns a company. The form, when completed, should be forwarded to the local Revenue District. Special care should be taken when completing the form to include the name, address, PPSN, business type and the relevant tax types. The form must also be signed and dated.

A trader who supplies goods and/or services is generally required to register for VAT, subject to turnover exceeding certain thresholds. The most common thresholds are €37,500 for the supply of services, and €75,000 for the supply of goods. Some traders are generally not required to register for VAT, although they may choose to do so. These include traders whose turnover does not exceed the thresholds above, and also farmers.

Invoice basis accounting for VAT

VAT-registered persons normally account for VAT on an invoice ('sales') basis. This means that VAT is due when the invoice is issued to the customer, rather than when the customer pays. Also, VAT is claimed by the trader when he/she purchases goods and services, that is, when the purchase invoice is received. However, certain persons may opt to account for VAT on the moneys received ('cash') basis, i.e. by reference to payments actually received by them (see 'Cash basis accounting for VAT' this section).

Right to claim VAT

In computing the amount of VAT payable in respect of a taxable period, a registered trader may deduct the VAT charged on most goods and services that are used for the purposes of the taxable business. No deduction may be made, however, for the VAT on goods and services used for any other purpose. To be entitled to the deduction, the trader must have a proper VAT invoice. These invoices and other records must normally be kept by the trader for six years.

A trader may not deduct VAT on any of the following, even when the goods and services in question are acquired or used for the purposes of a taxable business:

* expenditure incurred on food, drink or accommodation or other personal services for the trader or the trader's agents and/or employees
* entertainment expenses incurred by the trader or the trader's agents and/or employees
* the purchase or hiring of passenger motor vehicles generally (other than motor vehicles held as stock-in-trade, or hired for the purpose of a business, or for use in a driving school business)
* the purchase of petrol other than as stock-in-trade.

Importance of invoices and credit notes

In order for VAT-registered traders to claim VAT on purchases, they must receive a proper VAT invoice from their supplier. It is vital, therefore, that these invoices are properly drawn up and carefully retained. The checking of invoices and credit notes forms a very important part of the periodic examination, which revenue officers may make of a trader's VAT position.

VAT law contains specific requirements for the issue and retention of invoices, credit notes and related documents. Failure to comply with these requirements leaves a trader liable to penalties. Traders who issue invoices and credit notes, and persons to whom these documents are issued, should ensure that the documents accurately represent the transactions to which they refer.

Information required on a VAT invoice

The VAT invoice issued must show:

* date of issue
* invoice number
* full name, address and VAT registration number of the person who supplied the goods or services
* full name and address of the person to whom the goods or services were supplied

- quantity and nature of the goods supplied or the extent and nature of the services supplied
- date on which the goods or services were supplied
- unit price, exclusive of VAT, of the goods or services supplied
- amount of the consideration, exclusive of VAT taxable at each rate (including zero rate), and the rate of VAT chargeable
- VAT payable in respect of supply.

Electronic invoicing

It is open to traders to operate an electronic invoicing system, provided the particulars to be contained in such invoices or other documents are recorded, retained and transmitted electronically by a system that ensures the integrity of those particulars and the authenticity of their origin. The electronic system in use must be capable of producing, retaining and storing invoices and credit notes.

Cash basis accounting for VAT

Under the normal invoice basis for accounting, a trader is liable to account for VAT when an invoice is issued to a customer. Under the cash basis (also called the 'receipts' or 'moneys received' basis) of accounting, a trader is liable to account for VAT when payment is actually received.

A trader must fulfil one of two criteria to be on the cash basis. Either:

- annual turnover does not exceed €1.25 million (with effect from 1 May 2013); or
- supplies are almost exclusively (at least 90%) made to customers who are not registered for VAT, or are not entitled to claim a full deduction of VAT.

In practice, the cash basis of accounting is mainly used by shops, restaurants, public houses and similar businesses, and by any other person supplying goods or services directly to the public. A person or business applying for VAT registration, who wishes to use the cash rather than invoice basis, must apply for permission in writing at the time of registration.

VAT returns

A VAT-registered trader normally accounts for VAT on a two-monthly basis (e.g. January/February, March/April). The return is made on the Form VAT3, together with a payment for any VAT due, and remitted to the Collector-General on or before the 19th of the month following the end of the taxable period. In 2009, the Revenue introduced important changes regarding mandatory electronic filing and payment of taxes. From 1 June 2012, on Phase 4 of Revenue mandatory e-filing requirements, all traders must submit their VAT Return form and payment using the Revenue Online Service (ROS).

They must submit their VAT Return form and payment on or before the 23rd of the month following the end of the taxable period.

From 1 July 2007, the frequency of filing VAT returns was reduced for certain persons on the following criteria:

- For businesses with a yearly VAT liability of €3,000 or less, the option of filing returns on a six-monthly basis is available.
- For businesses with a yearly liability of between €3,001 and €14,400 the option of filing returns on a four-monthly basis is available.

How to complete a VAT3 Return form

The VAT3 Return form records the total value of transactions carried on by the trader over the course of a tax period. The figures representing the transactions carried out should be recorded in the boxes on the ROS system, as follows:

- **T1 Box – VAT on Sales**: This figure is the total **VAT** charged by the trader on sales to customers in the taxable period.
- **T2 – VAT on Purchases**: This figure is the total **VAT** incurred by the trader on purchases of goods for resale (if any) and on expenses incurred for business purposes in the taxable period.
- **T3 – VAT payable**: Where the figure in T1 is greater than that in T2, then the trader has a net liability to Revenue, which is calculated by subtracting T2 from T1.
- **T4 – VAT repayable**: Where the figure in T2 is greater than that in T1, then the trader is entitled to a net refund of VAT, which is calculated by subtracting T1 from T2.

Intra-EU transactions

Where the trader has made supplies of goods to customers in other EU countries, or purchased goods from suppliers in other EU countries, this must be reflected in the VAT3 as follows:

- **E1 – Intra-EU supply of goods:** This is the total value of goods sold to customers in other EU countries.
- **E2 – Intra-EU acquisition of goods:** This is the total value of goods purchased from suppliers in other EU countries.

Where the trader has supplied services to customers in other EU countries, or received services from suppliers in other EU countries, this must be reflected in the VAT3 as follows:

- **ES1 – Intra-EU supply of services:** This is the total value of services supplied to customers in other EU countries.

- **ES2 – Intra-EU acquisition of services:** This is the total value of services received from suppliers in other EU countries.

A Sample VAT3 Return is contained on your Student Resources, which represents the ROS e-filing system.

Review questions

1. Goods were sold at a price of €1,210 inclusive of VAT at 23%. The VAT amount is:
   a. €278.30
   b. €226.26
   c. €757.48.
2. List four situations in which VAT incurred by a taxable person is not recoverable.
3. A person must register for VAT if their annual turnover from the supply of goods exceeds or is likely to exceed:
   a. €37,500
   b. €75,000
   c. €41,000.
4. What information should normally be included in the E1 and E2 boxes of a VAT3 return?
5. VAT is an expense to be suffered by:
   a. companies dealing with goods
   b. all traders dealing with goods
   c. all traders, registered for VAT, dealing with goods
   d. the final consumer of the goods.
6. Aine paid €4,000 to buy equipment from Lorraine and sold it for €5,000 plus VAT at 23% to Sandra who, in turn, sold it for a VAT-inclusive price of €7,050 to James, a customer. Aine and Sandra are VAT-registered, while Lorraine is not. How much VAT would Aine and Sandra have to pay?
   a. Aine €1,150; Sandra €1,318
   b. Aine €1,150; Sandra €1,234
   c. Aine €168; Sandra €1,318
   d. Aine €1,150; Sandra €168

1.3 Manual Preparation of Accounts

Learning outcomes (Accounting Manual and Computerised 5N1348): 9 (part)
Learning outcomes (Bookkeeping Manual and Computerised 5N1354): 3, 4, 5 and 7

The system of preparing accounts on a manual basis involves collecting and processing transactions and communicating them as financial information to interested parties. We will now explore this in more detail, commencing with the basic transactions and ending with the preparation of financial statements, as demonstrated in Part 2.

The elements that make up the accounting system are:

- the transaction, e.g. purchasing, selling, receiving payment, making payments
- accounts prepared, i.e. daybooks (purchases, sales, bank/cash receipts, bank/cash payments)
- ledger accounts processed and balanced
- a Trial Balance produced
- financial statements prepared.

The transaction

In any business, the transaction may involve purchasing goods for resale, purchasing a vehicle for use, paying rent, selling goods to a customer, paying a supplier for goods purchased or a customer paying for goods. These are all financial transactions that occur in all businesses and so must be recorded in the accounting system. Each of these transactions has a **source document**, for example:

- Purchase invoice – received by a trader from the supplier when goods are purchased
- Sales invoice – issued to a customer by the trader when goods are sold
- Purchase credit note – received by a trader from the supplier when goods are returned
- Sales credit note – issued to a customer by the trader when the customer returns goods

- Cheque book stub – a record of all payments made by the trader to suppliers and other payments, e.g. rent, wages
- Lodgement record – a record of lodgements made by the trader to the bank account
- Petty cash voucher – a record of all petty cash payments made by the trader.

Accounts prepared

Accounts prepared are the daybooks of the business (purchases, sales, bank/cash receipts, bank/cash payments. All of these transactions must go through the recording process. This process uses a bookkeeping system that includes daybooks and ledgers.

The daybooks are used to compile lists of similar transactions and are totalled, usually at the end of the month. A trader can have daybooks for any type of transaction, but these are the most common:

- Sales daybook (including returns) – contains lists of sales invoices and sales credit notes
- Purchases daybook (including returns) – contains lists of purchase invoices and purchase credit notes
- Cash book – contains lists of cash/cheque lodgements and lists of cheque payments
- Petty Cash book – contains lists of small cash payments and receipts transferred from the bank account.

Ledger accounts processed and balanced

The daybooks have solved the problem of a large business that has many transactions, as these are now grouped together into similar transactions. But under the daybook system, there are no individual accounts for each customer or supplier. As a result, the trader has no information about individual debtors and these will need to be billed in order to collect the amount outstanding. Also, the trader has no information about individual suppliers, who will need to be paid the balance outstanding. This problem is solved by introducing ledger accounts, which are made up of **personal ledgers** (debtors ledger and creditors ledger) and **nominal ledgers** (all other general ledgers).

The procedure of transferring entries from the daybooks to the ledgers is called 'posting'. This involves a **double-entry system**. The double-entry system arises from the recognition that every time a transaction takes place, there must always be a two-sided effect – a debit and a credit.

One basic rule of bookkeeping when trying to understand the double-entry system is: *All assets and expenses go on the **debit** side of the ledger and all liabilities and income go on the **credit** side of the ledger.*

To apply this rule, therefore:

- *Debit*: Assets and expenses
- *Credit*: Liabilities and income.

A ledger account will look similar to the layout shown (fig. 1).

		Name of Account			
DEBIT					**CREDIT**
Date	Details	Amount	Date	Details	Amount

Figure 1

This T-account will have a debit balance when the total of the debit amounts exceed the total of the credit amounts, and vice versa. The basic rules for double-entry are:

- Calculate the ledger accounts involved, which are usually two or three ledger accounts.
- Decide which account to debit and which to credit, remembering the rule to:
  - *Debit assets and expenses.* This refers to increases in assets and expenses and also to decreases in liabilities or income.
  - *Credit liabilities and income.* This refers to increases in liabilities and income and also to decreases in assets and expenses.

Normally, assets and expenses will have a debit balance, whereas liabilities and income accounts will have a credit balance.

Trial Balance produced

A Trial Balance is a method of summarising ledger account balances, with debit balances grouped together and credit balances grouped together. It is essentially a summary of all the ledger account balances. If the double-entry system has been adhered to properly, then the total debit balances and the total credit balances should agree. The primary purpose of the Trial Balance is to prove the mathematical equality of the debits and the credits and to summarise the accounts and transactions of the business. The Trial Balance contains a list of the ledger account names and the closing balance – debit or credit. The Trial Balance will not prove that all transactions have been recorded or that the ledger is correct. Errors may exist, even though the Trial Balance may agree. For example, a transaction may be completely omitted, or a transaction may be recorded on both debit and credit with an incorrect amount, or debits and credits may be reversed or a transaction may be recorded twice. Despite this limitation, the Trial Balance is a useful tool for finding errors in the recording system.

Financial statements prepared

Once a Trial Balance has been prepared, final accounts can then be produced, i.e. a Profit and Loss account and a Balance Sheet. The Profit and Loss account will report the profit or loss that the business incurred for a given period. It is essentially the difference between expenses and income of the business over a given period. The Balance Sheet is a statement of the assets and liabilities of the business over the same period. The items referred to as post-trial balance items (accruals, prepayments, depreciation and bad debts) will be covered in Part 2.

The above system of accounting for transactions is best explained with a detailed example. Remember, business transactions originate from a source document and it is these source documents that form the starting point of our accounting system. We will go through each daybook and posting to the ledger, using the following business, Daly's Pharmacy Ltd.

Business name	Daly's Pharmacy Ltd
Address	Grattan Road
	Salthill
	Co Galway
Telephone	091-1234567
VAT reg. no.	IE4732206N

Daly's Pharmacy Ltd sells pharmaceutical products to a range of cash and credit customers. The business purchases pharmaceutical products on credit from a range of suppliers. It also incurs other expenses in order to run the business.

The business is registered for VAT and is accounted for on an invoice basis. VAT is charged on the sale of cosmetic goods at the rate of 23% and on the sale of medicines at the rate of 0%.

Purchases and purchases returns

Refer to your Student Resources for the Purchase invoices and Credit note of Daly's Pharmacy Ltd.

These Purchase Invoices and Credit note are firstly recorded as shown in the Purchases daybook for Daly's Pharmacy (fig.2).

VAT columns in the Purchases daybook need to be evident for each rate of VAT, showing net values at each rate and the VAT amount at each rate. Purchases of medicines and cosmetics are resale items, i.e. they are purchased in order to be sold to customers. Electricity is a non-resale item, that is, it is purchased for use in the business. Resale purchases and non-resale purchases need to be recorded separately in all daybooks. This distinction between resale and non-resale purchases is not necessarily needed for the completion of the business's VAT 3 Return, but is needed when a trader completes an annual return of trading (Form RTD) at the end of the accounting year.

Purchases Book – Daly's Pharmacy

Date	Inv. No.	Supplier	Net Purchases 23%	Resale VAT 23%	Net Purchases 0%	Net Light & Heat 13.5%	Non-resale VAT 13.5%	TOTAL
2-Nov	58	Alchemy Ltd	1,770.00	407.10	522.50			2,699.60
4-Nov	1259	United Drugs Ltd	3,885.00	893.55	930.00			5,708.55
15-Nov	1305	United Drugs Ltd	(84.00)	(19.32)	(93.00)			(196.32)
18-Nov	4589	Stafford Lynch	3,009.00	692.07				3,701.07
20-Nov		Electric Ireland				274.28	37.03	311.31
		TOTALS	**8,580.00**	**1,973.40**	**1,359.50**	**274.28**	**37.03**	**12,224.21**

Figure 2

When a trader purchases goods for resale, in this case, medicines and cosmetics, they are classified as 'Purchases', where they will be posted to the Purchases account in the ledger. When a trader purchases other non-resale items, e.g. electricity, the item is classified as a separate heading in the Purchases daybook. In summary, as well as recording the total amount of purchase transactions, the Purchases daybook includes an analysis of the *types* of purchases.

Posting the Purchases daybook to the ledger

The suppliers to Daly's Pharmacy are the business's **creditors**. These purchases are assumed to be on credit and have not as yet been paid. Therefore, Daly's Pharmacy owes the amount on the invoice to these suppliers – so they represent a **liability** to the business – and are, therefore, posted to the **credit** side of the ledger. These suppliers will be listed in the Creditors ledger. The term 'creditors' derives from the word 'credit', as they usually have a credit balance.

The total Purchases and Light & Heat above are regarded as **expenses**. This effectively means that these amounts should appear on the **debit** side of the ledger.

The VAT amounts above can be reclaimed by Daly's Pharmacy from the Revenue commissioners. This means that the business is owed VAT from the Revenue at this moment, as VAT is on an invoice basis. This represents an **asset** for the business, which effectively means that there will be a **debit** entry in the VAT ledger account. This may sound confusing, due to the fact that there are more than two accounts here having a debit entry. This still qualifies as a double-entry since the total debits will equal the total credits, as follows:

- *Debit*: Purchases/Light & Heat accounts with the *net* value of Purchases/ Light & Heat for the month.
- *Debit:* VAT account with the *VAT* on these purchases for the month.
- *Credit:* Suppliers/Creditors accounts with the *total* value of the invoices for the month.

Given that the *net* value and the VAT amount equal the *total* value of the invoices, our debits equal our credits. Technically, the term 'double-entry' refers to the amounts of money, not necessarily the number of accounts involved.

The Ledger Accounts of Daly's Pharmacy Ltd will be recorded as shown (fig. 3).

Creditors Ledger

Alchemy Ltd

DR						CR
Date	Details	Amount	Date	Details	Amount	
			2-Nov	Purchases	2699.60	

United Drugs Ltd

DR						CR
Date	Details	Amount	Date	Details	Amount	
15-Nov	Purchases Returns	196.32	4-Nov	Purchases	5708.55	

Stafford Lynch

DR						CR
Date	Details	Amount	Date	Details	Amount	
			18-Nov	Purchases	3701.07	

Electric Ireland

DR						CR
Date	Details	Amount	Date	Details	Amount	
			20-Nov	Purchases	311.31	

Nominal Ledger

Purchases A/C

DR						CR
Date	Details	Amount	Date	Details	Amount	
Nov	Purchases	8580.00				
Nov	Purchases	1359.50				

Light & Heat A/C

DR			Date	Details	CR
Date	Details	Amount	Date	Details	Amount
Nov	Purchases	274.28			

VAT A/C

DR			Date	Details	CR
Date	Details	Amount	Date	Details	Amount
Nov	Purchases	1973.40			
Nov	Purchases	37.03			

Figure 3

To summarise the double-entry for purchases and purchases returns:

- *Credit*: Each supplier/creditor with the *total* value of the purchase invoice; debit the supplier/creditor with the total value of credit notes with purchases returns.
- *Debit:* VAT account with the *VAT* amount on each purchase invoice. In the example shown, we use the monthly total for posting to the VAT account. The VAT on the VAT account of €1,973.40 has been reduced by the VAT on the credit note.
- *Debit:* Purchases account or relevant expense account with the *net* value of each purchase Invoice.

The individual entries are shown in the summary of ledger purchases for Daly's Pharmacy (fig. 4)

	Account	Debit	Credit	Type of Account
Credit	Alchemy Ltd		2699.60	Increase in Liability
Credit	United Drugs Ltd		5708.55	Increase in Liability
Debit	United Drugs Ltd	196.32		Decrease in Liability
Credit	Stafford Lynch		3701.07	Increase in Liability
Credit	Electric Ireland		311.31	Increase in Liability
Debit	Purchases A/c	8580.00		Increase in Expense
Debit	Purchases A/c	1359.50		Increase in Expense
Debit	Light & Heat A/c	274.28		Increase in Expense
Debit	VAT A/c	1973.40		Increase in Asset
Debit	VAT A/c	37.03		Increase in Asset
		12420.53	12420.53	

Figure 4

Sales and sales returns

Refer to your Student Resources for the Sales invoices and Credit note of Daly's Pharmacy Ltd.

These sales invoices and credit note are first recorded in the Sales daybook for Daly's Pharmacy (fig. 5).

Sales Daybook – Daly's Pharmacy

Date	Inv. No.	Customer	Net Sales 23%	VAT 23%	Net Sales 0%	TOTAL
8-Nov	225	James Mulcahy	2,024.82	465.71		2,490.53
10-Nov	226	Martha Downey	1,281.78	294.81	680.60	2,257.19
15-Nov	227	Cash Sales	220.14	50.63	62.10	332.87
19-Nov	228	Martha Downey	477.75	109.88	103.50	691.13
23-Nov	229	Martha Downey	(17.25)	(3.97)	(27.60)	(48.82)
		TOTALS	**3,987.24**	**917.06**	**818.60**	**5,722.90**

Figure 5

VAT columns in the Sales daybook need to be evident for each rate of VAT, showing net values at each rate and the VAT amount at each rate.

Posting the Sales daybook to the ledger

Daly's Pharmacy customers are the business's **debtors**. These sales are assumed to be on credit, except for the Cash sales. The money received from the Cash sale will be recorded later in the Cash book. The Sales daybook is a record of all sales, showing the details of all sales invoices (and credit notes as negative values) grouped together. Daly's Pharmacy customers owe the amount on the above invoices to the business – so they represent an **asset** to the business – and are, therefore, posted to the **debit** side of the ledger. These customers will be listed in the Debtors ledger. The term 'debtors' derives from the word 'Debit', as they usually have a debit balance.

The total of **sales** is regarded as **income**. This effectively means that this amount should appear on the **credit** side of the ledger.

The VAT amounts need to be paid by Daly's Pharmacy to the Revenue Commissioners. This means that the business owes VAT to the Revenue at this moment, as VAT is on an invoice basis. This represents a **liability** to the business, which effectively means that there will be a **credit** entry in the VAT ledger account. Total debits will equal the total credits, as follows:

Debit: Customers/Debtors accounts with the *total* value of the invoices for the month.
Credit: Sales account with the *net* value of sales for the month.
Credit: VAT account with the *VAT* on these sales for the month.

Given that the net value and the VAT amount equal the total value of the invoices, our debits equal our credits.

The Debtors ledger accounts of Daly's Pharmacy Ltd appear as shown (fig. 6).

Debtors Ledger

James Mulcahy

DR					CR
Date	Details	Amount	Date	Details	Amount
8-Nov	Sales	2490.53			

Martha Downey

DR					CR
Date	Details	Amount	Date	Details	Amount
10-Nov	Sales	2257.19	23-Nov	Sales Returns	48.82
19-Nov	Sales	691.13			

Cash Sales

DR					CR
Date	Details	Amount	Date	Details	Amount
15-Nov	Sales	332.87			

Nominal Ledger

Sales A/C

DR					CR
Date	Details	Amount	Date	Details	Amount
			Nov	Sales	3987.24
			Nov	Sales	818.60

VAT A/C

DR					CR
Date	Details	Amount	Date	Details	Amount
			Nov	Sales	917.06

Figure 6

The individual entries are shown in the summary of ledger sales (fig. 7).

	Account	Debit	Credit	Account Type
Debit	James Mulcahy	2490.53		Increase in Asset
Debit	Martha Downey	2257.19		Increase in Asset
Debit	Cash Sales	332.87		Increase in Asset
Debit	Martha Downey	691.13		Increase in Asset
Credit	Martha Downey		48.82	Decrease in Asset
Credit	Sales A/c		3987.24	Increase in Income
Credit	Sales A/c		818.60	Increase in Income
Credit	VAT A/c		917.06	Increase in Liability
		5771.72	5771.72	

Figure 7

Cash book/Bank account

The Cash book/Bank account as a 'daybook' records what money the trader keeps in the bank. It shows what has been lodged (usually in the form of cash and cheques) and what has been taken out (usually by cheque payments).

The Cash book/Bank account is looked upon as a **daybook** to record lodgements and withdrawals from the business bank account, but it has a debit and a credit side. As a result, it forms part of the double-entry system of recording.

If the trader **lodges** money to the business bank account, this will result in an increase in an asset for the business and, accordingly, the lodgement is recorded on the *debit* side of the business bank account.

If the trader **withdraws** money from the business bank account, this will result in a decrease in an asset for the business and, accordingly, the withdrawal is recorded on the *credit* side of the business bank account.

The source documents for lodgements for a business are records of lodgement slips kept when money is lodged to the business bank account. Withdrawals of money from the business bank account are evidenced by cheque book stubs, copies of remittance advices and withdrawal slips.

Refer to your Student Resources for the lodgements and withdrawals of Daly's Pharmacy Ltd.

All lodgements and withdrawals are first entered in the Cash book (fig. 8).

On the debit side of the Cash book, an analysis column is kept, labelled 'Debtors', which records amounts received. This total will be used to complete a debtors control account later. An analysis of 'Creditors' is also shown on the withdrawals side for a creditors control account. These accounts are analysis columns only and are not part of a double-entry system.

Cash Book/Bank Account

DR — Lodgements   CR — Withdrawals

Date	Description	Slip. No		Debtors	Date	Description	Chq. No		Creditors
1-Nov	Capital	1	5000.00		2-Nov	Petty Cash	1199	300	
15-Nov	Cash Sales	2	332.87	332.87	2-Nov	Insurance	1200	520.00	
29-Nov	Martha Downey	3	2257.19	2257.19	20-Nov	Alchemy Ltd	1201	2699.60	2699.60
					21-Nov	United Drugs Ltd	1202	500.00	500.00
					29-Nov	Wages	1203	1780.00	
					30-Nov	Balance c/d		1790.46	
			7590.06	2,590.06				7590.06	3199.60
1-Dec	Balance b/d		1790.46						

Figure 8

Posting the Cash book to the ledger

As you can see, there is a debit and credit side to the Cash book, so half the double-entry has been completed at this stage. When this book is posted to the ledger, it will look as shown (fig. 9). The Cash book items posted are shown in *italics* and follow on from the previous ledger accounts.

Debtors Ledger

Cash Sales

DR					CR
Date	Details	Amount	Date	Details	Amount
15-Nov	Sales	332.87	*15-Nov*	*Bank*	*332.87*

Martha Downey

DR					CR
Date	Details	Amount	Date	Details	Amount
10-Nov	Sales	2257.19	23-Nov	Sales Returns	48.82
19-Nov	Sales	691.13	*29-Nov*	*Bank*	*2257.19*

Creditors Ledger

Alchemy Ltd

DR					CR
Date	Details	Amount	Date	Details	Amount
20-Nov	Bank	2699.60	2-Nov	Purchases	2699.60

United Drugs Ltd

DR					CR
Date	Details	Amount	Date	Details	Amount
15-Nov	Purchases Returns	196.32	4-Nov	Purchases	5708.55
21-Nov	Bank	500.00			

Nominal Ledger

Capital

DR					CR
Date	Details	Amount	Date	Details	Amount
			1-Nov	Bank	5000.00

Petty Cash

DR					CR
Date	Details	Amount	Date	Details	Amount
2-Nov	Bank	300.00			

Insurance

DR					CR
Date	Details	Amount	Date	Details	Amount
2-Nov	Bank	520.00			

Wages

DR					CR
Date	Details	Amount	Date	Details	Amount
29-Nov	Bank	1780.00			

Figure 9

To summarise the double-entry in relation to bank lodgements and payments, take note of the table (fig. 10), where each individual transaction is recorded. This follows the main rule of double-entry, which is:

- *Debit*: Assets and expenses
- *Credit:* Liabilities and income.

Transaction		Account	Debit	Credit	Type of Account
Owner lodges from private funds	Debit	Bank	5000.00		Increase in Asset
	Credit	Capital		5000.00	Increase in Liability
Receipt of Cash Sales	Debit	Bank	332.87		Increase in Asset
	Credit	Cash Sales		332.87	Decrease in Asset
Receipt from Martha Downey	Debit	Bank	2257.19		Increase in Asset
	Credit	Martha Downey		2257.19	Decrease in Asset
Paid money into Petty Cash	Debit	Petty Cash	300.00		Increase in Asset
	Credit	Bank		300.00	Decrease in Asset
Paid Insurance	Debit	Insurance	520.00		Increase in Expense
	Credit	Bank		520.00	Decrease in Asset
Paid Alchemy Ltd	Debit	Alchemy Ltd	2699.60		Decrease in Liability
	Credit	Bank		2699.60	Decrease in Asset
Paid United Drugs Ltd	Debit	United Drugs Ltd	500.00		Decrease in Liability
	Credit	Bank		500.00	Decrease in Asset
Paid Wages	Debit	Wages	1780.00		Increase in Expense
	Credit	Bank		1780.00	Decrease in Asset
			13389.66	13389.66	

Figure 10

Petty Cash book

Every business keeps a certain amount of cash on hand to pay for small purchase items, for which it may not be practical to write cheques. These items are recorded in the Petty Cash book. The Petty Cash book is also considered a **daybook** to record lodgements and withdrawals from petty cash, but it has a debit and a credit side.

If the trader **lodges** money to the petty cash account, this will result in an increase in an asset for the business and accordingly the lodgement is recorded on the *debit* side of the Petty Cash book.

If the trader **withdraws** money from petty cash, this will result in a decrease in assets for the business and accordingly the withdrawal is recorded on the *credit* side of the Petty Cash book.

Money is withdrawn from the bank current account at regular intervals to have cash on hand for these items of expenditure. A cheque was written on 2 November for €300 to be lodged to the Petty Cash. The Petty Cash account in the ledger will now be considered as a daybook, where there is already €300 on the debit side.

Refer to your Student Resources for the Petty Cash vouchers of Daly's Pharmacy Ltd.

Usually, on each occasion where cash is needed from petty cash, a voucher is completed listing the details of the purchase.

The Petty Cash book has the existing receipt of €300 on the debit side from the corresponding credit entry in the bank account (fig. 11). On the credit side, the payments from petty cash are recorded. The Petty Cash book has analysis columns to record the breakdown of expenses. For the purchase of diesel, the net value is shown in the Motor Expenses account and the VAT amount in the VAT account. The VAT on diesel is a non-resale purchase and can be claimed by the business in its accounts. The stamps are similarly analysed in a Printing & Postage account. The total of these analysis columns will be used for posting to the ledger. Remember that we only need the corresponding debits in the ledger as the credit is shown in the Total column. The Petty Cash book is balanced, showing a debit balance of €145 still remaining in petty cash.

Petty Cash Book

DR – Lodgements   CR – Withdrawals

Date	Description		Date	Description	Voucher No.	Total	Motor Expenses	Printing & Postage	Non-resale VAT @ 23%
2-Nov	Bank	300.00	17-Nov	Diesel	133	100.00	81.30		18.70
			20-Nov	Stamps	134	55.00		55.00	
			30-Nov	Balance c/d		145.00			
		300.00				300.00	81.30	55.00	18.70
1-Dec	Balance b/d	145.00							

Figure 11

Posting the Petty Cash book to the ledger

To post the Petty Cash book, the double entries are:

Receipt of €300

Debit: Petty Cash account.
Credit: Bank account.

This has already been completed in the Bank ledger and Petty Cash book. Money withdrawn from the bank to lodge to Petty Cash is known as an inter-bank transfer, where money is being transferred from one bank account to another.

Payment for diesel

Debit: Motor Expenses account, with the *net* value.
Debit: VAT account, with the VAT amount.
Credit: Petty Cash, as in the Petty Cash book.

Payment for stamps

Debit: Printing & Postage account.
Credit: Petty Cash, as in the Petty Cash book.

The Motor Expenses, Printing & Postage and VAT accounts will appear as shown (fig. 12).

Motor Expenses A/c

DR					CR
Date	Details	Amount	Date	Details	Amount
Nov	Petty Cash	81.30			

Printing & Postage A/c

DR					CR
Date	Details	Amount	Date	Details	Amount
Nov	Petty Cash	55.00			

VAT A/c

DR					CR
Date	Details	Amount	Date	Details	Amount
Nov	Petty Cash	18.70			

Figure 12

Balancing the ledger

If we now assemble all of the ledgers we have completed so far that have recorded purchases, purchases returns, sales, sales returns, bank lodgements, bank payments, petty cash receipts and petty cash payments together, we get a better picture of the activities of Daly's Pharmacy.

Remember, the ledger is classified into three different categories:

1. **Debtors ledger:** Records all the sales, returns and money received from each customer. This ledger is also known as the Sales ledger.
2. **Creditors ledger:** Records all the purchases, returns and money paid to each supplier. This ledger is also known as the Purchases ledger.
3. **Nominal ledger:** Records all the details of other ledgers – income, expenses, assets and liabilities. This ledger is also known as the General ledger.

The Debtors and Creditors ledgers are balanced at the end of each month with a balance brought down for the beginning of the next month. They are continuous, that is, the next month's transactions are entered after the previous month is balanced, where a new balance is calculated after each month. In essence, each customer and supplier would have a separate ledger sheet, where closing balances for each month are calculated.

The nominal ledger may be balanced if the need arises, that is, where there are entries on both the debit and credit side. This usually refers to the VAT ledger account in particular. Other nominal ledger accounts may not need to be balanced as such, that is, where there are entries only on one side. In this instance, the amount is subtotalled at the end of the month. The transactions for the following month are added to this subtotal to determine a running total for the ledger account.

Refer to your Student Resources for the completed ledgers of Daly's Pharmacy Ltd.

Debtors ledger

These are the accounts of all customers (i.e. debtors):

- Sales invoices are on the *debit*.
- Sales returns are on the *credit*.
- Amounts received from customers are on the *credit*.

The result usually is a debit balance, showing the amount that the customers still owe to the business at the end of the month.

Creditors ledger

These are the accounts of all suppliers (creditors):

- Purchase invoices are on the *credit*.
- Purchase returns are on the *debit*.
- Cheque payments are on the *debit*.

The result usually is a credit balance, showing the amount still owed to these suppliers at the end of the month.

Nominal ledger

These are all the asset, expenses, liabilities and income accounts. Remember, the Bank and Petty Cash accounts are part of these nominal ledger accounts:

- Assets, e.g. Bank and Petty Cash, have a debit balance.
- Expenses, e.g. Purchases, Insurance and Wages, have a debit balance or subtotal.
- Liabilities, e.g. Capital, have a credit balance or subtotal.
- Income, e.g. Sales, has a credit balance or subtotal.

The VAT account above shows a debit balance, which represents the amount owed by the Revenue to the trader. VAT on purchases is greater than VAT on sales, so the trader is due a refund of VAT, which in this case is an asset to the business.

Debtors and creditors control accounts

Before we prepare a Trial Balance for Daly's Pharmacy, we need to introduce the concept of debtors and creditors control accounts. As a Trial Balance is a 'summary' of the ledgers, there could be numerous debtors (customers) and creditors (suppliers) in most businesses. It would not be practical to list each customer and supplier in the Trial Balance. They have their own individual accounts in the ledgers previously shown. We need a 'Total Debtors account' and a 'Total Creditors account'; these accounts are called Debtors control and Creditors control respectively. All transactions for the month are totalled and recorded in these accounts.

Debtors control

Information for the debtors control account is taken from the following sources:

- **Sales Book:** We can derive the total sales, less returns, to debtors for the month by taking the total of all the invoices (less credit notes), inclusive of VAT.
- **Cash Book/Bank account:** Our 'Debtors' analysis column records the total cash received from debtors for the month.

The difference between the two sums will equal the total amount owed by all debtors to the business. This should equal the sum of the individual balances in each customer's account.

Creditors control

Information for the Creditors control account is taken from the following sources:

- **Purchases book:** We can derive the total purchases, less returns, to creditors for the month by taking the total of all the invoices (less credit notes) inclusive of VAT.
- **Cash book/Bank account:** Our 'Creditors' analysis column records the total payments made to creditors for the month.

The difference between the two sums will equal the total amount the business owes to the creditors. This should equal the sum of the individual balances in each supplier's account (fig. 13)

Creditors Control A/c

DR						CR
Date	Details	Amount	Date	Details		Amount
Nov	Bank	3199.60	Nov	Purchases		12224.21
	from Cash Book			*from Purchases Book*		
30-Nov	Balance c/d	9024.61				
		12224.21				12224.21
			1-Dec	Balance b/d		9024.61

Debtors Control A/c

DR						CR
Date	Details	Amount	Date	Details		Amount
Nov	Sales	5722.90	Nov	Bank		2590.06
	from Sales Book			*from Cash Book*		
			30-Nov	Balance c/d		3132.84
		5722.90				5722.90
1-Dec	**Balance b/d**	**3132.84**				

Figure 13

The purpose of the Debtors and Creditors control accounts is twofold:

1. It summarises the Debtors and Creditors balances for the Trial Balance.
2. It checks the accuracy of entries, as the sum of the debtors' and creditors' personal accounts should equal the total of the control accounts (fig. 14).

Creditors	Balance
Alchemy Ltd	0.00
United Drugs Ltd	5012.23
Stafford Lynch	3701.07
Electric Ireland	311.31
Total Balances	9024.61
Equals Balance on Creditors Control	**9024.61**

Debtors	Balance
James Mulcahy	2490.53
Martha Downey	642.31
Cash Sales	0.00
Total Balances	3132.84
Equals Balance on Debtors Control	**3132.84**

Figure 14

Trial Balance

The Trial Balance can now be prepared, which is simply a summary of all of the ledger accounts of the business. We will not use the personal ledgers of the customers and suppliers; we use the debtors and creditors control account balances instead. Remember, the Cash book/Bank account and Petty Cash book are, as such, ledger accounts, and have a balance that is part of the Trial Balance.

It is traditionally a characteristic of a Trial Balance to list the ledger accounts in order of:

1. Income ledger accounts
2. Expenses ledger accounts
3. Asset ledger accounts
4. Liability ledger accounts.

This order of accounts allows for easier and consistent preparation of the Trading Profit and Loss account and Balance Sheet (fig. 15).

Trial Balance of Daly's Pharmacy as at 30 November

Account	Debit €	Credit €
Sales		4,805.84
Purchases	9,939.50	
Light & Heat	274.28	
Insurance	520.00	
Wages	1,780.00	
Motor Expenses	81.30	
Printing & Postage	55.00	
Debtors	3,132.84	
Bank	1,790.46	
Petty Cash	145.00	
Creditors		9,024.61
VAT	1,112.07	
Capital		5,000.00
	18,830.45	18,830.45

Figure 15

The Trial Balance is not an account, but merely proves the mathematical equality of the debits and credits entered in the accounts. However, as stated earlier in the section, the Trial Balance has its limitations. Although it can be prepared at the end of each month, the most important Trial Balance for any business is the one prepared at the end of the accounting year, before any adjustments have been made to the accounts at the end of the year.

A Trading Profit and Loss account and Balance Sheet are prepared from the Trial Balance at the end of the accounting year, subject to any adjustments made to the accounts. This is demonstrated in Part 2.

Entering opening balances for the following month

If you are preparing the accounts for a business that has been trading for some time, you need to know the opening balances in the various ledger accounts, in order to continue with the accounts for the period to follow. In this case you will need:

- the closing Trial Balance at the end of the period
- a list of customer balances that make up the debtors in the Trial Balance
- a list of supplier balances that make up the creditors in the Trial Balance
- the closing Bank Statement balance.

In the Trial Balance for Daly's Pharmacy Ltd as at 30 November, each amount would be the opening balance in the respective ledger accounts for 1 December. For example, the opening balance in the Sales account for 1 December would be €4,805.84 on the credit side, the opening balance in the Purchases account would be €9,939.50 on the debit side, and so on. You would need to know the individual customer balances that amount to total debtors of €3,132.84, and the individual supplier balances that amount to total creditors of €9,024.61.

VAT Return forms

Normally VAT Return forms are submitted every two months to the Revenue, but if we wanted to record the VAT payable or repayable for Daly's Pharmacy Ltd for the month of November, it would be as follows:

To calculate the VAT on Sales and the VAT on Purchases, refer to the VAT account of Daly's Pharmacy Ltd. The debit side records the VAT on Purchases (which represents an asset to the business) and the credit side records the VAT on Sales (which represents a liability to the business).

VAT on Sales €917.06, entered in T1 box
VAT on Purchases €2,029.13, entered in T2 box
VAT refund due €1,112.07, entered in T4 box

These amounts are rounded to the nearest € in the VAT3 Return.

Refer to your Student Resources for the completed VAT3 Return of Daly's Pharmacy Ltd.

Review assignments

Assignment 1

To check your understanding of the double-entry principle, complete the following assignment.

Business name	Watchworld Ltd
Address	Main Street
	Athlone
	Co Westmeath
Telephone	094-12336
VAT reg. no.	IE1288572N
Business activity	Watch sales to retail shops on credit; watch repairs

The company commenced business on 1 March 2014. The business is registered for VAT, which is charged on the sale of watches at 23% and on repairs of watches at 13.5%.

Refer to your Student Resources for the Source Documents of Watchworld Ltd.

Record the details given below for the month of March 2014 in the appropriate daybooks, post to the ledger, balance the ledger and complete a Trial Balance for March 2014. Extract the required VAT details from the records and complete a VAT3 Form.

Assignment 2

The following details relate to Equipment Supplies Ltd. The accounts are completed up to 30 November 2014. The accounting year is from 1 January to 31 December 2014.

Business name	Equipment Supplies Ltd
Address	108 Abbott Street, Dublin 1
Telephone	01-872 3456
VAT reg. no.	IE 4567823H
Business activity	Sales and repair of office equipment

VAT is charged on sales at the standard rate of 23%. VAT is charged on repairs at the lower rate of 13.5%.

The accounts are completed to 30 November 2014 as per the Trial Balance, customer and supplier balances as shown (fig. 16).

TRIAL BALANCE of Equipment Supplies Ltd as at 30 November 2014

	Debit	Credit
Sales of goods		337,148
Repair Income		13,033
Opening Stock 1 Jan 2014	16,448	
Purchases	164,300	
Salaries	36,960	
Printing, Postage & Stationery	9,600	
Delivery Costs	690	
Telephone	1,842	
Light & Heat	1,790	
Rent	15,000	
Miscellaneous Expenses	123	
Bank Charges	247	
Furniture	34,500	
Office Equipment	29,000	
Bank	27,450	
Petty Cash	1,600	
Debtors	102,630	
Creditors		66,852
VAT Payable		2,656
Capital		22,491
	442,180	**442,180**

Note: VAT Payable equals VAT on Sales €5,448 and VAT on Purchases €2,792 (for the month of Nov 2014)

Debtors Balances as at 30 November 2014

NAME	BALANCE
O'Sullivan's Office Centre	24,912.00
Cal Computing	23,339.00
Earls Office Supplies	37,479.00
Joe Malone	16,900.00
TOTAL	**102,630.00**

Creditors Balances as at 30 November 2014

NAME	BALANCE
Electric Ireland	434.53
Eircom	508.32
Pentech Office Ltd	52,269.00
Tech Supplies Ltd	13,640.15
TOTAL	**66,852.00**

Figure 16

Refer to your Student Resources for the Source Documents of Equipment Supplies Ltd.

1. Open ledger accounts and enter the opening balances in the nominal ledger, debtors ledger and the creditors ledger. Open a bank account and petty cash account and enter the opening balance.

   The following additional information is available: The customer, O'Sullivan's Office Centre, has gone into liquidation and the balance outstanding in the account is to be written off as a bad debt as of 31 December 2014. Enter this transaction in the appropriate ledger. *Note:* The company is entitled to claim a refund of VAT for a specific bad debt write-off, which is 23% for this customer.

2. Record the details given in (1) above for the month of December 2014 in the appropriate daybooks, post to the ledger, balance the ledger and complete a Trial Balance for 31 December 2014. Extract the required VAT details from the records and complete a VAT3 Form for November/ December 2014.

Review questions

1. Fill in the missing blanks in the following sentences:
   a. A debit entry goes on the _____-hand side of the ledger and a _____ entry goes on the right-hand side of the ledger.
   b. _____ compile lists of similar transactions and are usually totalled at the end of each month.
   c. A _____ is an individual or company who is owed money by one or more_____.
   d. All transactions in an account have a _____-fold effect.
   e. For every _____ entry, there must be a credit entry.
   f. The excess of income over expenses is called _____.
   g. A _____ is a separate legal entity distinct from its owners.
   h. Owners of a company are called _____.
   i. Ordinary shareholders are not entitled to a _____ dividend each year.

2. Which of the following is *not* an asset:
   a. debtors
   b. loan
   c. buildings
   d. Cash at Bank.

3. Which of the following is a liability:
   a. insurance
   b. creditors
   c. machinery.

4. The double-entry principle of bookkeeping involves at least:
   a. one entry
   b. two entries
   c. three entries.

1.4 Bank Reconciliation

Learning outcomes (Accounting Manual and Computerised 5N1348): 9 (part)
Learning outcomes (Bookkeeping Manual and Computerised 5N1354): 6

The bank account of a business contains a record of the transactions (e.g. cheques written, receipts from customers) that involve its bank current account. The bank also keeps a record of the current account of the business, when it processes cheques, receives lodgements, incurs service charges, and other items. Soon after the end of each month, the bank usually provides a bank statement to the business. The bank statement lists the activity in the bank account during the recent month, as well as the balance at the beginning and end of the month.

When it receives a bank statement, the business should verify that the amounts are consistent or compatible with the amounts in the bank current account in its general ledger and vice versa. This process of confirming the amounts is referred to as **bank reconciliation**.

Because most businesses write numerous cheques each month and make many lodgements, reconciling the amounts on its books with the amounts on the bank statement can be time consuming. The process is complicated, because some items appear in the business bank account in one month, but appear on the bank statement in a different month. For example, cheques written near the end of the month are deducted immediately on the business books, but those cheques are likely to be presented to the bank early the following month. Sometimes the bank reduces the bank account balance without informing the business of the amount. For example, a bank service charge might be deducted on the bank statement, but the business will not learn of the amount until it receives the bank statement.

From these two examples, you can understand why there is likely to be a difference between the balance on the bank statement and the balance in the bank account on the business books. It is also possible that neither balance is the true balance. Both balances may need adjustment in order to report the true amount of cash held in the bank current account at a particular date.

The steps in a bank reconciliation are:

* Step 1 – Adjust the balance per bank
* Step 2 – Adjust the balance per business books
* Step 3 – Compare the adjusted balances
* Step 4 – Finalise the double-entries.

Step 1 – Adjust the balance per bank

The first step is to adjust the balance on the bank statement to the true, adjusted or corrected balance. The items necessary for this step are listed below.

Balance as per bank statement

Add	Lodgements not credited to bank
Deduct	Cheques not presented for payment
Add/deduct	Bank errors

= Corrected bank balance.

Lodgements not credited to bank are amounts already received and recorded by the business, but are not yet recorded by the bank. For example, a retail store lodges its cash receipts of 31 July into the bank's night safe. The bank will process this deposit on the morning of 1 August. As of 31 July (the bank statement date) this is a deposit not yet credited to the bank's account.

Therefore, these lodgements need to be listed on the bank reconciliation as an increase to the balance per bank in order to report the true amount of cash.

Cheques not presented for payment are cheques that have been written and recorded in the business bank account, but have not yet cleared the bank's account. Cheques written during the last few days of the month plus a few older cheques are likely to be among those outstanding.

These outstanding cheques have not yet reached the bank or the bank statement. Therefore, outstanding cheques are listed on the bank reconciliation as a decrease in the balance per bank.

Bank errors are mistakes made by the bank. Bank errors could include the bank recording an incorrect amount, entering an amount that does not belong on a business bank statement, or omitting an amount from a business bank statement. The business should notify the bank of its errors. Depending on the error, the correction could increase or decrease the balance shown on the bank statement.

Step 2 – Adjust the balance per the business books

The second step is to adjust the balance in the business bank account so that it is the true, adjusted or corrected balance. Examples of the items involved are listed below.

Balance per business bank account

Deduct	Bank charges and fees
Deduct	Cheques dishonoured by the bank (bounced cheques)
Deduct	Direct debits and standing orders not recorded
Add	Credit transfers or electronic funds transfers not recorded
Add/deduct	Errors in the business bank account

= Corrected bank balance.

Bank charges and fees are deducted from the bank statement for the bank's processing of the current account (e.g. accepting lodgements, posting cheques, mailing the bank statement). Other types of bank service charges include the fee and interest charged when a business overdraws its current account, cheque printing charges and the bank referral fee for processing a stopped or bounced cheque. The bank deducts these charges or fees on the bank statement without notifying the business. When this occurs, the business usually learns of these amounts only after receiving its bank statement.

Because the bank charges and fees have already been deducted on the bank statement, there is no adjustment to the balance per bank. However, the charges will have to be entered as an adjustment to the business books. The business bank account will need to be decreased by the amount of these charges. The double-entry in the ledger accounts will be to:

Debit: Bank charges expense account
Credit: Bank account.

Cheques dishonoured are cheques that were rejected by the bank because an account did not have a sufficient balance. As a result, the cheque is returned without being honoured or paid. The bank usually describes these cheques in the bank statement as 'unpaid cheques'. When an unpaid cheque comes back to the bank in which it was deposited, the bank will decrease the bank account of the business that had deposited the cheque. The amount charged will be the amount of the cheque plus a referral fee.

If the business has not yet decreased its bank account balance for the returned cheque and the referral fee, the business must decrease the balance per books in order to reconcile. The double-entry in the ledger accounts will be as follows:

Debit: Customer (debtor) who paid the dishonoured cheque
Credit: Bank account

with the value of the cheque, *and*

Debit: Bank charges expense account
Credit: Bank account with the referral fee.

Direct debits and standing orders are instructions to the bank to make payments. A standing order is an instruction to make regular payments of a fixed amount, either to another person or to another account of the business. This would be common where a business may be transferring money from the current account to a savings account. A direct debit is an authority given by the business to allow a person or another business to claim money from its bank account to meet bills or repay loans. Direct debits are variable in amount and frequency. For example, many businesses arrange for telephone, gas and electricity bills to be paid in this way. The crucial difference is that with a direct debit, the retailer can make amendments without the need to obtain the customer's signature on each occasion.

The business may not have recorded these payments from its bank, or may decide to simply wait for the bank statement to record such items in the ledger accounts. These payments will decrease the bank balance of the business. The double-entry in the ledger accounts will be to:

Debit: Supplier (creditor)
Credit: Bank account
Or
Debit: Loan account if paying loan instalments
Credit: Bank account.

Credit transfers or electronic funds transfers are commonly known as 'EFT' or electronic funds transfers. This is the electronic exchange or transfer of money from one account to another through computer-based systems. Many customers presently pay the amount owed to the business by electronic funds transfer. The business may not be aware of this until receipt of the bank statement. Therefore, the business needs to increase its bank balance by the amount of money lodged by its customers. The double-entry in the ledger accounts will be to:

Debit: Bank account
Credit: Customer (debtor) who paid the money.

Errors in the business bank account are incorrect amounts entered, transactions that do not belong in the account, or omitted transactions that should be in the account. Since the business made these errors, the correction of the error will be either an increase or a decrease to the balance in the bank account on the business books.

Step 3 – Compare the adjusted balances

After adjusting the balance per bank (Step 1) and the balance per books (Step 2), the two adjusted amounts should be equal. If they are not equal, the process must be repeated until the balances are identical. The balances should be the true and correct amount of cash as of the date of the bank reconciliation.

Step 4 – Finalise the double-entries

If not already done, the double-entries must be prepared for the adjustments to the balance per books (Step 2). Adjustments to increase the bank balance will require a double-entry that debits the Bank account and credits another account. Adjustments to decrease the bank balance will require a credit to the Bank account and a debit to another account.

Example 1

The Bank account of Daly's Pharmacy was completed in section 1.3.(8) and is produced again here, along with the bank statement received from the bank (fig. 1).

Bank Statement

Irish Bank
Salthill, Galway

Your account name: Daly's Pharmacy Ltd

Current account

Account no: 19385298
Statement date: 30-Nov-13

Date	Transaction details	Payments out	Payments in	Balance
	Balance forward			0.00
1-Nov	Lodgement		5000.00	5,000.00
2-Nov	Cheque 1199	300.00		4,700.00
2-Nov	Cheque book Govt Duty	25.00		4,675.00
6-Nov	Cheque 1200	520.00		4,155.00
15-Nov	Lodgement		332.87	4,487.87
28-Nov	Cheque 1201	2699.60		1,788.27
29-Nov	Bank charges	25.63		1,762.64
30-Nov	James Mulcahy EFT		1000.00	2,762.64

Cash Book/Bank Account

DR – Lodgements   CR – Withdrawals

Date	Description	Slip. No		Debtors	Date	Description	Chq. No		Creditors
1-Nov	Capital	1	5000.00		2-Nov	Petty Cash	1199	300	
15-Nov	Cash Sales	2	332.87	332.87	2-Nov	Insurance	1200	520.00	
29-Nov	Martha Downey	3	2257.19	2257.19	20-Nov	Alchemy Ltd	1201	2699.60	2699.60
					21-Nov	United Drugs Ltd	1202	500.00	500.00
					29-Nov	Wages	1203	1780.00	
					30-Nov	Balance c/d		1790.46	
			7590.06	2,590.06				7590.06	3199.60
1-Dec	Balance b/d		1790.46						

Figure 1

Let us prepare a bank reconciliation for Daly's Pharmacy (fig. 2). The steps are:

Step 1: Adjust the balance per bank: to the true, adjusted or corrected balance.

Step 2: Adjust the balance per the business books so that the balance in the business bank account is the true, adjusted or corrected balance.

Adjusted Bank Balance	€
Balance as per Bank Statement	2,762.64
Add: Lodgements not credited to bank	
Martha Downey	2,257.19
Deduct: Cheques not presented for payment	
United Drugs – Cheque 1202	-500.00
Wages – Cheque 1203	-1,780.00
= Corrected Bank Balance	**2,739.83**

Corrected Bank Account	€
Balance as per business bank account	1,790.46
Deduct: Bank charges and fees	
Cheque book govt duty	-25.00
Bank charges	-25.63
Add: electronic transfers	
James Mulcahy	1,000.00
= Corrected Bank Balance	**2,739.83**

Figure 2

Step 3: Compare the adjusted balances so that, after adjusting the balance per bank and the balance per books, the two adjusted amounts are equal. As above, the true balance in the bank account of Daly's Pharmacy is €2,739.83.

Step 4: Complete the double-entries that must be prepared for the adjustments to the balance per books. Adjustments to increase the bank balance will require a double-entry that debits bank and credits another account. Adjustments to decrease the bank balance will require a credit to bank and a debit to another account.

The ledger accounts of Daly's Pharmacy to account for the above adjustments will be as shown (fig. 3).

Debtors Ledger

James Mulcahy

DR						CR
Date	Details	Amount	Date	Details		Amount
8-Nov	Sales	2490.53	30-Nov	Bank EFT		1000.00
			30-Nov	Balance c/d		1490.53
		2490.53				2490.53
1-Dec	Balance b/d	1490.53				

Nominal Ledger

Bank Charges A/c

DR						CR
Date	Details	Amount	Date	Details		Amount
2-Nov	Cheque book govt duty	25.00				
29-Nov	Bank charges	25.63				
		50.63				

Figure 3

James Mulcahy paid €1,000 by electronic funds transfer. The double-entry is:

Debit: Bank account
Credit: James Mulcahy, leaving a closing balance on his account of €1,490.53.

Cheque book duty and bank charges are recorded as:

Debit: Bank charges expense account
Credit: Bank account.

After these adjustments are entered in the ledger accounts, a revised Trial
Balance would then be prepared. The revised Trial Balance is shown (fig. 4).

Revised Trial Balance of Daly's Pharmacy as at 30 November

Account	Debit	Credit
Sales		4,805.84
Purchases	9,939.50	
Light & Heat	274.28	
Insurance	520.00	
Wages	1,780.00	
Motor Expenses	81.30	
Printing & Postage	55.00	
Bank Charges	50.63	
Debtors	2,132.84	
Bank	2,739.83	
Petty Cash	145.00	
Creditors		9,024.61
VAT	1,112.07	
Capital		5,000.00
	18,830.45	18,830.45

Figure 4

Example 2

The bank statement of Doyle Ltd, dated 31 December, showed a balance of €24,594.72. The business bank account on the same date showed a balance of €23,196.79. The following information is available after comparing the bank account with the bank statement:

- The following cheques were paid by the business, but are still outstanding:
  - Cheque 123 for €320.00
  - Cheque 128 for €49.21
  - Cheque 129 for €275.00
  - Cheque 136 for €186.50.
- A lodgement made on 31 December of €400 does not appear on the bank statement.
- The following items have *not* been recorded by Doyle Ltd:
  - There appears on the bank statement an unpaid cheque of €850. The bank charged a referral fee of €3.30.
  - Bank fees of €46.70 appear on the bank statement.
  - Interest income on the business's average bank balance was €187.22.
  - A customer paid by EFT an amount of €1,590 directly into the bank account.
  - A lodgement of €430 was incorrectly entered as €340 in the business's bank account.

Prepare a bank reconciliation statement for Doyle Ltd as at 31 December (fig. 5).

BANK RECONCILIATION of Doyle Ltd as at 31 December

Adjusted Bank Balance	€
Balance as per Bank Statement	24,594.72
Add: Lodgements not credited to bank	
Lodgement	400.00
Deduct: Cheques not presented for payment	
Cheque 123	-320.00
Cheque 128	-49.21
Cheque 129	-275.00
Cheque 136	-186.50
= Corrected Bank Balance	**24,164.01**

Corrected Bank Account	€
Balance as per business bank account	23,196.79
Deduct: Unpaid cheques:	
Unpaid Cheque	-850.00
Deduct: Bank charges and fees	
Referral fee	-3.30
Bank fees	-46.70
Add: Electronic transfers	
Interest income	187.22
Customer EFT	1,590.00
Add: Error by business	
Lodgement understated	90.00
= Corrected Bank Balance	**24,164.01**

Figure 5

The balances match to give a corrected bank balance of €24,164.01. The ledger accounts to record the omitted entries would be:

Unpaid cheque:
Debit: Customer €850
Credit: Bank account €850.

Bank charges and fees:
Debit: Bank charges €50
Credit: Bank account €50.

Electronic transfers:
Debit: Bank account €187.22
Credit: Interest income account €187.22.
Debit: Bank account €1,590
Credit: Customer €1,590.

Error by business:
Debit: Bank account (the lodgement was understated)
Credit: Account where error was found.

Review assignments

Assignment 1

The bank statement received by Watchworld Ltd is displayed below (fig. 6).
Prepare a bank reconciliation statement for Watchworld Ltd and a corrected
bank account. Use your bank account prepared for Watchworld Ltd in review
assignment 1, section 1.3.

Bank Statement

Irish Bank
Athlone
Co Westmeath

To: Watchworld Ltd
Main Street
Athlone
Co Westmeath
Your account name: Watchworld Ltd
Current account

Account no: 33312202
Statement date: 31-Mar-14

Date	Transaction details	Payments out	Payments in	Balance
	Balance forward			0.00
1-Mar	Lodgement		44,000.00	44,000.00
2-Mar	Cheque book Govt Duty	25.00		43,975.00
6-Mar	Cheque 1001	5,240.00		38,735.00
27-Mar	Cheque 1002	6,634.52		32,100.48
28-Mar	Lodgement		6,063.90	38,164.38
29-Mar	Bank charges	25.63		38,138.75
30-Mar	Cheque 1003	10,000.00		28,138.75

Figure 6

Enter the transactions that are not recorded by Watchworld Ltd into the
ledger accounts and produce a revised Trial Balance for the business as at
31 March 2014.

Assignment 2

Figure 7 shows the bank account and bank statement of Smart Designs at 30
September 2014.

Bank Statement

National Bank
6 Jones Square
Waterford

Account Name: Smart Designs
Account No: 55963154
Date: 30 September 2014

Date	Details	Debit	Credit	Balance
1-Sep	Balance			406.93
12-Sep	Cheque 653	256.36		150.57
13-Sep	Cheque 652	1,500.00		-1,349.43
15-Sep	Cheque book Govt Duty	25.00		-1,374.43
16-Sep	Lodgement		2,000.00	625.57
17-Sep	Lodgement		158.68	784.25
19-Sep	Jim Gordan EFT		600.00	1,384.25
22-Sep	Cheque 650	654.65		729.60
23-Sep	Lodgement		100.00	829.60
24-Sep	Loan repayment	2,029.00		-1,199.40
24-Sep	Lodgement		3,698.00	2,498.60
25-Sep	Unpaid cheque	100.00		2,398.60
25-Sep	Referral fee	3.30		2,395.30
26-Sep	Vodafone DD	564.20		1,831.10
26-Sep	Lodgement		5,600.00	7,431.10
30-Sep	Interest	5.60		7,425.50

Bank Account – Smart Designs

Date	Details	Ref No.	€	Date	Chq. No.	Details	€
1-Sep	Balance b/d		406.93	3-Sep	650	Axel Ltd	654.65
16-Sep	Mary Hudson	12	2,000.00	4-Sep	651	Insurance	4,000.00
17-Sep	Kelly Morris	13	158.68	5-Sep	652	Computer Supplies Ltd	1,500.00
23-Sep	Peter Hill	14	100.00	10-Sep	653	Time Solutions Ltd	256.36
24-Sep	Liam Potter	15	3,698.00	24-Sep	654	Rent	900.00
26-Sep	Walter Knight	16	5,600.00	30-Sep	655	Wages	500.00
30-Sep	John Corbett	17	580.00	30-Sep		Balance c/d	4,732.60
			12,543.61				12,543.61
1-Oct	Balance b/d		4,732.60				

Figure 7

1. Prepare a bank reconciliation statement for Smart Designs.
2. Prepare a corrected bank account, showing the corrected bank balance.
3. List the double-entries required in the ledger accounts for Smart Designs to take account of entries not already made in the accounts.

Part 2

Final Accounts

2.1 Trading, Profit and Loss Account and Balance Sheet

Learning outcomes (Accounting Manual and Computerised 5N1348): 7 (part) and 10 (part)

Once ledger accounts have been written up and a Trial Balance prepared, we can now prepare final accounts for a business. These final accounts are the Trading account, Profit and Loss account (usually referred to as 'Trading, Profit and Loss') and the Balance Sheet. However, before preparing these accounts, we must examine the role of stock.

Stock

To include the correct amount of stock in the final accounts, it would be useful to understand the mechanics surrounding the movements in stock. Stock represents the purchases of goods of a business that are for resale to its customers and are still on hand at the end of the accounting period. It is most unlikely that all of the purchases that have been made during the year will be sold by the end of the year, so some stock will almost certainly be carried forward to the next accounting year.

Trading account

The **Trading account** calculates the **gross profit** for the period and here it will be necessary to make some allowance for stock unsold at the end of the period, since we want to match the 'Cost of Goods Sold' and not the cost of all those goods actually purchased during the period, with the sales income for that same period. This adheres to the 'matching concept' discussed in Part 1. Consequently, we need to check the quantity of stock on hand at the end of the period and put some value on it; this is normally its cost value.

Stock on hand at the end of the accounting period, which is unsold, is referred to in accounts as 'closing stock'. This closing stock becomes the 'opening stock' for the next period. In calculating the Cost of Goods Sold, we have to allow for opening stock at the beginning of the period and closing stock at the end of the period. The cost of goods sold (also known as cost of sales) can be easily calculated by the following formula:

Cost of Sales = (Opening Stock + Purchases) – Closing Stock.

Example

Jacobs Ltd has been trading for a number of years. At the beginning of the year, it had stock of €8,000 (which will be sold this year). During the year it purchased stock to the value of €85,000. At the end of the year, it had closing stock of €11,500 (stock unsold during the year). Its sales for the year were €140,000. The table calculates the gross profit for the year.

	€	€
Sales		140,000
Less Cost of Sales:		
Opening Stock	8,000	
Add Purchases	85,000	
= Cost of Goods available for sale	93,000	
Less Closing Stock	-11,500	
= Cost of Sales/Cost of Goods Sold		
Gross Profit		81,500
		58,500

Sales are valued at 'retail price' to the customer. Purchases, opening stock and closing stock are valued at 'cost price'. Gross profit is essentially the difference between retail price and cost price of the goods that are sold for the period, that is, Sales *less* Cost of Sales. The Trading Account above matches the sales income for the year against the cost of those goods for the same period.

Profit and Loss account

A **Profit and Loss account** is prepared after the Trading account, where the gross profit is adjusted to include other income and expenses of the business. The difference between gross profit, *plus* other income, *less* other expenses, is known as **net profit**, (or net loss). We can use the following equations:

Sales – Cost of Sales = Gross Profit (or Loss)
Gross Profit + other income – other expenses = Net Profit (or Loss).

The Trading, Profit and Loss account are both accounts in their own right and form part of the double-entry system, so a corresponding entry has to be made in some other account. The expenses that are part of the Profit and Loss account are classified as revenue expenditure.

Balance Sheet

Once the Trading, Profit and Loss account balances have been extracted from the Trial Balance, the second stage in the preparation of final accounts is to summarise the balances that are left in the form of a statement called a Balance Sheet. It is simply a listing of all the remaining balances that are left in the ledger, following the preparation of the Trading, Profit and Loss account. The Balance Sheet does not form part of the double-entry system; it is merely a summary of remaining balances, these remaining balances are all the assets and liabilities of the business.

In summary, the Trading, Profit and Loss account records all the expenses and income from the Trial Balance to arrive at net profit. The balance of the Profit and Loss account (i.e. net profit) is carried to the Capital account in the Balance Sheet

The Balance Sheet lists all the assets and liabilities from the Trial Balance at the end of the period. The Balance Sheet also acts as a check on the mathematical accuracy of the accounts; assets should equal liabilities *plus* capital (including the net profit or loss).

Let us prepare a Trading, Profit and Loss account and Balance Sheet of Daly's Pharmacy from the Trial Balance extracted in section 1.3(15) reproduced below.

Trial Balance of Daly's Pharmacy as at 30 November

Account	Debit	Credit
Sales		4,805.84
Purchases	9,939.50	
Light & Heat	274.28	
Insurance	520.00	
Wages	1,780.00	
Motor Expenses	81.30	
Printing & Postage	55.00	
Debtors	3,132.84	
Bank	1,790.46	
Petty Cash	145.00	
Creditors		9,024.61
VAT	1,112.07	
Capital		5,000.00
	18,830.45	18,830.45

We will assume that 30 November is the end of the Daly's Pharmacy accounting year, as final accounts are normally prepared at the end of the accounting year. We will also assume that the business has no opening stock and that the closing stock at 30 November (goods purchased but not sold) is valued at €8,000 (fig. 1).

Trading Profit and Loss Account of Daly's Pharmacy as at 30 November

	€	€
Sales		4,805.84
Less Cost of Sales:		
Opening Stock	-	
Add Purchases	9,939.50	
= Cost of goods available for sale	9,939.50	
Less Closing Stock	-8,000.00	
= Cost of Sales		1,939.50
= Gross Profit		2,866.34
Less Expenses:		
Light & Heat	274.28	
Insurance	520.00	
Wages	1,780.00	
Motor Expenses	81.30	
Printing & Postage	55.00	
TOTAL expenses		2,710.58
= Net Profit		**155.76**

Balance Sheet of Daly's Pharmacy as at 30 November

	€	€
FIXED ASSETS		Nil
Current Assets:		
Closing Stock	8,000.00	
Debtors	3,132.84	
Bank	1,790.46	
Petty Cash	145.00	
VAT refund due	1,112.07	
TOTAL Current Assets	14,180.37	
Current Liabilities:		
Creditors	9,024.61	
Net Current Assets		5,155.76
		5,155.76
Financed by:		
Capital		5,000.00
Add Net Profit		155.76
		5,155.76

Figure 1

The main features of the Balance Sheet are classified as:

* **Fixed Assets:** the assets acquired for use within the business, which are not for resale, e.g. machinery, premises, land, vehicles. The expenditure on fixed assets is known as capital expenditure.
* **Current Assets:** the assets acquired for conversion into cash in the ordinary course of business. Such current assets include closing stock that will be sold in the next accounting year, debtors from whom payment will be received in the next accounting year, and closing bank and cash balances. VAT is a current asset in the Balance Sheet (fig. 1), as Daly's Pharmacy is due a refund of VAT from Revenue.
* **Current Liabilities:** the amounts owed by the businesses that are expected to be paid within a year from the Balance Sheet date, e.g. creditors, short loans and overdrafts, amounts owed to Revenue to include tax, PRSI (pay-related social insurance) and VAT. The difference between current assets and current liabilities is called Net Current Assets or Working Capital. When a business has excess current assets over current liabilities, it is able to pay its debts in the short term and has a positive working capital. The fixed assets amount (in fig. 1) is added to the net current assets to arrive at the total assets of the business, in this case €5,155.76.
* **'Financed by':** the owner's interest in the business. It is represented by the capital invested in the business increased by the net profit earned.

In almost all businesses, there are items listed after the Trial Balance. These are called post-trial balance adjustments, which will come to light after the ledger accounts have been balanced and closed and the Trial Balance is prepared. In other words, no entry has been made in the accounts for these items. Such items include depreciation, accruals, prepayments and bad debts, which will be covered later.

Before preparing further final accounts, a distinction needs to be made between a sole trader and a limited company.

Sole trader

Sole traders are the key contributors to our domestic economy. The term 'sole trader' describes a business owned by one person who is personally responsible for the debts of the business, so creditors can sue his/her personal assets. Sole traders are usually limited in resources, particularly capital. All profits made by sole traders belong to them and are added to capital at the end of the year. Any withdrawals of cash or assets for the sole trader's personal use are treated as drawings, which reduce the capital at the end of the year.

It is relatively simple to set up as a sole trader. The main legal obligation is that sole traders must register as self-employed persons with the Office of the Revenue Commissioners. If they wish to use a business name, other than their own true name, they must register the business name with the Companies Registration Office (CRO).

Many small businesses in Ireland began as sole traders, who have the day-to-day responsibility for operating their business.

Advantages and disadvantages of sole traders

The advantages of being a sole trader include:

- A sole trader business is the easiest business structure to start and maintain. Although sole traders have to comply with tax registration, there is no formal paperwork to establish the business.
- Sole traders own all the assets of the business and have full control over the business activities. They enjoy the profits alone and decision making is easy.

The disadvantages include:

- A sole trader has no existence apart from the individual. Sole traders may own all the assets of the business, but they also own all the liabilities. Many suppliers will require sole traders to provide a personal guarantee when purchasing stock. This means that if the business fails and cannot pay a supplier, the creditor can legally come after the sole trader's personal property. The sole trader has unlimited liability and also many responsibilities to take on alone.
- A sole trader also has limited sources of capital.

Limited company

A limited company is a business owned by more than one individual, where these individuals are called shareholders. The business is a separate legal entity, which means that if the company gets into debt, the creditors generally only have a claim on the assets of the company. The shareholders' losses are limited, hence the term 'limited company'.

The company name must be registered with the CRO and the company's reports and accounts must be returned to the CRO each year. The company is managed by directors, who need not be shareholders and who are appointed at the Annual General Meeting (AGM). Companies can be either:

- Public Limited Companies (PLC) – usually large entities whose shares are quoted on the stock exchange
- Private Limited Companies (Ltd) – whose shares are not traded on the stock exchange. These companies are usually medium or small in size and are often family businesses.

For a private limited company to form there must be at least two directors. Every limited company must have a Company Secretary. This may be one of the named directors or another person. The directors can be of any nationality but one of the company directors must be 'resident' in a member state of the European Economic Area (EEA). The directors who work in the company are employees of the company and receive a salary, which is taxed under the PAYE system.

To form a limited company, an application form (Form A1) is completed and submitted with a Memorandum and Articles of Association.

The **Memorandum of Association** states the objectives of the company and the type of trade it will engage in. The amount of share capital invested in the company by the shareholders will also be stated. It consists of clauses that state:

* the name of the company, including the address of the registered office
* the objects of the company, i.e. the business activities it intends to carry on
* the share capital of the company, divided into different classes of shares
* the limited liability clause, stating the company possesses limited liability.

The **Articles of Association** defines the right of the shareholders and the internal rules of operation of the company. It may deal with such matters as directors' duties, voting procedures, payment of dividends and raising of capital.

After incorporation, the company will need to register with the Revenue Commissioners for such requirements as corporation tax and VAT. It will also need to maintain the necessary statutory registers of the company – an Annual Return will need to be filed six months after incorporation, and every year thereafter. Accounts must be prepared and filed each year, and in certain cases, audited accounts may be required.

Share capital

Companies finance their operations in many ways, but limited companies raise money mainly by issuing shares. Purchasers of these shares pay money to the company and become owners as a result. The debt to the shareholders is called 'share capital' and is found in the 'Capital and Reserves' section of the Balance Sheet. As discussed in section 1.1, there are two types of shares, ordinary and preference shares.

The 'authorised' share capital of a company is the total number of shares that can be issued in the company. The 'issued' or paid-up share capital comprises the shares that have been allotted and paid for by the shareholders.

Advantages and disadvantages of limited companies

The advantages of limited companies are as follows:

* A limited company is a legal entity in its own right. The owners/ shareholders are not personally liable for the company's debts as long as it has not traded fraudulently or not given personal guarantees for bank

borrowings or to suppliers. Creditors can only look for payment from the company and this can only be settled out of the company assets.

- Once the company name is registered as a limited company, the name is legally protected and it cannot be used by other businesses.
- A limited company can expand the number of owners to acquire additional funding or to acquire new skills. It generally has greater access to banks.

The disadvantages of limited companies are as follows:

- To incorporate a company, Form A1 must be completed and submitted with a memorandum and articles of association to the CRO. This can incur costs to the business.
- Limited companies need to file an annual return (Form B1) and accounts with the CRO, which is openly available to the public.
- If a company makes a loss, the loss may not be set against personal income of any shareholder.
- There is a need for accounts to comply with Companies Acts together with auditing and accounting standards for larger companies.

Here is a comprehensive comparison between the two forms:

	Sole trader	Limited company
Need to register business name?	Yes, but only if different from own true name	Yes
Statutory regulation required?	No	Yes. A limited company must abide by the regulations of the *Companies Act*.
Who owns the business?	Sole trader	Shareholders
Who manages the business?	Sole trader	Board of directors appointed by shareholders
Has the business limited liability?	No	Yes
Is the business a separate legal entity?	No	Yes
Does the business change when the owners change?	Yes	No

	Sole trader	Limited company
What is the employment status?	Self-employed. A sole trader cannot be his/ her own employee.	A director is treated as an office holder of the company. If the director works in the company, he/she is also an employee.
How do the owners extract profits from the business?	By drawings, which will reduce capital of the business	By payment of dividends and/or salary, which will reduce profits of the business
How are profits taxed?	At sole trader's income tax rate	At corporation tax rate of 12.5%
What are the tax return obligations?	Pays tax at end of tax year under self-assessment by filing Form 11 with the Revenue.	Directors who work in the company are employees and are taxed during the year under the PAYE system. The company pays corporation tax on profits at end of the accounting year by filing Form CT1.
Is the business required to file accounts?	No	Yes. Must file Annual Return and accounts with CRO, which for larger companies need to be audited.

Review assignments

Assignment 1

Figure 2 shows the Trial Balance of James Farrell, a sole trader, for the year ended 31 December 2014.

Closing Stock at 31 December 2014 is valued at €4,400.

Prepare a Trading, Profit and Loss account and Balance Sheet of James Farrell for the year end.

Trial Balance of James Farrell as at 31 December 2014

	Debit	Credit
Sales		89,000
Opening Stock	9,500	
Purchases	26,200	
Rent and Rates	600	
Light & Heat	490	
Wages	15,000	
Discounts Allowed	45	
Motor Expenses	540	
Bank Charges	120	
Telephone	584	
Equipment	60,000	
Motor Vehicles	12,000	
Debtors	28,500	
Bank Current account	2,522	
Petty Cash	62	
Creditors		6,941
VAT Payable		222
Capital		85,000
Drawings	25,000	
	181,163	**181,163**

Figure 2

Assignment 2

Figure 3 shows the Trial Balance of Kelly Ltd, a private limited company, for the year ended 30 June 2014.

Closing Stock at 30 June 2014 is valued at €14,300.

Prepare a Trading, Profit and Loss account and Balance Sheet of Kelly Ltd for the year end.

Trial Balance of Kelly Ltd for year ended 30 June 2014

	Debit	Credit
Sales		150,000
Stock 1 July 2013	10,000	
Purchases	89,000	.
Carriage Inwards	555	
Director's fees	36,000	
Staff salaries	22,721	
Telephone	2,500	
Insurance	8,000	
Interest paid	590	
Bank Charges	364	
Motor Expenses	560	
Administration expenses	6,500	
Discounts Allowed	120	
Discounts Received		165
Plant & Machinery	89,000	
Debtors	36,000	
Bank Current Account		4,100
Administration expenses	870	
Creditors		52,114
VAT Payable	2,010	
Share Capital		50,000
Retained Profit		3,411
Long-term Loan		45,000
	304,790	**304,790**

Figure 3

Review questions

1. State whether each item below is included in the Trading, Profit and Loss Account or Balance Sheet:
   a. Costs incurred for insurance
   b. Amounts paid to directors of a company
   c. Income received for services performed
   d. Amounts paid to a sole trader
   e. Cash paid to purchase a new factory
   f. Amounts paid to employees
   g. Amounts paid for purchases of trading stock
   h. Loan from the bank
   i. Office supplies on hand at the end of the year
   j. Total debts outstanding at the end of the year
   k. Ordinary shares

l. Rent received from tenant using business premises

m. Cash taken by owner to finance private assets.

2. State three characteristics that distinguish a limited company from a sole trader.

3. Complete the following equations:

Sales – Cost of Sales = _____

Opening Stock + Purchases – _____ = _____

Opening Capital + _____ = Closing Capital

Current Assets – Current Liabilities = _____

Gross Profit – Expenses = _____

4. State in which section of a Balance Sheet the following items would be found:

a. Amounts owed for VAT from the Revenue

b. Amounts owed to suppliers

c. Bank overdraft

d. Cash on hand

e. Loan taken out by the business for 10 years

f. Stock of goods not sold at the end of the year

g. Motor vehicles

h. Drawings by the owner of the business

i. PAYE owed by the business.

2.2 Depreciation

Learning outcomes (Accounting Manual and Computerised 5N1348): 7 (part)

In the last section, we explained how a Trading, Profit and Loss account and Balance Sheet can be prepared from a Trial Balance. At the end of the accounting period, a number of various adjustments are usually required that are not normally incorporated into the Trial Balance. The final accounts will need to be amended and finalised and ledger accounts prepared. These types of post-trial balance adjustments comprise mainly:

* Depreciation
* Closing stock
* Accruals and prepayments
* Bad debts and bad debt provisions.

Depreciation

Depreciation is one of those expenses that are not prompted by a source document, such as an invoice or receipt, and therefore the accountant must remember to include it at the end of the accounting period.

Before going on to explain the meaning of depreciation, it is necessary to distinguish between capital and revenue expenditure.

* **Capital expenditure** is money spent on the purchase of fixed assets, e.g. plant, machinery, vehicles, furniture, premises. Fixed assets are assets used by the business itself, which are not for resale. They are bought by the business with a view to generating future profits and will normally last for a number of years. The cost of these fixed assets is not treated as an expense in the Profit and Loss account. The double-entry to record the purchase of fixed assets is:

  Debit: Fixed asset account, e.g. machinery
  Credit: Bank account or creditors (if the item is not yet paid for).

* **Revenue expenditure** represents the cost of running the business on a day-to-day basis. It is all the expenditure of a business other than capital expenditure, e.g. rent, rates, wages, and electricity. All such expenditure appears in the Profit and Loss account, whereas capital expenditure

appears in the Balance Sheet. The double-entry in relation to expenditure of a revenue nature is:

Debit: Expense account e.g. wages
Credit: Bank account.

Capital expenditure, i.e. expenditure on fixed assets, is necessary in order to provide a general service to the business. The benefit received from the purchase of fixed assets extends beyond more than one accounting period. The cost of these fixed assets must therefore extend beyond more than one accounting period and must be matched with the benefit from such assets. This is in line with the 'matching concept' discussed in section 1.1. The charge made to the accounts each year is known as depreciation. If the cost of fixed assets was not charged to accounts each year the profits would be overestimated. In practice, it is not easy to measure the benefit derived in each accounting year from the use of fixed assets, but the principle of allocating the cost of a fixed asset over its expected useful life seems to be an acceptable method of allocation.

Let us consider an example. A business purchases a machine for use at a cost of €20,000. This machine will last, say, 10 years. Rather than charging the full €20,000 to profits in the year of purchase, the business will spread the cost of this machine over its expected useful life. In this way, the cost of the machine will be spread over 10 years rather than just the first year. After all, the business will acquire the benefit of the machine for 10 years, not just one year! Thus the profit of the first year will not be understated. In this example, the business will charge €2,000 to profits each year for 10 years in the form of depreciation and so the cost of the machine will be written off over 10 years. Depreciation simply means the writing off of an asset over its expected useful life.

Another way to view this is that fixed assets have a limited useful life. While they are being used by the business they will fall in value every year due to wear and tear and obsolescence. Depreciation attempts to measure this and charge it against profits. To return to our example, we may assume that the machine falls in value by €2,000 each year so that after one year of use; it is no longer worth €20,000 but €18,000. At the end of year two, its value will be €16,000 and so on.

More formally, depreciation has been defined as a measure of wearing out, consumption or other reduction in the useful economic life of a fixed asset whether arising from use, lapse of time or obsolescence through technology and market changes.

In order to calculate the depreciation charge for a particular fixed asset, the following factors must be determined:

- **Cost:** The cost of an asset will include all amounts necessary in order to bring the asset to a state ready for use. This normally means the purchase price of the asset plus carriage and installation charges.
- **Useful life:** The useful life of the asset will have to be estimated, i.e. how long the fixed asset will last in the business. This can generally be

determined with reasonable accuracy. For example, a computer may have a useful life of five years, furniture may have a useful life of 15 years and premises may have a useful life of 50 years.

- **Residual value:** This is commonly called the 'scrap value' of the fixed asset. This may be difficult to estimate in practice. It is the amount that the business hopes to receive for the asset when its useful life is over. For some assets, the scrap value may be zero.

Of the three elements above, the original cost of the fixed asset is the only item that the accountant is sure of. The other items are estimates based on past experience.

Methods of depreciation

There are two main methods of depreciation, namely the straight-line method and the reducing-balance method.

- **Straight-line method:** This simply charges to profit the same amount of depreciation each year. It is usually expressed as a percentage of cost.

Example

A motor vehicle was purchased on 1 January for €15,000. It is estimated that its useful life is five years with nil residual value. Therefore we must spread €15,000 over five years and so €3,000 will be charged as depreciation each year. At the end of year 1, €3,000 will be written off the vehicle. The vehicle will then be worth €12,000. At the end of year 2, another €3,000 will be written off the vehicle and it will then be worth €9,000. At the end of five years, the vehicle will be totally depreciated and its value in the Balance Sheet will then be zero.

The annual depreciation charge is:

(Original cost of asset − estimated residual value) ÷ estimated life of the asset.

- **Reducing-balance method:** Some assets do not depreciate or fall in value by the same amount each year. For example, motor vehicles fall more in value in earlier years than they do in later years. For such assets it is inappropriate to use a straight-line method of depreciation, as it would not reflect the real fall in value. The reducing-balance method may be more suitable. It means that the depreciation is calculated as a percentage of **net book value** each year. Net book value is the cost of the asset less depreciation already charged.

Example

Assume that a motor vehicle costs €30,000 and that the depreciation rate is 25% of the reduced balance. The depreciation charge each year would be as shown in the following table.

	€
Year 1	
Cost	30,000
Deprecation for year 1 @ 25%	(7,500)
= Net Book Value end year 1	22,500
Year 2	
Depreciation for year 2 @ 25%	(5,625)
= Net Book Value end year 2	16,875
Year 3	
Depreciation for year 3 @ 25%	(4,218.75)
= Net Book Value end year 3	12,656.25

The reducing-balance method results in a much higher level of depreciation in the earlier years and a much lower charge in later years.

Comparison of the two methods

In the straight-line method, equal amounts of depreciation are charged each year. This is appropriate where assets tend to lose their value evenly throughout their life. The advantage of the straight-line method is that it is simple to operate. In the reducing-balance method, higher amounts of depreciation are charged in earlier years and lower amounts in later years. This would be appropriate where assets fall in value in that manner, e.g. motor vehicles. The advantage is that it may be more realistic for these types of assets, but it has the drawback of being more difficult to operate.

Accounting for depreciation

The annual depreciation of an asset is charged against profit for the year, i.e. it is an expense in the Profit and Loss account. You may think that the double-entry would be to debit the depreciation expense account and to credit the fixed asset account. This would be incorrect from the accounting point of view because valuable information about the original cost of the fixed asset would be lost. It is a legal requirement that a business must disclose separately in its Balance Sheets the original cost of all fixed assets and the related depreciation to date. To accomplish this, an accumulated depreciation account is opened, which records the depreciation of fixed assets year after year. Therefore, the annual depreciation will be entered in the ledger accounts as follows:

Debit: Depreciation Expense account (Profit and Loss)
Credit: Accumulated Depreciation account (Balance Sheet item) with the depreciation charge for the year. Each group of fixed assets will normally have its own accumulated depreciation account.

As far as the Balance Sheet is concerned, the following details for each group of fixed assets are disclosed:

- Original cost of fixed asset
- Accumulated depreciation to date
- Net book value (NBV).

The accumulated depreciation to date of each fixed asset is subtracted from the original cost to arrive at the respective NBV of each group of fixed assets.

Example 1

Mayfield Ltd purchases a new truck for €50,000 and pays by cheque on 1 January. The firm estimates that it will have a useful life of 10 years. Mayfield Ltd also estimates that the truck will have a residual or disposal value of €5,000 at the end of that time. We will calculate the depreciation charge for the first two years and provide all the ledger entries. We will also show the Profit and Loss and Balance Sheet at the end of each year. We assume a straight-line method of depreciation.

Firstly, figure 1 shows the ledger accounts for the purchase of the truck.

NOMINAL LEDGER

Motor Vehicles A/c

DR					CR
Date	Details	Amount	Date	Details	Amount
1-Jan	Bank	50,000			

Bank A/c

DR					CR
Date	Details	Amount	Date	Details	Amount
			1-Jan	Motor Vehicles	50,000

Figure 1

After year 1, the depreciation expense using the straight-line method would be calculated as follows:

$$\frac{\text{Cost of asset} - \text{disposal value}}{\text{Useful life of asset}} = \frac{€50,000 - €5,000}{10} = €4,500 \text{ depreciation expense}$$

The ledger accounts to record the depreciation expense for year 1 are as shown (fig. 2).

NOMINAL LEDGER

Depreciation Expense A/c					
DR					**CR**
Date	Details	Amount	Date	Details	Amount
31 Dec Year 1	Accumulated Depreciation	4,500			

Accumulated Depreciation A/c					
DR					**CR**
Date	Details	Amount	Date	Details	Amount
			31 Dec Year 1	Depreciation	4,500

Figure 2

The depreciation expense amount above will be transferred to the Profit and Loss account and will be listed among the expenses. The Accumulated Depreciation account, as the name suggests, will *accumulate* the depreciation expense year after year and will continue to exist as long as the asset exists. Its place will be in the Balance Sheet and will be balanced at the end of each year. From that we look at the Profit and Loss account and Balance Sheet as at the end of year 1 (fig. 3).

Profit and Loss Account of Mayfield Ltd – end year 1 (extract)

Expenses:
Depreciation: Motor Vehicles   4,500

Balance Sheet of Mayfield Ltd end year 1 (extract)

Fixed Assets	Cost	Acc. Dep.	NBV
Motor Vehicles	50,000	4,500	45,500

Figure 3

The accumulated depreciation is a credit balance in the ledger and it reduces the original cost of the motor vehicles in the Balance Sheet.

In year 2, the ledger accounts to record the depreciation would be similar to that shown in fig. 4.

NOMINAL LEDGER

Depreciation Expense A/c

DR					CR
Date	Details	Amount	Date	Details	Amount
31 Dec Year 2	Accumulated Depreciation	4,500			

Accumulated Depreciation A/c

DR					CR
Date	Details	Amount	Date	Details	Amount
31 Dec Year 1	Balance c/d	4,500	31 Dec Year 1	Depreciation	4,500
		4,500			**4,500**
			1 Jan Year 2	Balance b/d	4,500
31 Dec Year 2	Balance c/d	9,000	31 Dec Year 2	Depreciation	4,500
		9,000			**9,000**
			1 Jan Year 3	Balance b/d	9,000

Figure 4

The accumulated depreciation account is balanced at the end of each year and accumulates the expense of depreciation each year.

The Profit and Loss account and Balance Sheet at the end of year 2 will look as shown (fig. 5).

Profit and Loss Account of Mayfield Ltd – end year 2 (extract)

Expenses:
Depreciation: Motor Vehicles   4,500

Balance Sheet of Mayfield Ltd – end year 2 (extract)

Fixed Assets	Cost	Acc. Dep.	NBV
Motor Vehicles	50,000	9,000	41,000

Figure 5

The depreciation 'accumulates' year after year in the Balance Sheet and further reduces the NBV of the motor vehicle. This gives some idea of the age of the asset in the Balance Sheet.

Some comments may be appropriate at this moment. The original or historical cost is entered in the Balance Sheet as demanded by the historical cost concept, discussed in section 1.1, where it must be stated in the Balance Sheet when calculating the NBV. The NBV is defined as the historical cost, less the accumulated depreciation to date and is always shown the Balance Sheet. The accumulated depreciation ledger account balance will always be a credit balance and appears in the Balance Sheet under the heading 'Accumulated Depreciation'.

Example 2

Johnson Ltd purchased the following fixed assets on 1 January:

Equipment: Cost €51,000
Motor Vehicle: Cost €28,000.

The equipment is to be depreciated on a straight-line method, over three years, with a residual value of zero. The motor vehicle is to be depreciated on a straight-line method, over three years, with a residual value of €1,000. Calculate the depreciation on both assets and show the ledger accounts, Profit and Loss account and Balance Sheet for each of the three years.

- Depreciation of equipment

$$\frac{\text{Cost of asset} - \text{disposal value}}{\text{Useful life of asset}} = \frac{\text{€}51{,}000 - \text{€}0}{3} = \text{€}17{,}000 \text{ depreciation expense}$$

- Depreciation of motor vehicle:

$$\frac{\text{Cost of asset} - \text{disposal value}}{\text{Useful life of asset}} = \frac{\text{€}28{,}000 - \text{€}1{,}000}{3} = \text{€}9{,}000 \text{ depreciation expense}$$

- Figure 6 shows the Ledger accounts, Profit and Loss account and Balance Sheet, year 1.

NOMINAL LEDGER — Year 1

Equipment (Cost) A/c

DR					CR
Date	Details	Amount	Date	Details	Amount
Year 1	Bank	51,000			

Motor Vehicles (Cost) A/c

DR					CR
Date	Details	Amount	Date	Details	Amount
Year 1	Bank	28,000			

Bank A/c

DR					CR
Date	Details	Amount	Date	Details	Amount
			Year 1	Equipment	51,000
			Year 1	Motor Vehicles	28,000

The above recording the purchase of Equipment and Motor Vehicles and paid by cheque

Depreciation Expense A/c – Equipment

DR					CR
Date	Details	Amount	Date	Details	Amount
Year 1	Accumulated Depreciation	17,000			

Accumulated Depreciation A/c – Equipment

DR					CR
Date	Details	Amount	Date	Details	Amount
31 Dec Year 1	Balance c/d	17,000	Year 1	Depreciation	17,000
		17,000			**17,000**
			1 Jan Year 2	Balance b/d	17,000

The above recording the depreciation of Equipment

Depreciation Expense A/c – Motor Vehicles

DR					CR
Date	Details	Amount	Date	Details	Amount
Year 1	Accumulated Depreciation	9,000			

Accumulated Depreciation A/c – Motor Vehicles

DR					CR
Date	Details	Amount	Date	Details	Amount
31 Dec Year 1	Balance c/d	9,000	Year 1	Depreciation	9,000
		9,000			**9,000**
			1 Jan Year 2	Balance b/d	9,000

The above recording the depreciation of Motor Vehicles

Profit and Loss Account of Johnson Ltd – end year 1 (extract)

Expenses:

Depreciation: Equipment	17,000
Depreciation: Motor Vehicles	9,000

Balance Sheet of Johnson Ltd – end year 1 (extract)

Fixed Assets	Cost	Acc. Dep.	NBV
Equipment	51,000	17,000	34,000
Motor Vehicles	28,000	9,000	19,000

Figure 6

- Figure 7 shows Ledger accounts, Profit and Loss account, Balance Sheet, Year 2.

NOMINAL LEDGER — Year 2

Depreciation Expense A/c – Equipment

DR					CR
Date	Details	Amount	Date	Details	Amount
Year 2	Accumulated Depreciation	17,000			

Accumulated Depreciation A/c – Equipment

DR					CR
Date	Details	Amount	Date	Details	Amount
			1 Jan Year 2	Balance b/d	17,000
31 Dec Year 2	Balance c/d	34,000	Year 2	Depreciation	17,000
		34,000			**34,000**
			1 Jan Year 3	Balance b/d	34,000

The above recording the depreciation of Equipment

Depreciation Expense A/c – Motor Vehicles

DR					CR
Date	Details	Amount	Date	Details	Amount
Year 2	Accumulated Depreciation	9,000			

Accumulated Depreciation A/c – Motor Vehicles

DR					CR
Date	Details	Amount	Date	Details	Amount
			1 Jan Year 2	Balance b/d	9,000
31 Dec Year 2	Balance c/d	18,000	Year 2	Depreciation	9,000
		18,000			**18,000**
			1 Jan Year 3	Balance b/d	18,000

The above recording the depreciation of Motor Vehicles

Profit and Loss Account of Johnson Ltd – end Year 2 (extract)
Expenses:
Depreciation: Equipment   17,000
Depreciation: Motor Vehicles   9,000

Balance Sheet of Johnson Ltd – end Year 2 (extract)

Fixed Assets	Cost	Acc. Dep.	NBV
Equipment	51,000	34,000	17,000
Motor Vehicles	28,000	18,000	10,000

Figure 7

- Figure 8 shows the Ledger accounts, Profit and Loss account, Balance Sheet, Year 3.

NOMINAL LEDGER – Year 3

Depreciation Expense A/c – Equipment

DR					CR
Date	Details	Amount	Date	Details	Amount
Year 3	Accumulated Depreciation	17,000			

Accumulated Depreciation A/c – Equipment

DR					CR
Date	Details	Amount	Date	Details	Amount
			1 Jan Year 3	Balance b/d	34,000
31 Dec Year 3	Balance c/d	51,000	Year 3	Depreciation	17,000
		51,000			**51,000**
			1 Jan Year 4	Balance b/d	51,000

The above recording the depreciation of Equipment

Depreciation Expense A/c – Motor Vehicles

DR					CR
Date	Details	Amount	Date	Details	Amount
Year 3	Accumulated Depreciation	9,000			

Accumulated Depreciation A/c – Motor Vehicles

DR					CR
Date	Details	Amount	Date	Details	Amount
			1 Jan Year 3	Balance b/d	18,000
31 Dec Year 3	Balance c/d	27,000	Year 3	Depreciation	9,000
		27,000			**27,000**
			1 Jan Year 4	Balance b/d	27,000

The above recording the depreciation of Motor Vehicles

Profit and Loss Account of Johnson Ltd – end Year 3 (extract)

Expenses:

Depreciation: Equipment	17,000
Depreciation: Motor Vehicles	9,000

Balance Sheet of Johnson Ltd – end Year 3 (extract)

Fixed Assets:	Cost	Acc. Dep.	NBV
Equipment	51,000	51,000	-
Motor Vehicles	28,000	27,000	1,000

Figure 8

The annual depreciation of €17,000 for equipment and €9,000 for motor vehicles is debited to the Depreciation Expense account and credited to the Accumulated Depreciation account. At the end of each year, the Depreciation Expense account is transferred to the Profit and Loss account. In this way, the profits of the business are reduced to allow for the use and wear and tear of the fixed assets. The cost of the fixed assets is being written off against profits over their expected useful lives.

The annual depreciation is accumulated in the Accumulated Depreciation account and a balance is brought down on the credit side at the end of each year. This credit balance appears in the Balance Sheet under the heading 'Accumulated Depreciation' (Acc. Dep.).

The Fixed Asset account for equipment and motor vehicles remains untouched – no depreciation is entered in this account. It is balanced, of course, at the end of each year. If the business purchased assets, or sold any, the entries would appear in the Fixed Asset account.

The credit balance on the Accumulated Depreciation account is deducted from the debit balance on the Fixed Asset account to arrive at the NBV (net book value) of the asset. This information is recorded in the Balance Sheet.

Review assignments

Assignment 1

Fulton Ltd purchased a motor vehicle for €35,000 on 1 January. Its accounting year ends on 31 December. Depreciation is charged at 25%, reducing-balance.

Show the ledger accounts for the first two years and the entries in the Profit and Loss account and Balance Sheet.

Assignment 2

The following is an extract from the Trial Balance of Smith Ltd at 1 January:

Motor vehicles at cost: €30,000
Accumulated depreciation of motor vehicles: €10,800
Machinery at cost: €14,000
Accumulated depreciation of machinery: €1,400

Depreciation is calculated as follows:
Motor Vehicles: 20% per annum, reducing-balance
Machinery: 10% per annum, straight-line.

Show the Profit and Loss account and Balance Sheet extracts for the year end.

Assignment 3

On 1 January 2014, Langdale Ltd has in its books:

- Equipment: at cost €10,000
- Accumulated depreciation of equipment to date: €3,750
- Furniture: at cost: €12,000
- Accumulated depreciation to date: €4,800.

Depreciation of equipment is charged at 12.5% per annum, straight-line. Depreciation of furniture is charged at 10% per annum, straight-line.

Show the ledger accounts, Profit and Loss account and Balance Sheet entries for the year ended 31 December 2014.

2.3 Bad Debts and Bad Debt Provisions

Learning outcomes (Accounting Manual and Computerised 5N1348): 7 (part)

When a business sells goods on credit, there is a risk that some debtors will not pay the amount due. Here the business has to bear the loss and this loss is called a **bad debt**. Well-managed businesses take care not to sell to any customer where there is a high risk of non-payment. They are also likely to have a credit control system in operation to ensure that all debts are collected within a reasonable time. Even despite this, businesses must accept that inevitably some debts will turn out to be bad debts.

Accounting for bad debts

A bad debt is a normal business risk and it is written off to the Profit and Loss account as an expense. They are accounted for by removing the debtor from the accounts and indicating the lost amount in the Profit and Loss account by means of a Bad Debts expense account. The ledger account double-entry is:

Debit: Bad Debts expense account (Profit and Loss account)
Credit: Debtors account (Balance Sheet).

Example

On 1 May, goods were sold on credit to Mr Hynes for €800. On 8 June Mr Hynes paid €700 and then went bankrupt. The remaining €100 owing was written off as a bad debt.

Figure 1 shows the ledger accounts:

DEBTORS LEDGER

Mr Hynes

DR					CR
Date	Details	Amount	Date	Details	Amount
1-May	Sales	800	8-Jun	Bank	700
			8-Jun	Bad Debts	100
		800			**800**

NOMINAL LEDGER

Bad Debts A/c

DR					CR
Date	Details	Amount	Date	Details	Amount
8-Jun	Debtors – Mr Hynes	100			

Figure 1

The Bad Debts account is an expense and will be transferred to the Profit and Loss account, the entry being:

Debit: Profit and Loss account €100
Credit: Bad Debts expense account €100.

The occurrence of a bad debt means that what was believed to be, and had been treated as, an asset, i.e. debtors, is now known not to be an asset. Instead, an expense is recognised as soon as it has been incurred and is in accordance with the **prudence concept**. The prudence concept states that if a business has the possibility of suffering an expense, it should be immediately written off against profits (see section 1.1). Therefore the double-entry for bad debts written off reflects a reduction in an asset (debtors) and an increase in expenses (bad debts). In the above example, the debtors figure relating to Mr Hynes will not appear in the Balance Sheet as an asset since the account is closed off.

The debtors figure shown in the Balance Sheet will be the figure *after* deducting any bad debts that have been written off to the Profit and Loss account. The effect will also be shown in the Profit and Loss account where the net profit will be reduced by €100 as a result of the expense of a bad debt.

Provision for bad debts

After the business has written off the debts known to be bad, it must make provision for debts that are not yet bad but may be doubtful. At the end of each accounting period it is necessary to estimate the extent of doubtful debts. These are the debts outstanding at the end of the year that are uncertain of recovery. It is important that we do not overstate the value of debtors in the Balance Sheet by including debts that *may* prove to be bad, i.e. the doubtful debts.

At the end of the accounting year, the manager or accountant of the business examines all the debtors and makes a list of those he/she considers from experience to be unable or unwilling to pay. The total of this list represents the probable amount of bad debts in the next accounting period. A more simplistic method of estimating doubtful debts is to apply an overall percentage of the debtors figure, say, 5% of total debtors. This method may not be as accurate as going through each debtor in detail and ageing them.

The double-entry in order to create a provision for bad/doubtful debts is:

Debit: Profit and Loss account
Credit: Provision for Bad Debts account.

You should note that the amount created as a provision for bad debts does not go into the individual debtor's account. There is still a possibility this provision may need to be reversed. It is only when a bad debt is written off in full, as a specific bad debt, that the debtors account is credited.

A provision is usually defined as an amount set aside out of profits to provide for any known expense that cannot be determined with accuracy. The amount of the provision created is debited to the Profit and Loss account, thus creating an expense for the year. This is in accordance with the prudence concept. The business has the *possibility* of bad debts, so it is writing the amount off in the Profit and Loss account and so reducing profit for the year.

Example

Walls Ltd has completed its first year trading and has a €500,000 debtors balance at the end of the year. Even if individual doubtful debtors are not apparent, common sense and experience will conclude that some debtors are doubtful. The loss may not be apparent within the year of business but it may arise the following year. By availing of the prudence concept, the business makes a conservative guess as to the size of the loss. Then the business adheres to the matching principle by setting up a provision for bad debts at the end of its first year. It determines that 3% of these debtors are doubtful, that is, 3% of €500,000 equals €15,000.

Figure 2 shows the ledger accounts.

Debtors A/c

DR					CR
Date	Details	Amount	Date	Details	Amount
Year 1	Balance b/d	500,000			

Provision for Bad Debts A/c

DR					CR
Date	Details	Amount	Date	Details	Amount
			Year 1	Profit & Loss	15,000

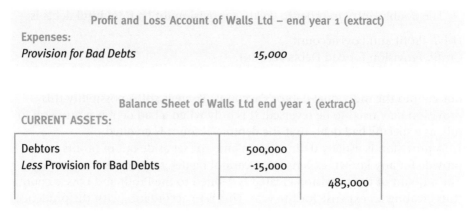

Profit and Loss Account of Walls Ltd – end year 1 (extract)

Expenses:

Provision for Bad Debts   *15,000*

Balance Sheet of Walls Ltd end year 1 (extract)

CURRENT ASSETS:

Debtors	500,000	
Less Provision for Bad Debts	-15,000	
		485,000

Figure 2

As shown, the debtors figure in the ledger remains untouched, still showing €500,000 owing. There is a credit entry in the Provision for Bad Debts account of €15,000 and the Profit and Loss account is debited with €15,000. The Provision for Bad Debts account is balanced at the end of the year and the balance (€15,000) is subtracted from the debtors figure in the Balance Sheet. The Balance Sheet now shows a reduced debtors balance of €485,000 representing a *true* amount of debtors that are *expected* to be converted into cash at the end of the accounting year. In other words, the provision for bad debts (credit balance) is presented as a deduction from debtors (debit balance) in the Balance Sheet.

A change in the provision balance

Management of Walls Ltd may decide in year 2 to increase the provision to 4% of the debtors balance at the end of the year. Let us assume the balance on the debtors account at the end of year 2 is €400,000 (sales for the year total €900,000 and receipts from debtors €1,000,000) and the provision for bad debts is calculated at 4% of this balance equals €16,000. Because a provision already exists for €15,000, management only needs to increase this by €1,000.

    The double-entry for an *increase* in the provision would be:

Debit: Profit and Loss account €1,000
Credit: Provision for Bad Debts account €1,000.

Figure 3 shows the ledger accounts.

If the provision for bad debts needed to be *reduced*, then very simply the business would:

Debit: Provision for Bad Debts
Credit: Profit and Loss account
with the amount of the reduction in the provision.

Debtors A/c

DR						CR
Date	Details	Amount	Date	Details		Amount
Year 1	Balance b/d	500,000	Year 2	Bank		1,000,000
Year 2	Sales	900,000	Year 2	Balance c/d		400,000
		1,400,000				**1,400,000**
Year 3	Balance b/d	400,000				

Provision for Bad Debts A/c

DR					CR
Date	Details	Amount	Date	Details	Amount
			Year 1	Balance b/d	15,000
Year 2	Balance c/d	16,000	Year 2	Profit & Loss	1,000
		16,000			**16,000**
			Year 3	Balance b/d	16,000

Profit and Loss Account of Walls Ltd – end year 2 (extract)

Expenses:
Provision for Bad Debts   1,000

Balance Sheet of Walls Ltd end year 2 (extract)

CURRENT ASSETS:

Debtors	400,000	
Less Provision for Bad Debts	-16,000	
		384,000

Figure 3

Example

Let us assume that in year 3, the Walls Ltd debtors balance was €350,000 (sales for the year totalled €800,000 and receipts from debtors €850,000) and management wants to create a provision for bad debts of 4% of this balance equals €14,000. As a provision of €16,000 already exists in the accounts, this balance needs to be reduced by €2,000.

The double-entry is:

Debit: Provision for Bad Debts €2,000
Credit: Profit and Loss account €2,000.

Figure 4 shows the ledger accounts.

Debtors A/c

DR					CR
Date	Details	Amount	Date	Details	Amount
Year 2	Balance b/d	400,000	Year 3	Bank	850,000
Year 3	Sales	800,000	Year 3	Balance c/d	350,000
		1,200,000			**1,200,000**
Year 4	Balance b/d	350,000			

Provision for Bad Debts A/c

DR					CR
Date	Details	Amount	Date	Details	Amount
Year 3	Profit & Loss	2,000	Year 2	Balance b/d	16,000
Year 3	Balance c/d	14,000			
		16,000			**16,000**
			Year 4	Balance b/d	14,000

Profit and Loss Account of Walls Ltd - end year 3 (extract)

Income:

Decrease in Provision for Bad Debts   *2,000*

Balance Sheet of Walls Ltd - end year 3 (extract)

CURRENT ASSETS:

Debtors	350,000	
Less Provision for Bad Debts	-14,000	
		336,000

Figure 4

The amount of the reduction, €2,000, is clawed back into the profits of the business as a credit in the Profit and Loss account and the Balance Sheet entry displays the new balance in the Provision for Bad Debts account, subtracted from debtors.

Review assignments

Assignment 1

On 1 January 2014 Liam Matthews had a debtors balance of €36,000 and a provision for bad debts of €1,200. During 2014 credit sales were €90,000 and receipts from debtors were €100,000. Also €200 was written off as a bed debt in a customer's account. The owner decided at the end of the year to create a provision of 3% for debtors. Show the following accounts for year end 2014:

a. Debtors
b. Bad Debts
c. Provision for Bad Debts
d. Profit and Loss extract
e. Balance Sheet extract.

Assignment 2

Michael Doyle commenced business on 1 January 2014 and figure 5 shows an extract from his accounts at the end of his first year.

	Debtors before Bad Debts	Provision for Bad Debts	Bad Debts
Year end 31 Dec 2014	110,000	1,700	5%
Year end 31 Dec 2015	96,000	2,000	5%

For the years 2014 and 2015, write up the Bad Debts account and Provision for Bad Debts account. Show extracts from the Profit and Loss account and Balance Sheet for the two years.

Assignment 3

On 1 January 2014 the balance on the Provision for Bad Debts account of Duffy Ltd was €4,000, being 5% of debtors on that date. During 2014 and 2015, bad debts written off were €2,000 and €2,800 respectively. Credit sales for 2014 and 2015 were €86,000 and €98,000 respectively. Payments by debtors for 2014 and 2015 were €81,000 and €112,000 respectively. The owner wishes to maintain a provision for bad debts of 5% of debtors at the end of each year.
    Write up the following accounts for the two years:

a. Debtors
b. Bad Debts
c. Provision for Bad Debts
d. Profit and Loss extract
e. Balance Sheet extract.

2.4 Accruals and Prepayments

Learning outcomes (Accounting Manual and Computerised 5N1348): 7 (part)

Final accounts are usually prepared for a definite accounting period, say one year. So far, when preparing our final accounts, we have assumed that expenses relate to the period in which they are paid and so there are no accruals or prepayments. Similar assumptions have been made regarding income. In practice, however, if we take the expenses paid or income received by a business, it is most unlikely that they will exactly match the accounting period. It is almost certain that some expenses due during the accounting year, e.g. electricity and telephone, will not have been paid at the end of the year. An adjustment in the final accounts will need to be made for these accruals. Other business expenses, e.g. insurance, rent and rates, may be overpaid in the accounting year. A prepayment will exist at the end of the year and again must be adjusted for.

Accruals concept

Accruals is one of the main accounting concepts discussed in Part 1. It essentially means that income and expenses should be matched together and dealt with in the Profit and Loss account for the period to which they relate, regardless of the period in which the cash was received or paid. So we are matching in two ways:

- **Matching by time:** recognising the expense during the period in which it was incurred
- **Matching of income and expenses:** matching the expense to its corresponding revenue.

In the ledger accounts, the expense accounts will record the amounts that have been paid by cheque or cash during the accounting year – but will not make an allowance for accruals and prepayments. In practice, the accruals concept means that, when preparing the Profit and Loss account, expenses charged to profit relate to the *full* accounting period, whether or not they have actually been paid. In other words, the expenses that relate to the full year are included in the Profit and Loss account. For example, the Profit and Loss account should charge one full year's rent, rates, wages and electricity.

The same principle applies to income in the Profit and Loss account. The income that is included in the Profit and Loss account is the income that relates to the *full* year, not necessarily what was actually received.

Accounting for accruals

An accrual is an amount owed by a business at the end of the accounting period. It is therefore a liability to the business. The amount owing at the end of the year appears as a credit balance brought down in the appropriate ledger account. It will require an adjustment to expenses in the Profit and Loss account and the liabilities in the Balance Sheet and at the end of the accounting year.

Example

From 1 January to 31 December, a business has to pay rent of €1,000. The rent is paid every quarter on 1 January, 1 April, 1 July and 1 October, being €250 per quarter. The amount due on 1 October is not paid and is still owing as at 31 December. The rent expense account is as shown (fig. 1).

Rent A/c – Expense

DR					CR
Date	Details	Amount	Date	Details	Amount
1-Jan	Bank	250			
1-Apr	Bank	250			
1-Jul	Bank	250			

Bank A/c

DR					CR
Date	Details	Amount	Date	Details	Amount
			1-Jan	Rent	250
			1-Apr	Rent	250
			1-Jul	Rent	250

Figure 1

The business paid €750 rent, where the double-entry is:

Debit: Rent expense account €750
Credit: Bank account €750.

A further €250 is due and should be included in the Profit and Loss account for the year. The rent expense in the Profit and Loss account should account for the full €1,000 and there exists an accrual (liability) of €250 at the end of the accounting year. To account for this accrual, the double-entry is:

Debit: Rent expense account €250
Credit: Rent accrued (liability) €250.

So the complete ledger accounts and Profit and Loss account and Balance Sheet for the year would be as shown (fig. 2).

Rent A/c – Expense

DR					CR
Date	Details	Amount	Date	Details	Amount
1-Jan	Bank	250			
1-Apr	Bank	250	31-Dec	Profit & Loss	1,000
1-Jul	Bank	250			
31-Dec	Rent Accrued	250			
		1,000			**1,000**

Rent Accrued A/c – Liability

DR					CR
Date	Details	Amount	Date	Details	Amount
			31-Dec	Rent	250

Profit and Loss Account (extract)

Expenses:
Rent   1,000

Balance Sheet (extract)

CURRENT LIABILITIES:
Rent accrued   250

Figure 2

The rent expense included in the Profit and Loss account is €1,000, that is the amount that relates to the full year, and not €750, being the amount paid for the year. The Balance Sheet records that the business has a current liability of €250 at the end of the accounting year. Again, it must be stressed that what is included in the Profit and Loss account is the *total* expense for the *full* year and not necessarily the amount actually paid.

Accrued income

Income relating to the accounting period, but not received by the end of the period, also needs to be accounted for in the final accounts. This accrued income is an asset to the business and therefore appears as a **debit** balance in the appropriate ledger account and as a current asset in the Balance Sheet. This is similar to debtors; the business is owed money at the end of the accounting year.

Example

Rent is received by a business for the accounting year January to December. The rent is received quarterly on 1 January, 1 April, 1 July and 1 October, being €700 each quarter. The rent was received on the due dates, except for the amount receivable on 1 October, which remains unpaid at the end of the year.

The Rent Receivable account is as shown (fig. 3).

Rent Receivable A/c – Income

DR						CR
Date	Details	Amount	Date	Details		Amount
			1-Jan	Bank		700
			1-Apr	Bank		700
			1-Jul	Bank		700

Bank A/c

DR					CR
Date	Details	Amount	Date	Details	Amount
1-Jan	Rent Received	700			
1-Apr	Rent Received	700			
1-Jul	Rent Received	700			

Figure 3

The business received €2,100 rent, where the double-entry is:

Debit: Bank account €2,100
Credit: Rent Receivable account €2,100.

A further €700 is owed to the business and should be included in the Profit and Loss account for the year. The rental income in the Profit and Loss account should account for the full €2,800 and there exists accrued income (asset) of €700 at the end of the accounting year. To account for this accrued income, the double-entry is:

Debit: Rent Receivable accrued (asset) €700
Credit: Rent Receivable (income) €700.

So the complete ledger accounts and Profit and Loss account and Balance Sheet for the year would be as shown (fig. 4).

Rent Receivable A/c – Income

DR					CR
Date	Details	Amount	Date	Details	Amount
			1-Jan	Bank	700
			1-Apr	Bank	700
31-Dec	Profit & Loss	2,800	1-Jul	Bank	700
			31-Dec	*Rent Receivable*	
				accrued	*700*
		2,800			**2,800**

Rent Receivable Accrued A/c – Asset

DR					CR
Date	Details	Amount	Date	Details	Amount
31-Dec	*Rent Receivable*	*700*			

Profit and Loss Account (extract)

Income:

Rent Receivable	2,800

Balance Sheet (extract)

CURRENT ASSETS:

Rent Receivable accrued	700

Figure 4

The rental income included in the Profit and Loss account is €2,800 – the amount that relates to the *full* year, and not €2,100, being the amount received for the year. The Balance Sheet records that the business has a current asset of €700 at the end of the accounting year.

Prepayments

Certain expenses of a business may be paid in advance, that is, when some of the expense paid relates to the next accounting year. These prepaid amounts are assets to the business and must therefore appear as **debit** balances brought down in the ledger accounts.

Similar to accruals, there are two categories of prepayments, both of which require adjusting at the end of the year:

- Prepaid expenses – expenses paid for services before they are used
- Prepaid income – money received by the business before it is earned.

Accounting for prepaid expenses

As stated, these are expenses paid in advance and will therefore benefit more than one accounting period. Examples include insurance that may need to be paid in advance and payments for office supplies.

Example 1

A business incurs an insurance expense of €6,000 for the year 1 January to 31 December. It pays the insurance on the following dates: 1 January, €3,000 for the first 6 months; 1 July, €3,000 for the remaining 6 months; and 20 December: €3,200 for the first 6 months of the following year.

Figure 5 shows the ledger accounts to record this.

Insurance A/c – Expense

DR						CR
Date	Details	Amount	Date	Details		Amount
1-Jan	Bank	3,000				
1-Jul	Bank	3,000				
20-Dec	Bank	3,200				

Bank A/c

DR					CR
Date	Details	Amount	Date	Details	Amount
			1-Jan	Insurance	3,000
			1-Jul	Insurance	3,000
			20-Dec	Insurance	3,200

Figure 5

The business paid €9,200 insurance, where the double-entry is:

Debit: Insurance expense account €9,200
Credit: Bank account €9,200.

It is apparent that the insurance expense in the Profit and Loss account should only represent €6,000 (which relates to the current year) and there exists a prepayment (asset) of €3,200, being the payment made on 20 December, which relates to the next accounting year. To account for this prepayment, the double-entry is:

Debit: Insurance prepaid account (asset) €3,200
Credit: Insurance expense account (expense) €3,200, thus reducing the expense charged for the year.

So the complete ledger accounts and Profit and Loss account and Balance Sheet for the year would be as shown (fig. 6).

Insurance A/c – Expense

DR					CR
Date	Details	Amount	Date	Details	Amount
1-Jan	Bank	3,000	*31-Dec*	*Insurance Prepaid*	*3,200*
1-Jul	Bank	3,000	31-Dec	Profit & Loss	6,000
20-Dec	Bank	3,200			
		9,200			**9,200**

Insurance Prepaid A/c – Asset

DR					CR
Date	Details	Amount	Date	Details	Amount
31-Dec	*Insurance Expense*	*3,200*			

Profit and Loss Account (extract)

Expenses:

Insurance   6,000

Balance Sheet (extract)

CURRENT ASSETS:

Insurance prepaid   3,200

Figure 6

The insurance that is included in the Profit and Loss account is €6,000 – only the amount that relates to the year – and not €9,200, being the amount paid for the year. The Balance Sheet records that the business has a current asset of €3,200 at the end of the accounting year.

Example 2

Assume a business prepares its accounts from 1 January to 31 December each year. It purchased a truck on 1 October in the accounting year and pays motor tax, recorded in the motor expenses account for 12 months, costing €1,200. This represents a motor tax cost of €100 per month.

Figure 7 shows the ledger accounts to record this.

Motor Expenses A/c – Expense

DR					CR
Date	Details	Amount	Date	Details	Amount
1-Oct	Bank	1,200			

Bank A/c

DR					CR
Date	Details	Amount	Date	Details	Amount
			1-Oct	Motor Expenses – Tax	1,200

Figure 7

The double-entry is:

Debit: Motor expense account €1,200
Credit: Bank account €1,200.

It is apparent that the motor expense in the Profit and Loss account should only represent three months' motor tax of €300 (that relates to the current year) and there exists a prepayment (asset) of €900, being the payment made on 1 October, which relates to the next accounting year. To account for this prepayment, the double-entry is:

Debit: Motor Expenses prepaid account (asset) €900
Credit: Motor Expenses account (expense) €900, thus reducing the expense charged for the year.

So the complete ledger accounts and Profit and Loss account and Balance Sheet for the year would be as shown (fig. 8).

Motor Expenses A/c – Expense

DR					CR
Date	Details	Amount	Date	Details	Amount
1-Oct	Bank	1,200	31-Dec	*Motor Expenses Prepaid*	900
			31-Dec	Profit & Loss	300
		1,200			**1,200**

Motor Expenses Prepaid A/c – Asset

DR					CR
Date	Details	Amount	Date	Details	Amount
31-Dec	*Motor Expense*	*900*			

Profit and Loss Account (extract)

Expenses:

Motor Expenses   300

Balance Sheet (extract)

CURRENT ASSETS:

Motor Expenses prepaid   900

Figure 8

It now becomes apparent that only the motor expenses that relate to the current year, i.e. €300 are included in the Profit and Loss account and the business has a prepayment of €900 at the end of the year, which is displayed in the Balance Sheet.

Prepaid income

This is deemed to be unearned income for a business and should therefore be recorded as a liability, which will result in a credit balance in the accounts. This is similar to customers paying in advance for goods/services that are not delivered at the end of the accounting year or rent received in advance by the business. Until the business delivers, it must regard these advance payments as liabilities, showing a credit balance.

Example

Rent is received in an accounting year 1 January to 31 December of €2,500 on 15 January covering 15 months from the period 1 January to 31 March in year 2. This shows that 15 months' rent has been received in a 12-month accounting period. Therefore, three months' rent of €500 is overpaid.

The ledger accounts to record this are as shown (fig. 9).

Rent Received – Income

DR					CR
Date	Details	Amount	Date	Details	Amount
			15-Jan	Bank	2,500

Bank A/c

DR					CR
Date	Details	Amount	Date	Details	Amount
15-Jan	Rent received	2,500			

Figure 9

The double-entry for the rent received is:

Debit: Bank account €2,500
Credit: Rent Received account €2,500.

Only €2,000 should be included in the Profit and Loss account for the year representing the amount actually *earned*, and there exists prepaid income (liability) of €500 at the end of the accounting year. To account for this prepaid income, the double-entry is:

Debit: Rent received (income) €500
Credit: Rent receivable prepaid (liability) €500.

So the complete ledger accounts and Profit and Loss account and Balance Sheet for the year would be as shown (fig. 10).

Rent Received – Income

DR						CR
Date	Details	Amount	Date	Details		Amount
31-Dec	Rent Receivable prepaid	500	15-Jan	Bank		2,500
31-Dec	Profit & Loss	2,000				
		2,500				2,500

Rent Receivable Prepaid A/c – Liability

DR						CR
Date	Details	Amount	Date	Details		Amount
			31-Dec	Rent Receivable		500

Profit and Loss Account (extract)

Income:
Rent Received   2,000

Balance Sheet (extract)

CURRENT LIABILITIES:
Rent Receivable prepaid   500

Figure 10

Review assignments

Assignment 1

During 2014, the following payments were made relating to rent:
- 1 January – €1,200 for 1 January to 31 March
- 15 March – €1,200 for 1 April to 30 June
- 8 July – €1,200 for 1 July to 30 September.

The accounting year ends on 31 December. Write up the Rent account for 2014 and show the Profit and Loss account and Balance Sheet extracts for the end of the year.

Assignment 2

Insurance is paid for 2014 as follows:

- 1 January – €250 for 1 January to 30 June
- 28 June – €250 for 1 July to 31 December
- 12 December – €280 for 1 January to 30 June 2015.

The accounting year ends on 31 December. Write up the Insurance account for 2014 and show the Profit and Loss account and Balance Sheet extracts for the end of the year.

Assignment 3

Property is rented to a tenant on 1 January 2014 at an agreed rent of €10,000 per year. The following cash receipts were received:

- 1 January – €2,500
- 1 April – €2,500
- 1 July – €2,500
- 8 January 2015 – €2,500.

The accounting year ends on 31 December. Write up the Rent Receivable account for 2014 and show the Profit and Loss account and Balance Sheet extracts for the end of the year.

Assignment 4

On 1 July 2014, a trader had a rates prepayment of €850. The charge for rates for the accounting year 1 July 2014 to 30 June 2015 is €12,000. Rates were paid as follows during the accounting year:

- 8 August – €890
- 10 November – €8,000
- 1 April – €2,000.

Write up the ledger accounts for Rates for the year ended 30 June 2015 and show the Profit and Loss account and Balance Sheet extracts for the year-end.

Assignment 5

A trader rents property at a quarterly rent of €3,000. The property was first rented on 1 March 2014 and the rent is payable by the tenant in advance. Rent is received by the trader on:

- 1 March – €3,000
- 1 June – €3,000
- 8 September – €3,000
- 12 December – €3,000.

The accounting year is from 1 January to 31 December 2014. Write up the ledger accounts for Rent for the year ended 31 December 2014 and show the Profit and Loss account and Balance Sheet extracts for the end of the year.

2.5 Stock

Learning outcomes (Accounting Manual and Computerised 5N1348): 7 (part)

It is most unlikely that all purchases made during the year will be sold by the end of the year, so some stock will almost certainly be in the stores at the end of the year. The stock not sold during the year is called closing stock, which will be available for sale the following year as opening stock.

We have already discussed the concept of cost of sales, which is purchases allowing for opening and closing stock.

$$\text{Cost of sales} = (\text{Opening stock} + \text{Purchases}) - \text{Closing stock}$$

The bookkeeping entries are not quite as easy to understand; these are explained below.

Accounting for opening stock

The opening stock in the Trading account is, as discussed in section 2.1, the closing stock of the previous year. To transfer the closing stock of the previous year to the opening stock of the current year, the double-entry is:

Debit: Opening stock (Trading account)
Credit: Closing stock (Current asset: Balance Sheet).

This entry creates an opening stock account for the Trading account and cancels the debit balance in the closing stock account by crediting it. The closing stock account now has a nil balance.

Accounting for closing stock

The business will perform a stocktake at the end of the accounting year to establish the closing stock on hand. This amount (which is valued at cost) will be the new closing stock at the end of the year. This will be a Current Asset in the Balance Sheet at the end of the year.

The double-entry to record this is:

Debit: Closing stock (Current Asset: Balance Sheet)
Credit: Closing stock (Trading account).

Example

Figure 1 shows that closing stock of a business last year (2013) was €1,000, which will be the opening stock of the current year (2014).

- Purchases for 2014 were €2,000.
- Sales for 2014 were €4,000.
- The business performed a stock take at the end of 2014 to determine its closing stock, where the value was €1,500.

To record the opening stock of 2014 (closing stock of 2013):

Debit: Opening stock (Trading account) €1,000
Credit: Closing stock (Current asset: Balance Sheet) €1,000.

To record the closing stock of 2014:

Debit: Closing stock (Current asset: Balance Sheet) €1,500
Credit: Closing stock (Trading account) €1,500.

Stock A/c – Current Asset – Balance Sheet

DR						CR
Date	Details	Amount	Date	Details		Amount
1-Jan-14	Balance b/d – closing stock of 2013	1,000	31-Dec-14	Opening Stock		1,000
31-Dec-14	Closing Stock	1,500	31-Dec-14	Balance c/d		1,500
		2,500				**2,500**
1-Jan-15	Balance b/d	1,500				

Opening Stock – Trading A/c

DR					CR
Date	Details	Amount	Date	Details	Amount
31-Dec-14	Stock	1,000			

Closing Stock – Trading A/c

DR					CR
Date	Details	Amount	Date	Details	Amount
			31-Dec-14	Stock	1,500

Figure 1

The balance on the Stock account is recorded in the Balance Sheet as a current asset. The opening and closing stock of the current year (2014) are transferred to the Trading account. The Trading account also records Purchases and Sales for the year (fig. 2).

Stock A/c – Current Asset – Balance Sheet

DR					CR
Date	Details	Amount	Date	Details	Amount
1-Jan-14	Balance b/d – closing stock of 2013	1,000	31-Dec-14	Opening Stock	1,000
31-Dec-14	Closing Stock	1,500	31-Dec-14	Balance c/d	1,500
		2,500			**2,500**
1-Jan-15	Balance b/d – Current Asset Balance Sheet	1,500			

Sales A/c

DR					CR
Date	Details	Amount	Date	Details	Amount
31-Dec-14	To Trading A/c	4,000	31-Dec-14	Sales	4,000

Purchases A/c

DR					CR
Date	Details	Amount	Date	Details	Amount
31-Dec-14	Purchases	2,000	31-Dec-14	To Trading A/c	2,000

Opening Stock – Trading A/c

DR					CR
Date	Details	Amount	Date	Details	Amount
31-Dec-14	Stock	1,000	31-Dec-14	To Trading A/c	1,000

Closing Stock – Trading A/c

DR					CR
Date	Details	Amount	Date	Details	Amount
31-Dec-14	To Trading A/c	1,500	31-Dec-14	Stock	1,500

Trading A/c for year end 2014

DR				CR
Details	Amount	Details		Amount
Opening Stock	1,000	Sales		4,000
Purchases	2,000	Closing Stock		1,500
Gross Profit c/d	2,500			
	5,500			**5500**
		Gross Profit b/d		2,500

Balance Sheet (extract) for year end 2014

CURRENT ASSETS:

Stock   1,500

Figure 2

There are numerous double-entry ledger accounts to absorb at this stage, but an understanding is necessary in order to fully understand the concept of opening and closing stocks and how they have an effect on the profit of the business. To summarise, let us take each entry individually:

- **Sales for year (ignore VAT)**
  Debit: Debtors €4,000
  Credit: Sales €4,000
  Transfer the Sales account to the Trading account:
  Debit: Sales €4,000
  Credit: Trading account €4,000.

- **Purchases for year (ignore VAT)**
  Debit: Purchases €2,000
  Credit: Creditors €2,000
  Transfer the Purchases account to the Trading account:
  Debit: Trading account €2,000
  Credit: Purchases €2,000.

- **Opening stock (closing stock of last year)**
  Debit: Opening stock €1,000
  Credit: Closing stock €1,000
  Transfer the Opening stock to the Trading account:
  Debit: Trading account €1,000
  Credit: Opening stock €1,000.

- **Closing stock**
  Debit: Stock account: Balance Sheet €1,500
  Credit: Closing stock €1,500
  Transfer the closing stock to the Trading account:
  Debit: Closing stock €1,500
  Credit: Trading account €1,500.

The Trading account then calculates the following:

	€	€
Opening stock	1,000	
Add Purchases	2,000	
Less Closing stock		(1,500)
= Cost of sales	1,500	
Sales	4,000	
Less Cost of sales		(1,500)
= Gross profit	2,500	

As you can see, the closing stock figure appears twice in the final accounts; once in the Trading account (referred to as 'Closing stock') and also in the Balance Sheet (referred to as 'Stock'). This is the same stock figure. These adjustments may become clearer when final accounts with adjustments are completed in the next section.

Review assignment

From the following information, show the ledger accounts and prepare a Trading account and Balance Sheet extract for Grassroots Ltd for the year ended 31 December 2014.

Opening stock	€3,500
Purchases	€18,000
Sales	€27,500
Closing stock	€2,700

2.6 Final Accounts with Adjustments

Learning outcomes (Accounting Manual and Computerised 5N1348): 7 (part)

So far we have learned about double-entry accounting and the completion of a Trial Balance. Also, we are aware of end-of-year adjustments that are usually made to financial accounts, namely closing stock, depreciation, accruals and prepayments and bad and doubtful debts. These are items that are usually not part of the double-entry process and entries that do not appear in the Trial Balance. In preparation of final accounts, these items need to be taken into consideration and accounted for in order to show a more realistic profit for the business. It is also a fundamental part of the accruals concept of accounting.

Accounts of companies and sole traders

The business activity of sole traders is separate from their own private transactions. For example, the sole trader maintains a separate bank account to record business transactions. All money introduced by a sole trader into his/her business is treated as capital. Any profit made belongs to the sole trader and is added to the capital at the end of the accounting period. Any withdrawals of cash or assets for the sole trader's personal use are treated as drawings, which reduce the capital at the end of the accounting period. Drawings are not treated as expenses in arriving at the profit or loss for the accounting period.

Figure 1 shows how the Profit and Loss account of a sole trader might look.

Gross Profit	€10,000
Less Expenses	-€6,000
Equals Net profit, which is transferred to the Capital account	€4,000

Figure 1

Figure 2 shows how the Profit and Loss account of a company might look.

Gross profit	10,000
Less Expenses	-6,000
Net profit	4,000
Less Dividends	-1,500
Retained profit	2,500
Add Retained profit at beginning of year	600
Retained profit at end of year	3,100

Figure 2

It is obvious, when comparing the two Profit and Loss accounts, that the main difference arises after calculating the net profit figure. In a sole trader's situation, the net profit is added to the capital in the Balance Sheet. In other words, all of the net profit earned belongs to the sole trader and increases his/her capital.

In a company situation, some of the net profit is used to pay dividends to the shareholders. Here the shareholders get a proportion of the profit each year. Usually, not all of the profit each year is distributed in the form of dividends to shareholders. Some of the net profit is 'retained' by the company. The main advantage in retaining some profit is that it can be used to improve the business, for example:

- to expand
- to pay off a long-term loan
- to pay a dividend to shareholders in future years, when profit is scarce.

In the example we just looked at, €2,500 profit is retained by the company. The company would normally have retained profits from the last accounting period (in this example, €600) and this is added to this year's retained profits. The resultant figure of €3,100 represents the total retained profit of the company which is carried forward to the Balance Sheet.

The Balance Sheet of a company is similar to that of a sole trader, except for the 'Financed by', or Capital, section. Figure 3 shows how the 'Financed by' section of a sole trader's Balance Sheet might look.

Capital	50,000
Add Net profit	4,000
	54,000
Less Drawings	-1,000
Equals Capital at end of year	53,000

Figure 3

In the case of a limited company, the Capital section might look as shown (fig. 4).

Share capital	Authorised	Issued
50,000 ordinary shares @ €1 each	€70,000	€50,000
Reserves:		
Share Premium		€6,000
Profit & Loss balance (retained profit)		€3,100
Long term liabilities:		
5% Debenture loan		€80,000
		€139,100

Figure 4

Let us look separately at each of the entries in the Capital section of a company's accounts:

- **Share capital**: The ownership of a company comprises shares that have been issued by the company. A company may, for example, issue 10,000 shares at €1 each to an investor who wishes to purchase a stake in the company. The total amount of share capital a company can issue is governed by its Memorandum of Association. This maximum amount of share capital a company can issue is called the 'authorised share capital'. This authorised figure may be increased with the agreement of shareholders. The issued share capital represents that proportion of the authorised share capital that has been taken up by the shareholders. In the Balance Sheet of a company, the authorised share capital is stated for information purposes only, that is, it is not part of the calculations to arrive at the total figure in the Balance Sheet. It is the *issued share capital* that forms part of the Balance Sheet calculations.
- **Share premium**: It is common for companies to issue shares at a price in excess of their nominal or par value, which may be €1. The difference between the value at which shares are issued and the nominal value is referred to as the 'share premium'. The share premium account is, in fact, a capital reserve of the company.
- **Reserves**: This is a gain or profit that has been retained within the company. Reserves may be divided into two main categories:
  - **Revenue** reserves: These represent undistributed or retained trading profits. They can be used by the directors of the company to pay dividends in the future, or for any other reason they think fit. Revenue reserves are shown under various headings, the most common being the Profit and Loss account balance (retained profits).
  - **Capital** reserves: These represent profits that are not associated with the normal course of trading, e.g. share premium account. These reserves cannot be distributed in the form of dividends to shareholders. They can be used to finance future expansion of the company.

- **Profit and Loss balance**: this is the figure that has been extracted from the Profit and Loss account. It represents the retained profit of the company for this year plus any retained profit brought forward from last year. This is a revenue reserve and will appear with other reserves in the Balance Sheet at the year end.
- **Debentures**: It is common for companies to borrow funds on a long-term basis. One important form of a long-term loan normally associated with limited companies is a debenture loan. The institution from which this loan is borrowed is known as a 'debenture holder'. The debenture is for a fixed period of time, e.g. 20 years, and a fixed rate of interest attaches to it. Debenture holders are often offered security for the amount owed, in the form of a charge on the assets owned by the company. An example of this may be the company's freehold land. If the company defaults on interest or capital repayments, the debenture holder, under the debenture deed, would be entitled to sell the assets on which the debenture had been secured in order to reclaim the amount owed. Debenture interest is usually a fixed amount and represents a business expense in the Profit and Loss account. If a debenture loan is for a period of 20 years the company will pay a fixed interest each year and at the end of the 20 years, it will pay back the capital sum borrowed. In this case, the company may use some of its reserves to repay the capital sum. So, it should be obvious that a company needs retained profits for such purposes as this.

Example 1

Let us take the Trial Balance of a sole trader at year end 31 December 2014 and prepare final accounts. The adjustments after the Trial Balance are items that have not been accounted for in the preparation of the accounts during the year and now need to be taken into account to arrive at a profit or loss figure.

The Trial Balance in figure 5 was extracted from the ledger of Tim Corley, a sole trader, for the year ended 31 December 2014.

	Debit	Credit
Sales		452,000
Opening Stock	60,000	
Purchases	168,000	
Wages	82,000	
Advertising	12,300	
Repairs and Maintenance	7,400	
Loan interest	2,000	
Discounts Allowed	240	
Discounts received		196
Telephone	654	
Light & Heat	1,265	
Premises at cost	130,000	(contd)

Accumulated depreciation: Premises		20,000
Furniture at cost	70,000	
Accumulated depreciation: Furniture		14,000
Debtors	49,000	
Provision for Bad Debts		1,200
Cash at bank	8,900	
Cash on hand	125	
Creditors		45,000
VAT Payable		3,988
Capital		12,000
Drawings	25,000	
Long-term loan		68,500
	616,884	**616,884**

Figure 5

At the end of the year the following adjustments need to be accounted for:

- Closing stock is valued at €38,000.
- Light and heat outstanding is €180.
- The provision for bad debts is to be increased by €250.
- Depreciation for the year end is to be provided for:
  – Premises: 2% of cost
  – Furniture: 10% of cost.
- There is a prepayment in the advertising expense account of €2,300.

We will now prepare a Trading, Profit and Loss account and Balance Sheet of Tim Corley for 31 December 2014 (fig. 6).

Trading, Profit and Loss Account of Tim Corley for year end 31 Dec 2014

Sales			452,000
Less Cost of Sales:			
Opening Stock		60,000	
Purchases		168,000	
Cost of goods available for sale		228,000	
Less Closing Stock		-38,000	
Cost of Sales			190,000
Gross Profit			**262,000**
Less Expenses:			
Wages		82,000	
Advertising	12,300		
Less Prepayment	-2,300	10,000	
Repairs and Maintenance		7,400	
Loan Interest		2,000	
			(contd)

Discounts Allowed		240
Discounts Received		-196
Increase in provision for Bad Debts		250
Telephone		654
Light & Heat	1,265	
Add due	180	1,445
Dep: Premises 2% cost		2,600
Dep: Furniture 10% cost		7,000
TOTAL Expenses		113,393
Net Profit		**148,607**

Balance Sheet of Tim Corley for year end 31 Dec 2014

FIXED ASSETS	COST	ACC DEP	NBV
Premises	130,000	22,600	107,400
Furniture	70,000	21,000	49,000
TOTAL Fixed Assets			156,400
CURRENT ASSETS:			
Stock		38,000	
Debtors	49,000		
Less Provision for Bad Debts	-1,450	47,550	
Cash at Bank		8,900	
Cash on Hand		125	
Advertising prepaid		2,300	
TOTAL Current Assets		96,875	
CURRENT LIABILITIES:			
Creditors	45,000		
VAT Payable	3,988		
Light & Heat due	180		
TOTAL Current Liabilities		49,168	
Net Current Assets:			47,707
TOTAL NET ASSETS			**204,107**
Financed by:			
Capital	12,000		
Add Net Profit	148,607		
Less Drawings	-25,000		
			135,607
Long-term Liabilities:			
Long-term Loan			68,500
TOTAL CAPITAL EMPLOYED			**204,107**

Figure 6

- The **closing stock** at the end of the year is deducted from the purchases, as it represents unsold purchases, to arrive at the cost of sales. This figure is also a Current Asset in the Balance Sheet.
- Payment for **light & heat** of €180 is due. The light and heat expense shown in the Profit and Loss account has to be increased by €180, so the expense reflects the *full* expense for the accounting period, and not what was actually paid. This figure is a Current Liability in the Balance Sheet.
- The **provision for bad debts** is increased by €250. The double-entry for this is to *debit* the Profit and Loss account, so reducing the profit, and *credit* the bad debts provision account. The new balance in the bad debts provision account is now increased by €250. This is deducted from debtors in the Balance Sheet. The debtors figure, less the bad debts provision, is the amount of money the business expects to be converted into cash. This is in accordance with the prudence concept.
- **Depreciation** is writing off part of the cost of assets into profits over the expected useful life of each asset. As a result, 2% of the cost of the premises and 10% of the cost of the furniture is written off in the form of depreciation to the Profit and Loss account. Both of these use the straight-line depreciation method. The double-entry is to *debit* the Depreciation expense account and *credit* the Accumulated Depreciation account. The Depreciation account is then transferred to the Profit and Loss account, thus reducing profits, and the accumulated depreciation account balance is increased. The accumulated depreciation balance (which is a credit balance) is deducted from the cost of the asset to arrive at net book value in the Balance Sheet.
- **Advertising prepaid** of €2,300 represents a payment for advertising, which relates to the following accounting year. It needs to be deducted from the advertising paid as the amount does *not* relate to this accounting year. This complies with the accruals/matching concept. The advertising paid is reduced accordingly to reflect only the expense that relates to *this year*. This is a Current Asset in the Balance Sheet.
- Note that **discounts received** are income and therefore a credit in the Profit and Loss account. It is included in the expenses list as a negative amount. This has the same effect as treating discounts received as a positive in the income column. This will be particularly relevant when doing computerised accounts later on.

Example 2

Let us look at the Trial Balance of a limited company and prepare final accounts.

The Trial Balance was extracted from Deegan Print Ltd, a limited company, for the year ended 31 December 2014 (fig. 7).

	Debit €	Credit €
Sales		970,000
Opening Stock	85,000	
Purchases	558,250	
Wages	169,000	
Directors' fees	85,000	
Loan Interest	8,000	
Bank Charges	5,452	
Advertising	15,000	
Rent	20,800	
Rates	6,400	
Discounts Allowed	280	
Discounts received		200
Telephone	3,900	
Light & Heat	14,000	
Plant & Machinery at cost	350,000	
Accumulated depreciation: Plant & Machinery		80,000
Debtors	168,000	
Provision for Bad Debts		6,000
Cash at bank	9,600	
Cash on hand	1,500	
Creditors		185,500
VAT Payable		8,362
Issued Share Capital 5,000 ordinary shares @ €1 each		5,000
(Authorised Share Capital €300,000)		
Profit and Loss Balance (retained profit)		65,120
Debenture loan 6%		180,000
	1,500,182	1,500,182

Figure 7

At the end of the year, the following adjustments need to be accounted for:

- Closing stock is valued at €89,420.
- There is interest outstanding on the debenture loan of €2,800.
- A customer has gone into liquidation, owing the company €2,600. This balance needs to be written off as a bad debt.
- The provision for bad debts is to be adjusted to 3% of debtors.
- Rates are outstanding to the value of €600.
- The amount paid for advertising of €15,000 represents a 15-month period, where there is a prepayment of 3 months for the next accounting period.
- Depreciation is to be provided on the plant and machinery at 10% of cost.

Figure 8 shows the final accounts of Deegan Print Ltd.

Trading Profit and Loss Account of Deegan Print Ltd as at year end 31 Dec 2014

Sales			970,000
Less Cost of Sales:			
Opening Stock		85,000	
Add Purchases		558,250	
Cost of goods available for sale:		643,250	
Less Closing Stock		-89,420	
Cost of Sales:			553,830
Gross Profit			**416,170**
Less Expenses:			
Wages		169,000	
Directors' fees		85,000	
Loan Interest	8,000		
Add interest due	2,800	10,800	
Bank Charges		5,452	
Advertising	15,000		
Less prepaid	-3,000	12,000	
Rent		20,800	
Rates	6,400		
Add due	600	7,000	
Discounts allowed		280	
Discounts received		-200	
Telephone		3,900	
Light & heat		14,000	
Bad debt written off		2,600	
Reduction in Bad Debts provision		-1,038	
Dep: Plant & Machinery		35,000	
Total Expenses			364,594
Net Profit			**51,576**

Balance Sheet of Deegan Print Ltd as at year end

FIXED ASSETS:	COST	ACC DEP	NBV
Plant & Machinery	350,000	115,000	235,000
CURRENT ASSETS:			
Closing Stock		89,420	
Debtors	165,400		
Less Bad Debt provision	-4,962	160,438	
Bank		9,600	
Cash on hand		1,500	
Advertising prepaid		3,000	
Total Current Assets:		263,958	
CURRENT LIABILITIES:			
Creditors	185,500		
VAT payable	8,362		
Loan interest due	2,800		
Rates due	600		
Total Current Liabilities:		197,262	
Net Current Assets:			66,696
TOTAL NET ASSETS:			**301,696**
Financed by:		Authorised	Issued
Share Capital			
5,000 ordinary shares @ €1 each		300,000	5,000
Profit & Loss balance		65,120	
Add Net Profit		51,576	
Retained Profit:			116,696
Long term liabilities:			
6% Debenture loan			180,000
TOTAL CAPITAL EMPLOYED:			**301,696**

Figure 8

- **Debenture interest** of €2,800 is due. The interest calculated on the loan is 6% of the amount borrowed, which equals 6% of €180,000 – €10,800. The interest paid was €8,000, which results in a further €2,800 outstanding. The Profit and Loss account records the *full* expense for the accounting period, and not what was actually paid. The interest due is a Current Liability in the Balance Sheet.
- A **bad debt** of €2,600 needs to be written off at the end of the year. The double-entry is to *debit* the bad debts expense account (which is transferred to the Profit and Loss account) and *credit* the debtors. This reduces the debtors balance by €2,600, (€168,000 – €2,600) resulting in a debtors balance of €165,400. The new provision for bad debts is calculated

as 3% of €165,400 = €4,962. There already exists a bad debts provision of €6,000 and this needs to be reduced by (€6,000 – €4,962) = €1,038.

- The **provision for bad debts** is reduced by €1,038. The double-entry for this is to *credit* the Profit and Loss account, therefore increasing the profit, and *debit* the bad debts provision account. Note again that the amount in the Profit and Loss account is treated as a negative amount in the expenses column, which has the same effect as a positive amount in the income column. The new balance in the bad debts provision account is now €4,962. This is deducted from debtors in the Balance Sheet. The debtors figure less the bad debts provision is the amount of money the business expects to be converted into cash.
- **Rates outstanding** are €600. The double-entry is to *debit* the rates expense account (which is transferred to the Profit and Loss account) and *credit* the rates accrual (due) account. The rates in the Profit and Loss account now record the *full* expense of rates for the year and the amount outstanding is a Current Liability in the Balance Sheet.
- **Advertising prepaid** of €15,000 represents a payment for advertising that relates to 15 months. Three months relate to next year and €3,000 needs to be deducted from the advertising paid as the amount does *not* relate to this accounting year. This complies with the accruals/matching concept. The advertising paid is reduced accordingly by €3,000 to reflect only the expense that relates to the 12 months of *this year*. The prepayment is a Current Asset in the Balance Sheet.
- **Depreciation** of 10% of the cost of the plant and machinery is written off to the Profit and Loss account. The double-entry is to *debit* the depreciation expense account and *credit* the accumulated depreciation account. The depreciation account is then transferred to the Profit and Loss account, therefore reducing profits, and the accumulated depreciation account balance is increased. The accumulated depreciation balance (which is a credit balance) is deducted from the cost of the asset to arrive at net book value in the Balance Sheet.
- Note again that **discount received** is income and a credit in the Profit and Loss account. It is included in the expenses list as a negative amount. This has the same effect as treating discount received as a positive in the income column.
- The net profit for the year is added to the **profit and loss balance** to arrive at a new retained profit figure of €116,696 in the Balance Sheet.
- The **authorised share capital** is recorded in the Balance Sheet but is for information purposes only. It is not part of the calculations.

Review assignments

Assignment 1

Figure 9 shows a Trial Balance of James Mulhall, a sole trader, as at 30 June 2014.

Trial Balance of James Mulhall as at 30 June 2014

	Debit	Credit
Sales		268,000
Purchases	95,000	
Opening Stock	12,000	
Discounts	480	690
Carriage In	200	
Rent	13,500	
Wages	24,000	
Motor expenses	2,600	
Advertising	560	
Repairs	2,180	
Bad Debts written off	250	
Premises at cost	170,000	
Accumulated Dep: Premises		34,000
Motor Vehicles at cost	23,000	
Accumulated Dep: Motor Vehicles		3,200
Debtors	13,000	
Bank		1,260
Cash on hand	180	
Provision for Bad Debts		800
Creditors		11,200
VAT Payable		2,300
Capital		40,000
Drawings	4,500	
	361,450	**361,450**

Figure 9

The following additional information is available:

- The stock at 30 June 2014 is valued at €15,000.
- The rent figure is for a 15-month period to 30 September 2014.
- Depreciation is to be provided as follows:
  - Premises: 2% per annum straight-line method.
  - Motor vehicles: 20% per annum reducing-balance method.
- The provision for bad debts is to be adjusted to 5% of debtors.

Prepare a Trading, Profit and Loss account and Balance Sheet for the year end 30 June 2014.

Assignment 2

Figure 10 shows a Trial Balance of Ann Dolan, a sole trader, as at 31 December 2014.

Trial Balance of Ann Dolan as at 31 Dec 2014

	Debit €	Credit €
Sales		255,000
Purchases	106,000	
Stock 1/1/14	31,500	
Light & Heat	1,550	
Rates	6,800	
Salaries	65,000	
Discounts		250
Telephone	2,100	
Miscellaneous Expenses	580	
Bank Interest	1,300	
Bank Charges	231	
Interest in investments		160
Office Equipment	25,000	
Accumulated Dep: Office Equipment		5,000
Furniture	23,000	
Debtors	46,000	
Bank	25,500	
Cash on hand	1,159	
Creditors		6,000
VAT Payable	2,690	
Capital		55,000
Drawings	42,000	
Long-term loan – 3% p.a.		59,000
	380,410	**380,410**

Figure 10

The following additional information is available:

- The stock at 31 December 2014 is valued at €35,200.
- Rates due at the end of the year are €600.
- Depreciation is to be provided as follows:
  - Office equipment: 10% per annum straight-line.
  - The furniture was purchased on 1 July 2014 and is to be depreciated at a rate of 20% per annum. It is the owner's policy to apportion the depreciation charge from the date of purchase.
- A specific bad debt of €960 is to be written off.
- A provision for bad debts needs to be created, equal to 4% of debtors (to the nearest €).
- Provide for interest outstanding on the long-term loan.

Prepare a Trading, Profit and Loss account and Balance Sheet for the year ended 31 December 2014.

Assignment 3

Figure 11 shows a Trial Balance from the books of Bella Ltd, a private limited company, as at 30 September 2014.

Trial Balance Bella Ltd as at 30 Sept 2014

	Debit	Credit
Sales		332,520
Stock 01/10/2013	45,670	
Purchases	128,950	
Carriage Inwards	800	
Director's fees	69,000	
Staff wages	84,200	
Audit & legal fees	2,300	
Bank Charges	962	
Light & Heat	3,600	
Rent received		5,000
Rates	8,900	
Discounts Allowed	180	
Discounts received		250
Insurance	3,900	
Bad Debts	2,600	
Machinery at cost	70,000	
Accumulated depreciation: Machinery		13,500
Debtors	44,000	
Provision for Bad Debts		980
Cash at bank	29,600	
Cash on hand	1,500	
Creditors		52,000
VAT Payable		4,912
Issued Share Capital 1,000 ordinary shares @ €1 each		1,000
Profit and Loss Balance 01/10/2013		46,000
Long-term Loan		40,000
	496,162	**496,162**

Figure 11

The following additional information is available:

- Closing stock at 30 September 2013 is valued at €63,200.
- The provision for bad debts is to be adjusted to 2% of debtors.
- Rent received is for the 10-month period to 31 July 2014. Provide for the amount outstanding.
- Depreciation is to be provided on the machinery at 25% per annum, straight-line method.
- Insurance prepaid amount is €1,250.
- Provision is to be made for interest due of €1,200.

Prepare a Trading, Profit and Loss account and Balance Sheet for the year ended 30 September 2014.

Assignment 4

Figure 12 shows a Trial Balance from the books of Lakeland plc as at 31 December 2014. The authorised share capital of the company is 200,000 ordinary shares at €1 each.

Trial Balance Lakeland plc as at 31 Dec 2014

	Debit	Credit
Sales		393,000
Opening Stock	85,100	
Purchases	145,320	
Director's fees	167,000	
Staff wages	189,200	
Carriage Outwards	540	
Audit fees	3,600	
Selling expenses	4,832	
Hire of office equipment	3,000	
Telephone	2,500	
Administration expenses	15,000	
Rates	1,800	
Loan interest	1,100	
Discounts Allowed	98	
Discounts received		140
Insurance	1,650	
Investment income		11,000
Premises at cost	370,000	
Accumulated Depreciation: Premises		103,600
Plant at cost	95,000	
Accumulated Depreciation: Plant		65,000
Debtors	19,500	
Provision for Bad Debts		1,500
Cash at bank	22,000	
Cash on hand	400	
Creditors		16,900
VAT and Tax Payable		28,500
Issued Share Capital 100,000 ordinary shares @ €1 each		100,000
Profit and Loss Balance 01/01/2014		348,000
Share Premium account		5,000
Long-term Loan		55,000
	1,127,640	1,127,640

Figure 12

The following additional information is available:

* Closing stock at 31 December 2014 is valued at €55,000.
* Included in the debtors figure is a bad debt of €1,400, which is to be written off.
* The provision for bad debts is to be adjusted to 5% of debtors.
* Depreciation is to be provided on the premises at 2% per annum straight-line and on the plant at 10% per annum straight-line.
* The long-term loan is provided at an interest rate of 3% per annum. Provide for any interest outstanding.
* Provide for investment income due of €250.
* The amount in respect of the hire of the office equipment covers the 18-month period ending 30 June 2015.
* Provision is to be made for insurance prepaid of €250.

Prepare a Trading, Profit and Loss account and Balance Sheet for the year ended 31 December 2014.

Assignment 5

From the Trial Balance prepared by you of Equipment Supplies Ltd in assignment 2, section 1.3, prepare a Profit and Loss account and Balance Sheet for the year ended 31 December 2014.
The following additional information is available:

* The closing stock at 31 December 2014 is valued at €5,640.
* There is stock of stationery on hand valued at €672.
* There are salaries outstanding of €410 at the end of the year.
* The company wishes to create a provision for bad debts at the end of the year, equal to 2% of the debtors balance.
* Depreciation is to be provided on the furniture at 20% per annum straight-line and on the office equipment at 10% per annum straight-line.
* The rent of €15,000 in the accounts is for the period 1 January 2014 to 31 March 2015.

2.7 Interpretation of Final Accounts

Learning outcomes (Accounting Manual and Computerised 5N1348): 7 (part)

We have spent a considerable amount of time discussing the preparation and presentation of final accounts. The preparation of final accounts is not an end in itself; we need to be able to analyse and interpret the financial results. This makes sense, particularly when we consider the users of financial information, e.g. bankers, investors, directors, employees and creditors. Their particular interests will vary and it is important that individual users are able to draw their own conclusions from the financial statements.

Interpreting anything calls for analysis, which allows us to look at the accounts in a different way. For example, if a company's Balance Sheet shows a bank balance of €100,000, it may seem large – and it is! However, if the bank balance on average was €1,000,000 over the past number of years, then it may indicate that the company has a cash-flow problem. Consider also that if the company's Profit and Loss account showed profit as a percentage of sales at 10%, that would appear satisfactory; but if the industry average was 30%, the situation would look worrying for the company.

Ratio analysis

The main technique in interpreting financial information is ratio analysis. The main emphasis here will be on using financial information as a means of drawing logical conclusions from the Profit and Loss account and Balance Sheet, enabling more informed decisions to be made by users of accounts.

A ratio is a relationship in quantity, number or degree between one thing and another. It is a measure, often expressed in percentage terms. Ratios, once calculated, should be subject to comparison. For example, to state that a company's net profit percentage is 10% is meaningless in itself. We need the net profit percentage for the past years of the company to compare, or the net profit percentage of other companies in the same industry. Once ratios are calculated, they need to be compared to past performance or similar companies in the industry.

There are many problems with ratios from one period to another. Just because the result is currently better than the result in the past, this does not necessarily mean that it is acceptable now. The past result may be totally unsatisfactory. Another problem of comparison with past periods is that the economic environment may have changed dramatically.

To counteract these drawbacks, some businesses compare their financial performance with planned performance. This means that a business's future plans are expressed in terms of ratios, where actual results are compared with forecast results.

One of the most useful methods of comparison is for a business to compare its results with that of another business in the same industry. But, of course, the other business may also have its own problems. Comparisons with the industry average provide useful information about the business's relative position within the industry.

Despite all these problems, ratios are a good guide to the performance of a business. Ratio analysis provides quantitative insight into the financial position of the business. They are divided into three groups that reflect the fundamental concerns of any business:

1. Profitability ratios
2. Liquidity ratios
3. Efficiency ratios.

Profitability ratios

This measures the income or operating success of the business over a given period of time. Profitability reflects the fundamental performance of the business. It inspires confidence in its day-to-day operations and in its future plans for growth. Profitability ratios are explained below.

Gross profit percentage

This expresses the gross profit as a percentage of sales. It is also called the gross margin. The ratio is:

$$\text{Gross profit \%} \quad = \quad \frac{\text{Gross profit}}{\text{Sales}} \quad \times \ 100 \ = \ X\%$$

It measures how much profit the business has earned relative to the amount of sales. It indicates the efficiency of the production or purchasing department as well as the pricing policy. A low gross profit percentage would be a sign of inefficiency of operation and/or poor pricing policy.

If we find that the gross profit margin decreases substantially over a period, this could be attributable to a number of factors:

- The cost of buying stock has increased faster than selling prices.
- Selling prices have fallen due to increased competition.
- The product mix has changed to include goods with lower profit margins.
- Theft of stock may be taking place.

Like all ratios, it is difficult to comment on a particular result. It would need to be compared with previous results or the industry average. The type of activity the business is carrying on would also need to be known. For example, if the business was a food supermarket, we would expect a low gross profit percentage. However, if it were a jewellery trade, a high gross profit percentage would be expected.

Mark up

This ratio expresses gross profit as a percentage of cost of sales.

$$\text{Mark up} \quad = \quad \frac{\text{Gross profit}}{\text{Cost of sales}} \quad \times \text{ 100} \quad = \quad X\%$$

This measures the amount of profit added to the cost price of goods. As you are already aware, the cost of sales = (opening stock + purchases) – closing stock, and the cost of sales + profit = sales revenue.

   The mark up and the gross profit percentage are linked; if one ratio is low, the other ratio is also low and vice versa. In other words, the gross profit percentage expresses gross profit as a percentage of the selling price and mark up expresses gross profit as a percentage of the cost price of goods sold.

Net profit percentage

This ratio expresses the net profit as a percentage of sales. It indicates the efficiency of the business after deducting all expenses. If taxation is involved, the net profit is usually taken before tax. If there is a large gap between the gross profit percentage and the net profit percentage, it suggests that expenses are high in relation to all other figures. A more detailed analysis of the expenses may be needed in this case. The ratio is:

$$\text{Net profit \%} \quad = \quad \frac{\text{Net profit}}{\text{Sales}} \quad \times \text{ 100} \quad = \quad X\%$$

Again, it is difficult to fairly compare the net profit ratio of different businesses. Operations vary so much that businesses are bound to have different levels of expenditure. Thus this ratio is really only useful for making internal comparisons within the same business.

Return on capital employed (ROCE)

This is perhaps the most important ratio of all in assessing the efficiency of a business in generating profits. It relates the net profit to the level of investment used to earn it, i.e. the capital of the business. There are several variations of this ratio, some take net profit before tax, while others take net profit after tax. Some take capital employed as including long-term liabilities, while others exclude long-term liabilities. The definition depends on the use to which the ratio is to be put. The important matter is consistency in the application of the ratio. The most common ratio for the ROCE is:

$$\text{Return on capital employed} \ = \ \frac{\text{Net profit before tax}}{\text{Total capital employed}} \ \times\ 100 \ =\ \text{X\%}$$

The higher the ratio, the better. It shows that the business is efficient in generating profit from the capital available to it. The return should be higher than the return on a bank deposit account, as there is a greater degree of risk in running a business. The higher the level of risk, the higher the expected return should be. The return on capital employed can also be called the return on investment ratio.

Return on assets ratio

This measures the overall profitability of assets. It is calculated by:

$$\text{Return on assets} \ = \ \frac{\text{Net profit}}{\text{Average total assets}} \ \times\ 100 \ =\ \text{X\%}$$

The percentage derived is the return earned by each euro invested in assets. The strength of the number is only useful when comparing it with a competitor or the industry average. This ratio may be useful if the business is considering investing highly in fixed assets, by determining if it will generate more profit over a period of time to pay for the investment in fixed assets.

Liquidity ratios

Liquidity ratios measure the short-term ability of the business to pay its current obligations and meet unanticipated cash needs. These ratios would be of keen interest to creditors and bankers. Bankers will access the liquidity position so that they can be certain that loans can be repaid. A look at the Balance Sheet of a business will allow us to determine the liquidity of the business. Liquidity ratios are explained below.

Current ratio or working capital ratio

This shows the relationship between current assets and current liabilities. The ratio is:

$$\text{Current ratio or working capital ratio} \ = \ \frac{\text{Current assets}}{\text{Current liabilities}}$$

Or the ratio can be expressed as:

Current assets : Current liabilities

It determines the extent to which the current assets cover the current liabilities in the short term. It answers the question for the business: If current assets were converted into cash, would they be sufficient to pay all the current liabilities?

A current ratio in the region of 2:1 is generally considered acceptable. This suggests that a business has twice as many current assets as current liabilities and should be able to pay its current liabilities if the need arose. On the other hand, too high a current ratio may be an indication of poor management with too many resources tied up in current assets. Here, debtors' balances may be too high, indicating a poor credit-control policy for collection of debt. Stock levels may be too high, resulting in storage costs and the risk of obsolescence. Before we can make judgements on the current ratio of any business, we would need to know the type of trade it conducts. For example, a food supermarket may have a low current ratio because it turns stock over quickly and has few credit customers. A manufacturing business may have a high current ratio as it tends to hold quite a large amount of stock and mostly sells on credit. The weakness in the current ratio is that it does not consider the composition of current assets. For example, what is the actual amount of cash in the business? Is too much tied up in slow-paying customers or is the level of stock excessive? The acid test, or quick ratio, addresses this shortcoming.

Acid test ratio

This is also called the 'liquidity ratio' or 'quick ratio'. The ratio is:

$$\text{Acid test ratio} \quad = \quad \frac{\text{Current assets} - \text{Stock}}{\text{Current liabilities}}$$

Or the ratio can be expressed as:

(Current assets – Stock) : Current liabilities

This tests the ability of the business to meet its current liabilities without having to sell its stock. Stock is excluded from current assets as it is generally the most difficult of all current assets to convert quickly into cash. The generally accepted acid test ratio is 1 : 1, meaning that current assets, less stock, should equal current liabilities. Too high an acid test ratio may imply poor management and under-utilisation of working capital.

Both the current ratio and acid test ratio are always expressed as X : 1 as this allows for easy comparison from year to year and from business to business.

Efficiency ratios

Traditional accounts do not tell us how efficiently a business has been managed or how well its resources are being looked after. These ratios try to assess the effectiveness of the business in using its assets to the full. Efficiency or activity ratios are explained below.

Stock turnover ratio

This indicates how many times a business turns over its stock in a given period of time. The ratio is:

$$\text{Stock turnover} = \frac{\text{Cost of sales}}{\text{Average stock}} = \text{X times}$$

Or

$$\frac{\text{Average stock}}{\text{Cost of sales}} \times 365 = \text{X days}$$

The average stock is calculated by adding the opening and closing stocks and dividing by two. It indicates how many times a year the stock is replaced. It is difficult to comment on any ideal result here; it depends on the nature of the business. For example, in a food supermarket, the stock turnover would be high, indicating that the stock remains on the premises for a short period before it is sold. In the jewellery trade, the stock turnover would be low, suggesting that stock is only purchased a few times during the year.

A high stock turnover is not necessarily better than a low stock turnover or vice versa. A high stock turnover indicates that the business keeps small amounts of stock in comparison with sales, and makes frequent purchases. A lot of small businesses tend to adopt this procedure of purchasing stock only when needed. It saves having money tied up in stock, storage costs and also the risk of damage. But having too little stock may mean that the business loses on trade discounts from suppliers and loss of custom through inadequate stock levels.

It is important that each business keeps its stock at an optimum level, bearing in mind the customer's needs and the cost of holding stock.

Debtor collection period (debtors ratio)

This expresses the average length of credit given to customers, or the average length of time it takes to convert debtors into cash. The ratio is:

$$\text{Debtor collection period} = \frac{\text{Debtors}}{\text{Credit sales}} \times 365 = \text{X days}$$

The credit sales only are taken into account as these are the only sales that create debtors. In some businesses, depending on their accounting methods, it may be difficult to distinguish between credit and cash sales. In this case, a reasonable estimate can be taken.

An acceptable debtor collection period cannot be suggested, as much depends on the type of trade. High-volume, high-turnover businesses, such as food supermarkets, have short collection periods as they mostly sell for cash. Here it is important to establish a trend and, if the trend is upwards, it might suggest that the company's credit control is weakening. The business must remember that giving credit is expensive in terms of money tied up in debtors and it also carries the risk of bad debts. If the debtors are slow in paying, the business might find it has run into cash flow problems. Customers may be encouraged to pay more quickly by lowering the selling price and giving cash discounts.

Selling on credit is, of course, necessary for many businesses. Each business must achieve a balance between the costs of giving credit and the rewards associated with increased custom.

Creditor payment period (creditors ratio)

This expresses the average length of credit taken by the business in paying its creditors. The ratio is:

$$\text{Creditors payment period} = \frac{\text{Creditors}}{\text{Credit purchases}} \times 365 = \text{X days}$$

Again, credit purchases only are taken into account as these purchases generate creditors. A high payment period may suggest that the business is receiving maximum benefit from free credit and using its creditors as a source of finance in the short term. However, there is a danger associated with a high payment period – suppliers will not give cash discounts for prompt payment. An upward trend in the payment period would suggest that the business is having some difficulty in finding the cash to pay its creditors.

Again, the business must strike a balance between the costs of losing discounts for early payment and the rewards associated with free credit.

Example

The Profit and Loss account and Balance Sheet completed in section 2.6(8), and reproduced on the next page, will now be analysed to determine profitability, liquidity and efficiency.

As the name implies, this is a company that provides printing services and produces brochures for local businesses. Assume all its sales and purchases are on credit. As we only have one-year financial accounts, we cannot make value judgements as we cannot compare with other years to determine a trend.

Trading Profit and Loss Account of Deegan Print Ltd as at year end 31 Dec 2014

Sales			970,000
Less Cost of Sales:			
Opening Stock		85,000	
Add Purchases		558,250	
Cost of goods available for sale:		643,250	
Less Closing Stock		-89,420	
Cost of Sales:			553,830
Gross Profit			**416,170**
Less Expenses:			
Wages		169,000	
Directors' fees		85,000	
Loan Interest	8,000		
Add interest due	2,800	10,800	
Bank Charges		5,452	
Advertising	15,000		
Less prepaid	-3,000	12,000	
Rent		20,800	
Rates	6,400		
Add due	600	7,000	
Discounts allowed		280	
Discounts received		-200	
Telephone		3,900	
Light & heat		14,000	
Bad debt written off		2,600	
Reduction in Bad Debts provision		-1,038	
Dep: Plant & Machinery		35,000	
Total Expenses			364,594
Net Profit			**51,576**

Balance Sheet of Deegan Print Ltd as at year end

FIXED ASSETS	COST	ACC DEP	NBV
Plant & Machinery	350,000	115,000	235,000
CURRENT ASSETS			
Closing Stock		89,420	
Debtors	165,400		
Less Bad Debt provision	-4,962	160,438	
Bank		9,600	
Cash on hand		1,500	
Insurance prepaid		3,000	
Total Current Assets:		263,958	
CURRENT LIABILITIES			
Creditors	185,500		
VAT payable	8,362		
Loan interest due	2,800		
Rates due	600		
Total Current Liabilities:		197,262	
Net Current Assets:			66,696
TOTAL NET ASSETS			**301,696**
Financed by:			
Share Capital		Authorised	Issued
5,000 ordinary shares @ €1 each		300,000	5,000
Profit & Loss balance		65,120	
Add Net Profit		51,576	
Retained Profit:			116,696
Long term liabilities:			
6% Debenture loan			180,000
TOTAL CAPITAL EMPLOYED			301,696

1. ## Profitability ratios analysed

$$\text{Gross profit \%} = \frac{\text{Gross profit}}{\text{Sales}} \times 100$$

$$\frac{416,170}{970,000} \times 100 = 42.9\%$$

$$\text{Mark up} \; = \; \frac{\text{Gross profit}}{\text{Cost of sales}} \times 100$$

$$\frac{416,170}{553,830} \times 100 \; = \; 75.1\%$$

$$\text{Net profit \%} \; = \; \frac{\text{Net profit}}{\text{Sales}} \times 100$$

$$\frac{51,576}{970,000} \times 100 \; = \; 5.3\%$$

The above results indicate that Deegan Print Ltd has a relatively high gross profit percentage and mark up. Its relationship between cost price and selling price is high. Obviously, this would be the case in a printing company. Its cost of materials (paper, ink) would be a small proportion of its total expenses relative to sales, which are mostly labour intensive.

The net profit percentage is significantly less than the gross profit percentage as expenses are taken into account. The main overhead of a printing company would be labour, where a skilled workforce qualified in design and publishing would be needed. A net profit percentage of 5.3% does seem low, but we would need to compare it to other years of the business or the industry average to make a valued judgement.

$$\text{Return on capital employed} \; = \; \frac{\text{Net profit before tax}}{\text{Total capital employed}} \times 100$$

$$\frac{51,576}{301,696} \times 100 \; = \; 17\%$$

$$\text{Return on assets} \; = \; \frac{\text{Net profit}}{\text{Average total assets}} \times 100$$

$$\frac{51,576}{235,000} \times 100 \; = \; 21.9\%$$

The ROCE of 17% seems a high percentage for this business. It means that for every euro invested, it earns 17 cents profit. This would be a much better return than any business would receive from a bank or other financial institution. This would need to be the case, as there is risk attached to running any business. Also the return on assets is a comfortable percentage. In the printing industry, the cost of printing equipment would be high and it constantly needs updating due to technological changes. For the amount invested in machinery, the company is generating a healthy level of profit. Again these figures are only relevant when comparisons are made with other years or other businesses in the same industry.

Overall, the company is in a profitable position, taking into account the level of investment and the level of sales.

2. **Liquidity ratios analysed**

$$\text{Current ratio or Working capital ratio} = \frac{\text{Current assets}}{\text{Current liabilities}}$$

Or

Current assets : Current liabilities = 263,958 : 197,262 = 1.3 : 1

$$\text{Acid test ratio} = \frac{\text{Current assets} - \text{stock}}{\text{Current Liabilities}}$$

Or

(Current assets − Stock) : Current Liabilities = (263,958 − 89,420) : 197,262 = 0.88 : 1

The current asset and acid test ratio are below the accepted average of 2 : 1 and 1 : 1 respectively. The company may not be able to pay its debts in the short term. Loan interest of €2,800, Rates of €600 and VAT of €8,362 will most likely fall due in the next month or so. The company, at the moment, does not have enough funds in the bank to meet these short-term debts and will be relying on receipts from debtors. Of course, the company will have to pay at least some of its creditors in the next month or so. The business is in a tight liquidity position and paying insurance in advance for 15 months has worsened its short-term liquidity.

3. **Efficiency ratios analysed**

$$\text{Stock turnover} = \frac{\text{Cost of sales}}{\text{Average stock}} = \times \text{ times}$$

Or

$$\frac{\text{Average stock}}{\text{Cost of sales}} \times 365 = \text{X days}$$

$$\frac{553,830}{(85,000 + 89,420) / 2} = 6.3 \text{ times or 57 days}$$

The company replenishes its stock approximately six times a year, or every 57 days. This would seem appropriate for a printing business where the value of its stock would be low in comparison to the level of output. Although this can be viewed positively we should also be aware that there are costs involved with increased frequency in purchasing and taking delivery of stock. Also the company should be aware of trade discounts for buying in bulk.

$$\text{Debtors collection period} = \frac{\text{Debtors}}{\text{Credit sales}} \times 365 = \text{X days}$$

$$\frac{160,438}{970,000} \times 365 = 60 \text{ days}$$

$$\text{Creditors payment period} = \frac{\text{Creditors}}{\text{Credit purchases}} \times 365 = \text{X days}$$

$$\frac{185,500}{558,250} \times 365 = 121 \text{ days}$$

A collection period of 60 days seems appropriate and suggests that the company has a good credit control policy. But, 121 days to pay suppliers seems excessive. If Deegan Print Ltd continues to take such an extended time to settle its invoices, there is a risk that suppliers will refuse credit, impose late payment charges or even resort to legal action. There also could be a significant loss of goodwill with the suppliers.

The overall comment on Deegan Print Ltd would be: *The company is profitable, but has a liquidity problem in that it does not have adequate funds to meet creditors and other current liabilities.*

Review assignments

Assignment 1

Figure 1 shows the results of two companies, A and B, for the year ended 31 December 2014.

	Company A	Company B
Sales	80,000	50,000
Cost of Sales	36,000	14,000
Administration expenses	14,000	8,000
Selling expenses	2,000	1,500
Wages	4,000	3,500

Figure 1

Which of the above companies is the most profitable?

Assignment 2

The information in figure 2 was extracted from two companies, both engaged in the same retail business of selling footwear.

	Company X	Company Y
Opening Stock	18,000	31,500
Closing Stock	19,200	27,000
Cost of Sales	246,000	288,000
Sales	294,000	336,000
Expenses	15,000	20,100
Debtors	45,000	29,400

Figure 2

From the above, which of the companies do you consider to be in a better trading position? Use ratios to support your answer.

Assignment 3

Refer to the chapter 'Final Accounts with Adjustments' (section 2.6) and calculate the following ratios on the Trading, Profit and Loss account and Balance Sheet of Tim Corley for the year ended 31 December 2014. Assume all sales and purchases are on credit.

a. Gross profit %
b. Net profit %
c. Return on capital employed
d. Current ratio
e. Acid test ratio
f. Stock turnover
g. Debtors collection period
h. Creditors payment period

Assignment 4

The amounts in figure 3 were taken from the final accounts of Sophie Murphy on 31 December 2014.

	€
Stock 1 January 2014	42,000
Purchases	360,000
Sales	440,000
Stock 31 December 2014	38,000
Current assets	56,000
Current liabilities	36,000
Expenses	32,000
Total capital employed	500,000

Figure 3

Calculate the following ratios.

a. Gross profit %
b. Net profit %
c. Return on capital employed
d. Current ratio
e. Acid test ratio
f. Stock turnover

Assignment 5

The amounts in figure 4 are the results of a small electrical engineering business for the year ended 31 December 2013 and 2014.

Profit and Loss account year ended 31 December

	2014	2013
Sales	160,000	150,000
Less Cost of sales	-42,000	-34,000
Gross Profit	118,000	116,000
Less expenses	-85,200	-98,200
Net Profit	**32,800**	**17,800**

Balance Sheet (extract) for year ended 31 December

	2014	2013
FIXED ASSETS	12,500	11,000
CURRENT ASSETS:		
Stock	14,000	13,000
Debtors	90,000	85,000
Bank	1,500	1,250
CURRENT LIABILITIES:		
Creditors	24,000	18,000

Figure 4

The stock at 1 January 2013 is €10,000. Calculate the following ratios and comment on the position of the business.

a. Gross profit %
b. Net profit %
c. Return on capital employed
d. Current ratio
e. Acid test ratio
f. Stock turnover

Assignment 6

Figure 5 shows the final accounts of John Glenn, a small food retailer, for the last two years.

Trading, Profit and Loss Account of John Glenn for year end December

	2014	2013
Sales	62,000	54,500
Less Cost of Sales	-34,500	-31,500
Gross Profit	27,500	23,000
Less Expenses	-21,500	-15,500
Net Profit	**6,000**	**7,500**

Balance Sheet for year end December

	2014		2013	
FIXED ASSETS (cost less dep)				
Land and Buildings	130,000		125,000	
Plant and Equipment	14,500		10,500	
		144,500		135,500
CURRENT ASSETS				
Stock	9,000		13,000	
Debtors	9,500		11,500	
Cash	950		500	
	19,450		25,000	
CURRENT LIABILITIES				
Creditors	7,000		5,000	
Accruals	1,600		1,000	
Bank overdraft	9,000		15,000	
Net Current Assets		1,850		4,000
TOTAL NET ASSETS		146,350		139,500
Financed by:				
Capital		127,500		140,000
Net Profit		6,000		7,500
Less Drawings		-10,000		-20,000
Long-term Liabilities:				
Long-term Loan		22,850		12,000
		146,350		139,500

Figure 5

The opening stock as at 1 January 2013 is valued at €10,000. Calculate the following ratios for 2013 and 2014.

a. Gross profit %
b. Net profit %
c. Return on capital employed
d. Current ratio
e. Acid test ratio
f. Stock turnover
g. Debtors collection period, assuming all sales are on credit
h. Creditors payment period, assuming all purchases are on credit

Part 3

Forecasts and Budgets

3.1 Types and Purpose of Budgets or Forecasts

Learning outcomes (Accounting Manual and Computerised 5N1348): 5

A budget allocates funds based on forecasts. A forecast is an approximate comparison made between future income and expenses. Forecasting and budgeting are perhaps most commonly understood in the context of preparing household budgets for household expenses, a process that contains all the ingredients for preparing budgets in any business.

Types of budgets

There are many types of budgets prepared by a business, in which estimates of future income and expenses are calculated. The main types of budgets are:

- Sales budgets
- Production budgets
- Administration expenses budgets
- Cash budgets.

These budgets would then be combined into an overall budget, known as a master budget, to compile a Budgeted Profit and Loss Account and Budgeted Balance Sheet. This master budget would be examined by management to make sure it is in line with the overall plan of the business. For example, if the sales budget indicates an increase in sales for the forthcoming year, this would lead to an increase in production and purchases of raw materials (if the business was producing its own goods) or an increase in purchases of finished goods (if the business was not producing its own goods). Management must then have the facilities and cash available to accommodate this increase. This would mean that the business needs additional finance and personnel for the future. A cash budget would need to be produced to ensure that management has access to additional finance when required for the future.

Purpose of budgets

Budgets help the management of a business to not spend more than it can earn. They form a plan of the incoming and outgoing cash for a given period of time and the income and expenditure for a given period of time.

Budgets and forecasts help to aid the planning of actual operations by highlighting to managers how conditions might change in the future and what steps should be taken now to consider problems before they arise. Other purposes of budgets and forecasts are to:

- help management control its resources and cash
- help management communicate its plans to various departments within the organisation
- motivate management to achieve its budgeted goals
- evaluate the performance of managers, where actual performance can be measured against planned performance.

Types of budgets

There are many different types of budgets that can be prepared by management, depending on what management needs the budgeted information for. The main types are explained below.

Sales budget

A sales budget is an estimate of expected future sales and this is usually the first budget to be prepared. It indicates the expected number of units of a product to be sold, the expected selling price and the expected costs associated with sales for the future. A sales budget allows management to budget production and/or purchases of goods to meet expected sales. This is usually the first budget to be prepared; all other budgets are prepared from the results of this budget.

Production budget

The production budget shows the number of units that must be produced. To budget for annual production, three things must be known: the number of units to be sold, the required level of stock at the end of the year and the number of units, if any, in the beginning stock.

Operational budget

An operational budget is a budget of income and day-to-day expenses of the business. Income represents sales of products and services. Expenses represent the cost of goods sold as well as overhead and administration expenses directly related to producing goods and services.

Capital budget

A capital budget estimates all fixed asset purchases and summarises all expenses and costs of major purchases for the budgeted period. Capital assets include items that have useful lives of more than one year, such as buildings, land, furniture, equipment and motor vehicles.

Cash budget

A cash budget projects all cash inflows and outflows for the budgeted period. This is a very important budget as it allows management to identify potential periods with cash surpluses and shortages so they can take necessary remedial action.

Labour budget

A labour or personnel budget is a budget of costs associated with labour and wages. It forecasts costs such as recruitment, hiring, training, wages and overtime.

Master budget

The master budget consists of all the individual budgets required to prepare budgeted financial statements, i.e. the Profit and Loss account and Balance Sheet. Although different textbooks group the budgets differently, the main components of this budget are: operating budgets for income and expenses, capital expenditure budgets, cash budgets and finally the budgeted financial statements, which include the Profit and Loss account, Balance Sheet and Cash Flow Statement. The master budget may be viewed as the most important budget for a business as it is an aggregate of all the other budgets.

The budget period

The timeframe of the budget will depend on the business. For example, a government's budget may extend over a five-year period, whereas a retail shop may have a budget extending over a one-year period. The 'budget period' is the length of time for which a budget is prepared and used, which may then be subdivided into control periods, which usually correspond to calendar months. The most common period for a budget is one year, but there is no reason why this cannot be shorter or longer, depending on the requirements of the business.

Drawbacks of budgets

While budgets are an important aid to management in planning for the future, they do have their drawbacks:

- Budgets can be inflexible. A fixed budget does not facilitate any unexpected change in circumstances for the business. If an opportunity arises that has not been budgeted for, it may have to be passed over. It is therefore necessary that all budgets should have flexibility.
- Budgets can be time consuming and costly to produce. It may absorb a considerable amount of a manager's time, such as the time spent attending budget meetings, and drafting and redrafting the budget.
- Budgets can quickly become outdated. If a budget covers a calendar year, by the time November or December comes around, the information in the budget may be 15 months old, as the budget process would have to be started at least three months before the budget period begins.
- Budgets can create conflict between managers and staff if the targets are unrealistic. Staff may consider the targets too high and may lose motivation as a result. Budgets can be seen as pressure devices imposed by management, resulting in negative consequences such as bad labour relations or inaccurate record keeping.
- Waste may arise if managers adopt the view: 'We'd better spend it or we'll lose it.'
- Managers may overestimate costs so that they will not be blamed in the future, should they overspend.

Characteristics of a good budget

A good budget is characterised by the following:

- *Participation*: Involve as many people as possible in drawing up a budget.
- *Comprehensiveness*: Embrace the whole business.
- *Standards*: Base the budget on established standards of performance.
- *Flexibility*: Allow for changing circumstances.
- *Feedback*: Constantly monitor actual performance against the budget.

Review questions

1. Name four different types of budgets and briefly describe each type.
2. What are four main purposes of budgets?
3. What is the term used to describe the overall forecasted Profit and Loss and forecasted Balance Sheet?
4. Which of the following budgets is most likely to be prepared first?
   - ❏ Sales budget
   - ❏ Purchases budget
   - ❏ Cash budget
   - ❏ Stock budget

3.2 Cash Budgets, or Cash Flow Forecasts

Learning outcomes (Accounting Manual and Computerised 5N1348): 7 (part)

A cash budget, or cash flow forecast, is concerned with liquidity, rather than profitability. A business needs to not only earn profits, but also be able to pay debts as they fall due. A budget or forecast of cash requirements is therefore advisable in the ordinary course of trading and is essential when the company wants to make a decision regarding the expansion of capital expenditure.

A cash budget is concerned with cash inflows and outflows. No account is taken of sales until the debtor pays, or of purchases or other expenditure until the business pays the creditor. As the budget deals with future events, an estimate has to be made as to the average period of credit given to debtors and taken from creditors. A decision also has to be made as to the time span of the budget. Some companies may want a weekly cash budget but for others, a monthly budget would be adequate.

Cash inflows and outflows are netted off against each other to show the net cash inflow or outflow at a given point in time. This is especially useful for indicating the maximum bank overdraft a business will require during a period of expansion, pinpointing when this will occur. Similarly, it is advantageous to know whether the business will have a cash surplus for its requirements. Surplus cash can then be invested profitably in short-term or long-term projects.

The method used in preparing a cash budget is to take the information available and convert it into a cash basis, that is, identify cash inflows and outflows. These cash transactions are then listed for the shortest time basis being used. The totals are then summarised in the following format:

- Columns for months
- Rows for cash receipts and payments.

Example 1

Potter Ltd commenced business on 1 January with a cash balance of €4,000. From the following forecast information, prepare a monthly cash budget from January to June. Indicate the maximum overdraft required and when it will occur.

Purchases: €12,000 in January, €6,000 per month thereafter. One month's credit is taken from suppliers.

Sales: €15,000 per month. Two months' credit is given to customers.

Expenses: €600 per month, payable in the month incurred.

Figure 1 shows the cash budget for the period.

Cash Budget of Potter Ltd for 6 months to June

	January	February	March	April	May	June
Cash Inflow:	€	€	€	€	€	€
Receipts from Sales	0	0	15,000	15,000	15,000	15,000
Total Cash Inflow	0	0	15,000	15,000	15,000	15,000
Cash Outflow:						
Payment for Purchases	0	-12,000	-6,000	-6,000	-6,000	-6,000
Other expenses	-600	-600	-600	-600	-600	-600
Total Cash Outflow	-600	-12,600	-6,600	-6,600	-6,600	-6,600
Net Cash Inflow (Outflow)	**-600**	**-12,600**	**8,400**	**8,400**	**8,400**	**8,400**
Opening Balance	4,000	3,400	-9,200	-800	7,600	16,000
= Closing Balance	3,400	-9,200	-800	7,600	16,000	24,400

Figure 1

The maximum overdraft required will be in the region of €9,200 and will occur in February. The sales or purchases figures are not part of the budget until money is received from customers or paid to suppliers. For example, sales in January will not produce a cash inflow until March when the customers pay. Note that the closing balance of cash at the end of each month is the opening balance of cash at the beginning of the following month.

Example 2

Peter Lee started his own business on 1 July and wants to prepare a budget for the first four months of trading. He has opened a small hardware shop and invested €13,000 capital into the business, which he lodged to his business bank account. He estimates the following for the first four months of trading:

Total sales per month:

July	€8,000
August	€8,000
September	€9,500
October	€9,500

He expects that 80% of his sales will be on a cash basis and the remaining 20% of customers will be allowed one month's credit.

Total purchases per month (where one month's credit is allowed from suppliers):

July	€7,000
August	€6,000
September	€3,500
October	€3,500

He expects to hire specialised machinery at a cost of €100 per month, payable in the month incurred. He intends to purchase shop fittings in August at a cost of €28,000, payable at time of purchase. Other running costs are expected to be €200 per month, payable in the month incurred.

Figure 2 shows the cash budget for the four months.

Cash Budget of Peter Lee for 4 months to October

	July	August	September	October
Cash Inflow:	€	€	€	€
Receipts from Cash Sales 80%	6,400	6,400	7,600	7,600
Receipts from Credit Sales 20%	0	1,600	1,600	1,900
Total Cash Inflow:	6,400	8,000	9,200	9,500
Cash Outflow:				
Payment for Purchases	0	-7,000	-6,000	-3,500
Hire of Machinery	-100	-100	-100	-100
Purchase of shop fittings		-28,000		
Other expenses	-200	-200	-200	-200
Total Cash Outflow	-300	-35,300	-6,300	-3,800
Net Cash Inflow (Outflow)	6,100	-27,300	2,900	5,700
Opening Balance	13,000	19,100	-8,200	-5,300
= Closing Balance	19,100	-8,200	-5,300	400

Figure 2

An overdraft will be required in August, mainly to finance the purchase of shop fittings.

Review assignments

Assignment 1

Prepare a cash budget for John Kelly from the following information for the six months, January to June: The opening balance of cash on 1 January is to be €38,000. The sales and purchases forecasts are as follows:

	Jan	Feb	Mar	Apr	May	Jun
Cash Sales	€41,000	€45,000	€52,000	€52,000	€56,000	€56,000
Credit Sales	€15,000	€12,000	€13,000	€13,000	€18,000	€20,000
Purchases	€65,000	€52,000	€45,000	€45,000	€45,000	€45,000

- The business hopes to receive payment from credit sales in the month after sale. Credit sales for December of last year were €9,000. All purchases are on credit and the business hopes to receive one month's credit from its suppliers. Purchases for December of last year were €42,000.
- The business expects to purchase machinery in March costing €80,000 and will receive one month's credit from its supplier.
- Wages are to be paid in on the 1st of every month, costing €4,000.
- Other expenses are estimated to be €1,000 per month payable in the month incurred.

Assignment 2

Allen Ltd wishes to prepare a cash budget on a quarterly basis and has provided the following forecasted information:

	Quarter 1	Quarter 2	Quarter 3	Quarter 4
Sales	€42,000	€30,000	€35,000	€53,000
Purchases	€28,000	€25,000	€33,000	€26,000
Wages	€3,500	€3,500	€3,500	€6,000
Other expenses	€1,000	€1,000	€1,000	€2,500

- Cash sales are estimated to be 20% of total sales, the remainder being credit sales received in the following quarter. The total sales in quarter 4 of the previous year were €65,000.
- For purchases, 75% are paid in the same quarter, the remaining purchases being paid in the following quarter. Total purchases in quarter 4 of the previous year were €20,000.

- Wages and other expenses are paid in the quarter incurred.
- The bank balance at the beginning of quarter 1 was €9,250.

Prepare a cash budget of Allen Ltd on a quarterly basis.

Assignment 3

Maria Jones decided to commence business on 1 January, with capital of €50,000 lodged to her business bank account. Prior to commencing trading, she requires you to produce a Cash budget for the first three months of trading. She provides you with the following information:

Projected sales income:

January	€15,000
February	€13,500
March	€35,000

All sales are for cash.

Projected purchases:

January	€25,000
February	€10,000
March	€25,000

- All purchases are on credit, payable in the month following purchase.
- Drawings each month are expected to be €2,200.
- Rent amounts to €24,000 per annum, payable quarterly in advance.
- Furniture is expected to be purchased on 1 February, costing €34,000 payable immediately.
- Net wages are expected to be €2,000 per month payable in the month incurred. PAYE, PRSI and USC are expected to be €800, payable to the Revenue on the 23rd of the following month.
- Depreciation of furniture is to be calculated at 25% per annum straight-line and is provided for from the date of purchase.
- The advertising budget is €3,600, spread equally over the year, payable monthly with one month in arrears.

Review question

In a cash flow forecast, what is meant by the closing balance?

❏ How much cash the business is expected to have at the end of the budgeted time period.

❏ How much cash the business has at the start of the budgeted time period.

❏ The total cash outflows during the budgeted time period.

❏ The total cash inflows during the budgeted time period.

3.3 Forecasted Profit and Loss and Balance Sheet

Learning outcomes (Accounting Manual and Computerised 5N1348): 7 (part)

Once budgets are prepared, management can then calculate the effect of meeting them on the profit (or loss) and on the assets and liabilities of the business. Once it has an idea of the budgeted sales and related costs, management is in a position to prepare forecasted financial statements. This will show whether management is likely to achieve its first key financial requirement of making a profit.

Forecasted Profit and Loss

The Profit and Loss account records all income and expenses of the business for a given period of time, the difference being profit or loss. A profit or loss forecast is simply the difference between future or forecasted income and expenses. Here, estimated income and expenses are used instead of actual amounts. The responsibility lies with the management of a business to produce a forecasted Profit and Loss account, where they need to know the future profitability of the business.

Example 1

From the Cash Budget of Potter Ltd in example 1, section 3.2, it is possible to construct a forecasted Profit and Loss account. Here Potter Ltd needs to know what percentage of the selling price is gross profit.

Assume the gross profit of Potter Ltd is 60%. This means that 60% of his sales represents gross profit. Knowing this, we can prepare a forecasted Profit and Loss Account of Potter Ltd for the six months ending 30 June as shown (fig. 1):

Forecasted Profit and Loss of Potter Ltd for 6 months to 30 June

	€	€
Sales		90,000
Less Cost of Sales:		
Opening Stock	0	
Add Purchases	42,000	
= Cost of goods available for sale	42,000	
Less Closing Stock	-6,000	
= Cost of Sales		36,000
= Gross Profit		54,000
Less Expenses		-3,600
= Net Profit		**50,400**

Figure 1

Note: Gross profit percentage is 60%, i.e. gross profit is 60% of sales.

Sales €90,000
Gross Profit 60% €54,000

Therefore Cost of Sales = Sales less Gross Profit: €36,000

Closing Stock = (Opening Stock + Purchases) less Cost of Sales: €6,000.

There is no opening stock as the business commenced trade on 1 January. The Profit and Loss account records the income *earned* for the 6 months and the expenses *incurred* for the 6 months, regardless of when they were paid.

Example 2

From the cash budget of Peter Lee in example 2, section 3.2, we can prepare a forecasted Profit and Loss account (fig. 2). Peter expects that his gross profit percentage will be 45%.

Forecasted Profit & Loss of Peter Lee for 4 months to 31 October

	€	€
Sales		35,000
Less Cost of Sales:		
Opening Stock	0	
Add Purchases	20,000	
= Cost of goods available for sale	20,000	
Less Closing Stock	-750	
= Cost of Sales		19,250
= Gross Profit		15,750
Less Expenses:		
Hire machinery	400	
Other expenses	800	
		-1,200
= Net Profit		**14,550**

Figure 2

Note: Gross profit percentage is 45%.

Sales   €35,000
Gross Profit 45%   €15,750

Therefore Cost of Sales = Sales – Gross Profit: €19,250

Closing Stock = (Opening Stock + Purchases) less Cost of Sales: €750.

There is no opening stock as the business commenced trade on 1 July. The purchase of the shop fittings is a fixed asset and is not an expense in the Profit and Loss account.

Forecasted Balance Sheet

A Balance Sheet is a statement of the assets and liabilities of a business, to include owner's equity. Owner's equity represents the capital invested in the business plus any profits that are retained in the business. A forecasted Balance Sheet is simply a statement of future assets, liabilities and owner's equity.

Example 1

From the cash budget and forecasted Profit and Loss of Potter Ltd we can draw up a forecasted Balance Sheet for the six months ending 30 June. Firstly, the debtors and creditors balances as at 30 June would be calculated.

Debtors:
Two month's credit is given to customers. The debtors balance represents the forecasted sales for May and June that are unpaid at the end of the period. This amounts to €15,000 × 2 months = €30,000.

Creditors:
One month's credit is taken from suppliers. The creditors balance represents the forecasted purchases for June that are unpaid at the end of the period. This amounts to €6,000.

Bank balance:
This is the forecasted closing balance in the cash budget as at 30 June: €24,400.

Capital:
This is the amount invested by the owner, plus the forecasted net profit at the end of the period.

Figure 3 shows the forecasted Balance Sheet.

Forecasted Balance Sheet of Potter Ltd for 6 months ending 30 June	€	€
FIXED ASSETS		Nil
CURRENT ASSETS:		
Closing Stock	6,000	
Debtors	30,000	
Bank	24,400	
Total Current Assets	60,400	
CURRENT LIABILITIES:		
Creditors	6,000	
Net Current Assets		54,400
Total Net Assets		54,400
Financed by:		
Capital		4,000
Add Net Profit		50,400
Total Capital employed		54,400

Figure 3

Example 2

A forecasted Balance Sheet of Peter Lee can also be prepared from his cash budget and forecasted Profit and Loss (fig. 4).

Forecasted Balance Sheet of Peter Lee for 4 months ending 31 October

	€	€
FIXED ASSETS		
Shop Fittings		28,000
CURRENT ASSETS:		
Closing Stock	750	
Debtors	1,900	
Bank	400	
Total Current Assets	3,050	
CURRENT LIABILITIES:		
Creditors	3,500	
Net Current Assets		-450
Total Net Assets		27,550
Financed by:		
Capital		13,000
Add Net Profit		14,550
Total Capital employed		27,550

Figure 4

Note:
Debtors: 20% of October sales remain unpaid = €9,500 × 20% = €1,900.
Creditors: October purchases remain unpaid = €3,500.
Bank: Closing balance as per cash Budget = €400.

Example 3 (Comprehensive)

Lakeview Ltd intends commencing business on 1 July. During the month of June, the owners lodged €150,000 into the business bank account. Also during June, the company purchased machinery for €30,000 and stock for €25,000, and paid by cheque from the business bank account. This leaves a bank balance of €95,000 on I July. Forecasts for the year beginning 1 July are:

- Purchases of stock each month will be €18,000 and will be sold each month at a mark-up of 25%.
- Debtors will be allowed two months' credit.
- Creditors will allow one month's credit.
- Wages will be €2,800 per month and payable in the month incurred.
- Other operating expenses total €1,500 per month and are payable in the month incurred.

Figure 5 provides a comprehensive example for the following three tasks:

1. Prepare a cash budget for the 6 months July to December.
2. Prepare a forecasted Profit and Loss account for the 6 months ending 31 December.
3. Prepare a forecasted Balance Sheet for the 6 months ending 31 December.

Cash Budget of Lakeview Ltd for 6 months to December

	Jul	Aug	Sep	Oct	Nov	Dec
Cash Inflow:	€	€	€	€	€	€
Receipts from Sales	0	0	22,500	22,500	22,500	22,500
Total Cash Inflow:	0	0	22,500	22,500	22,500	22,500
Cash Outflow:						
Payment for Purchases	0	-18,000	-18,000	-18,000	-18,000	-18,000
Wages	-2,800	-2,800	-2,800	-2,800	-2,800	-2,800
Other expenses	-1,500	-1,500	-1,500	-1,500	-1,500	-1,500
Total Cash Outflow:	-4,300	-22,300	-22,300	-22,300	-22,300	-22,300
Net Cash Inflow (Outflow)	-4,300	-22,300	200	200	200	200
Opening Balance	95,000	90,700	68,400	68,600	68,800	69,000
= Closing Balance	90,700	68,400	68,600	68,800	69,000	69,200

Forecasted Profit & Loss of Lakeview Ltd for 6 months to 31 Dec

	€	€
Sales		135,000
Less Cost of Sales:		
Opening Stock	25,000	
Add Purchases	108,000	
= Cost of goods available for sale	133,000	
Less Closing Stock	-25,000	
= Cost of Sales		108,000
= Gross Profit		27,000
Less Expenses:		
Wages	16,800	
Other Expenses	9,000	
		-25,800
= Net Profit		1,200

Forecasted Balance Sheet of Lakeview Ltd for 6 months to 31 Dec

	€	€
FIXED ASSETS		
Machinery		30,000
CURRENT ASSETS:		
Closing Stock	25,000	
Debtors	45,000	
Bank	69,200	
Total Current Assets:	139,200	
CURRENT LIABILITIES:		
Creditors	18,000	
Net Current Assets:		121,200
Total Net Assets:		**151,200**
Financed by:		
Capital		150,000
Add Net Profit		1,200
Total Capital employed:		**151,200**

Figure 5

Review assignments

Assignment 1

Prepare a forecasted Profit and Loss and Balance Sheet for John Kelly from the information supplied in assignment 1, section 3.2. John forecasts a gross profit percentage of 40%. John's opening stock on 1 January is €8,500.

Assignment 2

Prepare a forecasted Profit and Loss and Balance Sheet for Allen Ltd from the information supplied in assignment 2, section 3.2. Allen forecasts a gross profit percentage of 25%. The opening stock of the business at the beginning of quarter 1 was €12,500.

Assignment 3

Using the information supplied for the cash budget of Maria Jones in assignment 3, section 3.2, she requires you to produce a forecasted Profit and Loss account and a forecasted Balance Sheet for the first three months of trading. Maria anticipates a gross profit margin of 30%.

Part 4

Introduction to Computerised Accounts

4.1 Introduction to Computerised Accounts

Learning outcomes (Accounting Manual and Computerised 5N1348): 6 and 11 (part)
Learning outcomes (Bookkeeping Manual and Computerised 5N1354): 1 (part) and 2

Accounting is a necessary function for any business, in order to keep a record of income, expenses, assets and liabilities. These records should be as detailed as possible. The concept of keeping records on spreadsheets, daybooks and ledgers on a manual basis is very time consuming. Computerised accounting is for many businesses a welcome relief.

Computerised accounting comprises application software that records and processes accounting transactions within functional ledgers such as creditors, debtors and bank. It can vary greatly in its complexity and cost. The software may be developed in-house by the company using it. It may be purchased from a third party, or may be a combination of a third-party application software package with local modifications.

Computerised accounting software consists of core modules or ledgers. The main modules in all types of software usually consist of:

- **Purchases or creditors** – where the company enters purchases and returns, and pays money it owes to suppliers
- **Sales or debtors** – where the company enters sales, returns and money received from customers
- **Bank or cash book** – where the company enters other bank current account payments and receipts and petty cash book payments and receipts
- **Purchase orders** – where the company orders stock
- **Sales orders** – where the company records customer orders for the supply of stock
- **Stock** – where the company keeps control of its stock
- **Nominal** – where the company processes adjustments to the accounts.

Computerised accounting has replaced manual-based accounting in virtually all businesses, providing accountants, managers and employees with access to vital accounting information at the touch of a button. Computerised accounting automates the process, improves efficiency and cuts down costs for the company or business. Financial reports are automatically generated at the end of each accounting period. Computerised accounting eliminates paper work making it easier and faster to collect, store and trail all transactions as they occur.

The manual accounting process includes the following steps:

1. Records the transactions in a daybook.
2. Posts the transactions to ledger accounts, where a double-entry is completed.
3. Balances the ledger accounts.
4. Prepares the Trial Balance from the balances in the ledger.
5. Makes adjustment entries for items such as depreciation, bad debts and accruals.
6. Prepares the adjusted end-of-period Trial Balance.
7. Prepares the financial statements, such as the Profit and Loss account and Balance Sheet.

From a first look this does not appear to be difficult, but when there are thousands or millions of transactions the situation dramatically changes. A lot of transactions are routine but even a little mistake or inaccuracy in the accounting process can mean that the whole process needs be rechecked from the very beginning in order to find and correct the error.

Computerised accounting makes this much simpler. The only thing that is required is to input transactions into the computer, which then processes the other steps automatically or by request.

Advantages and disadvantages of computerised accounting

Advantages

Computer accounting software calculates faster but it cannot meet your business needs unless you are clear about your purpose. Good computerised accounting software is expensive, depending on the complexity and size of the company or business. Its main advantages are:

- **Speed:** Computerised accounting software allows the user to enter the transaction into the program once, and all accounts are updated as necessary. For example, if the company sells €1,000 worth of goods to a customer, plus VAT of €230, the transaction is entered in the sales ledger as a single transaction. The customer's account, VAT account and sales account are updated simultaneously. The Trial Balance is updated also, along with the Profit and Loss account and Balance Sheet. This is much faster as far as entering information is concerned.

  What could take several minutes manually takes only seconds with computerised accounting software. Also, because only one entry needs to be made with a computerised system, the likelihood of an incorrect entry is greatly reduced.

- **Report generation:** Computerised accounting software will automatically pull all relevant ledger entries for the period to produce reports. With a manual system, each general ledger entry would have to be posted to the financial statements by hand. With computerised accounting software, each computerised transaction is automatically posted to both the general journal and the respective ledgers. This makes producing balance sheets, trial balances, and end-of-period financial reports as simple as selecting the desired report from the menu. Although manual accounting takes longer, it does help a bookkeeper better understand the posting and end-of-period process. This is one reason why it is very unwise for accounting students to take a computerised accounting course until they fully understand the manual accounting system.
- **Data manipulation:** With a computerised accounting system, information for a particular period of time can be compiled quickly. With a manual system, it can take time to locate the information from each book and compile it into a report.
- **Up-to-date information:** Because each entered transaction is automatically posted to its respective account, all account information is always up-to-date.
- **Easy document production:** Purchase orders, sales receipts, sales invoices, stock lists and other items can be printed in moments.
- **Increased security:** A computerised system can be protected by logging in user names and passwords, which will eliminate any unauthorised persons viewing sensitive financial information.
- **Legibility:** Computerised accounting software eliminates the need to decipher poor or odd handwriting, eliminating much of the possibility of error due to misreading a handwritten line item.
- **Automatic accounting for taxation:** This makes paying taxes such as VAT easier since the computerised system will keep a running total of all taxes owed.

Disadvantages

Although the advantages of computerised accounting are many, it does have its disadvantages, which should also be considered:

- **Cost:** Computerised accounting incurs extremely high costs for developing, introducing and using the system. The costs will vary depending on the size of the company and the software used. Special training is required for personnel, which increases labour costs.
- **Dependency on machines:** There is a high dependence on computers. If there is a computer or network malfunction, users are unable to process the accounts.
- **Undetected errors:** Computerised accounting software is not entirely error-free. Computers are liable to inaccurately record transactions and/or

fail to record transactions. It is not uncommon for computerised accounting software to record transactions in incorrect accounts, make multiple records of a transaction or enter incorrect information in the credit and debit parts of a transaction. These errors can be reduced and/or eliminated by manual checks of all recorded transactional data.

Advantages and disadvantages of manual accounting

The main advantages of manual accounting are:

* It requires fewer resources.
* It is mostly reliable.
* It is independent of machines and technical malfunctions.
* It does not rely on highly skilled IT personnel.

The main disadvantages of manual accounting are:

* It is slow compared to computerised accounting.
* It creates more effort for accountants, due to relatively slower internal control reporting.
* It is subject to frequent human error. Common errors are: entering information into incorrect accounts, transposing figures or recording information backwards. While these errors are also in computerised accounting systems, manual systems have no internal checks and balances to detect them. Accountants researching errors will often spend several hours locating and correcting entries.
* It lacks security. Compared to computer accounting, which is password protected, companies may be unable to prevent employees from reviewing sensitive data in paper ledgers and journals.

Obviously both computerised and manual accounting have advantages and disadvantages but they perform the same task and the final result is the same.

Accounting software currently available

There are several accounting software packages available. Some companies use software developed in-house. Others purchase from a third party or a combination of a third-party application software package with local modifications. Computerised accounting software can vary greatly in its complexity and cost. Some of the most common software packages available from third parties are described below.

TASBooks Accounting Plus, Version 2

TASBooks is for small and medium-sized Irish businesses. It maintains all the books of account, including payments, receipts, sales and purchases. It also provides quick journal entries, bank reconciliations and cash flow forecasts; converts sales orders into sales invoices; uses the e-payments facility to pay suppliers with ease; holds project records and marketing records; and creates product and service invoices to print and post or email to customers. It also has a simple backup facility and VAT returns can be submitted online. It keeps all the key information at hand, including month-by-month summaries, for three years. It is a complete accounting package capable of producing final accounts.

TASBooks Version 3

TASBooks Version 3 has all the accounting functionality of *TASBooks* Version 2 with the added benefit of stock control and purchase orders. This uses the stock additions to control purchasing, by creating purchase orders and matching purchase invoices to stock received. It streamlines stock control and allows easy monitoring of stock levels, back orders and stock valuations. It controls purchasing by ordering only what is needed. Purchase orders can be customised, printed or emailed. It has added features such as stock reports, which show how much stock is on hand, what is on back order and the level of re-orders.

Sage Accounts (Sage 50 Accounts Professional)

This is ideal for established small and medium-sized businesses that need to consolidate their finances across a number of companies or trade overseas. It has all the characteristics of *TASBooks*, with the added benefit of processing large volumes of financial data across a number of companies, and allows multi-currency banking, foreign trading and sales and purchase-order processing. It is relatively easy to set up and use. It has all the functions of *TASBooks* above with a full stock control system. It has the added benefit for companies who wish to trade in different currencies, raise invoices, pay suppliers and set up foreign bank accounts. It also produces final accounts and automatically calculates VAT and can submit returns online to Revenue Online Services.

Thesaurus Accounts (Solutions Plus)

This is a complete accounting package, which also processes all the books of account as per *TASBooks* and *Sage*. File structures are kept basic for ease of entry and it has full integration with *Thesaurus* (payroll).

Big Red Book Accounts

Big Red Book Accounting Software is simple and practical and is a full accounts software package.

Pegasus Accounts

Pegasus Opera 3 is also a complete business solution and allows full integration of accounts like all other software above.

Data accuracy

Data accuracy can be defined as how closely the results derived from accounts resemble the truth. As money continually goes in and out of a business, it needs to produce accurate accounts. For example, if a bank made an error that caused their records to show false balance figures in their customers' account, the customers would switch to a different bank. If the business does not produce accuracy in its accounting records, it could be potentially ruined. Take, for example, if an employee is entering figures into the accounts and accidentally adds an extra zero to a figure of €5,000 for VAT. The figure would then be €50,000. While the problem would eventually be picked up, it could cause mass confusion and loss of confidence in the business as a whole.

There is also the importance of tracking expenses, debtors, creditors, VAT and bank transactions. If there were a problem when processing the accounts, e.g. showing out-of-date figures, it might cost the business in the long run. All businesses should observe the most stringent standards in the keeping of accounts and records. Accurate disclosures are also essential to the operations and compliance with laws on accounting, taxation, filings, public disclosures and other important obligations.

It is the obligation of all businesses to keep books, records, accounts and financial statements in reasonable detail, appropriately reflecting the business's transactions, and to conform to both accounting standards and appropriate legislation.

Accounting and financial reporting practices must comply with applicable, generally accepted accounting principles and other criteria, such as local legislation and Revenue requirements. There must be internal controls to enable businesses to demonstrate that entries in financial records are accurate and complete and made in accordance with applicable regulations.

Keeping data accuracy in mind, remember that accounting systems follow a double-entry system and process the information in the same manner as a manual system. So you must follow the rule in computerised accounts that every entry has an amount on the debit side to correspond with a similar amount on the credit side. The totals of the debits must match the totals of the credits to the last cent, otherwise the entry will not be valid and will not balance.

Anti-virus protection software

A computer virus is a program that spreads from one computer to another by replicating itself. Viruses are also known as 'malware', which means malicious software. They are transferred via a number of means, without the host's knowledge. These include email attachments and downloading from the internet.

Anti-virus protection software can perform the following functions:

- It can automatically or manually scan a computer to search for computer viruses. If it finds a virus, it may remove it without the host knowing or alert the host and ask to clean the computer to get rid of the virus.
- Some anti-virus software can prevent click fraud. This is where a malicious piece of software records credit card numbers or other personal information. Anti-virus software will increase security for your computer to stop this from happening.
- It keeps up with the latest threats. This is achieved by daily updates of the anti-virus software, which counteract the latest threats to provide constant protection.
- The software may run in the background at all times, and should be kept updated so that it recognises new versions of malicious software.

The main type of virus that can damage files on a computer is Spyware. This is specifically designed to infect a computer and spy on its user. The spyware seeks and steals all personal information stored on a computer. This can include financial data, passwords, PPS numbers and credit card numbers. It can be so sophisticated that it can record and save data in real time and can run silently in the background. As the user of a computer enters a credit card number to pay for a purchase, the spyware records and saves the payment information and often transfers the personal data to its designer in a remote location.

Computerised accounts software can be run with an internet connection to perform updates automatically. As a user of computerised accounts, it is vital that the computer is protected with anti-virus software at all times.

Part 5
TASBooks

5.1 Using *TASBooks*

Learning outcomes (Accounting Manual and Computerised 5N1348): 11 (part)

The *TASBooks* computerised software used throughout this section is *TASBooks* Version 3.01.

Before you start entering company details in *TASBooks*, the following are some notes that you should be aware of before you start.

Selection of the program

S1

Menus

To select a program, the menu option is mainly used (see screens s1 and s1a). The main menus that you will be using are:

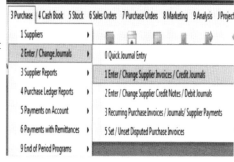

s1a

- **Purchase** – records purchase invoices, credit notes and payments to suppliers; creates supplier records and prints reports. Here, select the menu option, as displayed.
- **Sales** – records sales invoices, credit notes and receipts from customers; creates customer records and prints reports.
- **Cash book** – records other payments and receipts, excluding payments to suppliers and receipts from customers. This is used mainly to record payments of business expenses, such as wages and insurance. This menu is also used for petty cash payments and receipts.
- **Nominal** – the menu you will use to set up ledger accounts. This menu is also used to process adjustments to final accounts such as depreciation, bad debts, accruals and prepayments. The Trial Balance, Profit and Loss account and Balance Sheet are also printed from this menu.
- **Central** – sets up the company's details and configuration settings. VAT records and reporting is also in this menu.
- **File** – closes the *TASBooks* program and sets toolbars. You can also exit *TASBooks* by clicking on the **X** at the top right-hand corner of the window.

The other menus in *TASBooks* concern purchase ordering, sales orders, marketing and analysis reports and are not part of this course.

Toolbars

The toolbars in *TASBooks* that you can use are as follows:

- **Customers** – produces a customer-interactive flow chart, which can be used to access the programs and print reports of customers.
- **Sales** – produces the sales book, which is a list of the sales and returns for a particular period. This also produces the cash daybook, which is a list of sales receipts from customers.
- **Suppliers** – produces a supplier-interactive flow chart, which can be used to access the programs and print reports of suppliers.
- **Purchases** – produces the purchases book, which is a list of the purchases and returns for a particular period. This also produces the cash daybook, which is a list of payments made to suppliers.
- **Bank** – produces a bank-interactive flow chart that can be used to create an account, record receipts and payments and print reports.
- **Cash daybook** – prints cash book payments and receipts from any bank account selected.

Fields

All the data in the system is contained in fields, each of which contains one piece of data. Some fields are displayed in blue, such as Customer Code (s2). This indicates that it is a key field and allows the look-up facility (F2 or click on blue area) to be used. This is very useful in locating codes of customers that cannot be remembered.

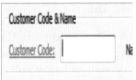

s2

Some fields display a down arrow, where you select your choice from the drop-down list (s3). The option needed can also be selected by pressing the up and down arrows on your keyboard.

Tab key

s3

The **Tab** key is a very important key in *TASBooks*. Pressing the **Tab** key moves the cursor from one field to the next. This is the method used to enter the data on almost all occasions. Some fields, such as an address of a customer or supplier, will have a number of lines in the same field. In this instance, use the **Enter** key to move from line to line in the same field.

Function keys

When you are working in *TASBooks*, you will need to make selections, for example, to select a customer or supplier, to select a nominal ledger account to make an entry or to print a report. In these situations, if you know your selection, such as a customer code or supplier code, you can simply enter it into the relevant field, but if you do not remember the code, use the **F2** key on your keyboard. This presents you with a look-up list of all the available codes, which you can simply pick from.

If you prefer to use the keyboard when entering your data in *TASBooks*, you can use the following shortcut keys:

F1 opens the *TASBooks* help system.
F2 displays the look-up list. (This will be the most used function key.)
F3 clears the screen.
F4 deletes the current record.
F5 moves to the first record.
F6 moves to the last record.
F7 moves the previous record.
F8 moves to the next record.
F9 searches for a record.
F10 saves the current record.
F11 is Smart Field – pop-up spell-checker, calendar or calculator.

ESC exits the window without saving.
Tab moves to the next field or box.
SHIFT + **Tab** moves back to the previous field or box.
END moves the cursor to the last character of the field or box.
HOME moves the cursor to the start of the field or box

ALT + **S** saves the current record.
ALT + **A** exits the window without saving.
ALT + **D** deletes the current record.
ALT + **O** is 'OK'.
ALT + **P** is Print.
ALT + **H** opens the *TASBooks* help system.
CTRL + **Insert** inserts a line in journal.
CTRL + **Delete** deletes a line from journal.

Onscreen instructions

You will notice that each time you are required to enter data or perform a certain task, there are onscreen instructions at the bottom of the screen that may be of help to you.

Customising the company

It would be useful to amend the company's name to include your own name or initials, especially if working in a classroom situation. This will help in the identification of printouts if other students are printing from the same printer. This can be done in the **(0)Central > (1)General Company Information > (1)Company Configuration**.

Customising reports

s4

s4a

It may be useful to customise reports in *TASBooks* in order to show only the information that is relevant to a particular report (s4). If you need to do this, select 'customise' on each report from the toolbar in the report menu. Change the font size if necessary. Uncheck the columns that you do not want displayed in the report and increase the width between the displayed columns so that they are fully visible in the report. The Trial Balance is customised to show only the necessary displayed columns (s5). When finished, click **OK** and refresh the report by using the appropriate icon from the toolbar. You may need to customise again if the report is not displayed correctly.

s5

Users and passwords

The default user code for *TASBooks* is **SPV** and the default password is SPV. This is the abbreviation for the user name 'Supervisor', where the user has all privileges and can use all menus and run all the reports. It may be necessary in some instances to restrict users to certain parts of the menu system. For example, a junior clerk may not be granted access to the bank account details or the Profit and Loss and Balance Sheet reports. Other users may be set up in *TASBooks* and their access can be restricted to certain menus if required.

A user account should ideally be set up for every person who uses *TASBooks*. Here, you can specify the level of access for each user, the information they can view and the menus they have access to. You can also edit existing users' accounts, for example, to change their password, or to add access to additional areas.

To add or edit a user, select **(0)Central > (4)User Password Maintenance > (1)Maintain Users**. The User Manager is displayed (s6). To add a new user, click on **Add**.

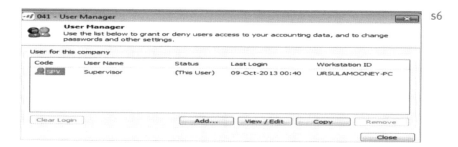

The 'Maintain User Settings' window is then displayed. Enter a user code and then name of the user. Check the box 'Needs Password to login'. Set the password in the 'Set Password' window. In the Options tab, check or uncheck the boxes for the required access. In the Access Rights tab, double-click on the options to grant access right to different menus.

To edit an existing user, select the user from the users' list and click **View/ Edit**. To create a user with the same settings as an existing user, click **Copy**. Choose the user you want to copy and click **OK**. If you want to delete a user, select the user and click **Remove**.

Exiting *TASBooks*

At the end of your session, you must exit the program completely. When you exit the main window by using the File menu or the **X** at the top right-hand of the screen, you must also exit the *TASBooks* Company Manager that is minimised on the taskbar.

In order to demonstrate the menus in *TASBooks* and how the software works, the accounts of Daly's Pharmacy Ltd that were completed in the manual accounts sections will be used. All other functions that are not part of this exercise will be demonstrated later.

5.2 Installing *TASBooks* and Creating a New Company

Learning outcomes (Accounting Manual and Computerised 5N1348): 8 (part)
Learning outcomes (Book-keeping Manual and Computerised 5N1354): 8 (part)

The first step in *TASBooks* is to install the software on your computer, if not already installed. Follow the installation instructions that are available with the *TASBooks* program.

Installation

After installation, select the program from your desktop. The Product Activation Assistant will be displayed (s1). You will need to activate the software with the serial number and company name supplied with the licence. This information will be supplied by your college or the holder of the licence agreement.

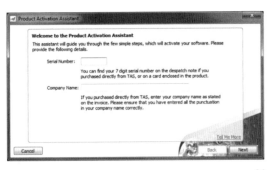

S1

The program will attempt to activate automatically if connected to the internet. If not, enter the serial number, licence name, company ID and activation code supplied with the licence.

Creating a company from scratch

Once *TASBooks* has been licensed, the screen is displayed as shown (s2). *Note: TASBooks* will have a demonstration company set up, but it is preferable to create a company from scratch. In this way, you can set up your own structure of nominal ledger accounts.

We will create a new company. To do so, we will set up the company 'Daly's Pharmacy Ltd', which you completed on a manual basis in Part 1.

After clicking **Next**, enter the details of Daly's Pharmacy Ltd (s3). Click **Next** again and the screen will display as shown (s4).

Click **Close** and the new company 'Daly's Pharmacy Ltd' will appear on the *TASBooks* Company Manager.

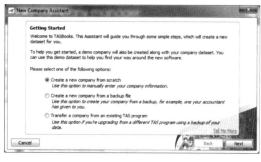

S2

S3

S4

S5

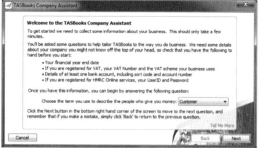

S6

Select **Daly's Pharmacy Ltd** from the company window by double-clicking on it or clicking on **Start TASBooks** (s5).

A *TASBooks* Company Assistant will be displayed (s6). After clicking **Next**, enter the default password SPV (s7). *Note:* You can change the password, but we will use the default password SPV throughout this section. It will display the strength as 'weak', but accept this password for the present.

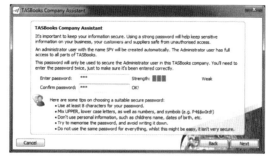

S7

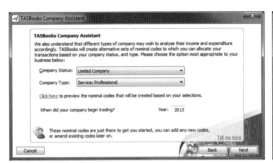

s8

s9

After clicking **Next**, the Company Status/Type and Year fields are displayed (s8). Enter the start year of your accounts. For demonstration purposes, 2013 is displayed. Accept the company status and company type. This will not be relevant as you will be setting up your own company from scratch.

After clicking **Next**, the Financial Year details are displayed (s9). Set the start year as 'January' on a monthly-based financial year. After clicking **Next**, the VAT details are displayed (s10). Select 'I am registered for VAT' and enter the VAT registration number of Daly's Pharmacy Ltd, as shown.

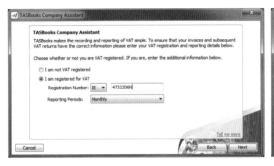

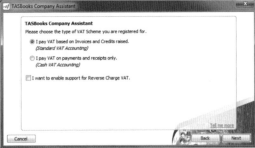

S10

S11

After clicking **Next**, select 'I pay VAT based on Invoices and Credits raised' (s11). *Note:* Refer to Part 1 for an explanation of the Invoice Basis for VAT.

After clicking **Next**, click **Next** again on the remaining two screens. You have now created the company Daly's Pharmacy Ltd. Click **Finish** (s12). You will now be asked to log onto Daly's Pharmacy Ltd. Enter the password SPV and Login (s13).

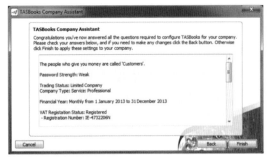

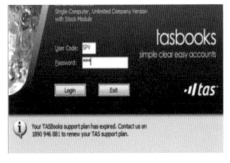

S12

S13

If a number of information windows are displayed after logging in, close these.

For the purposes of setting up Daly's Pharmacy Ltd, you will mainly be using the Menu options. You can use the interactive flow charts if you prefer.

You are creating Daly's Pharmacy Ltd from scratch. At this time, Daly's Pharmacy Ltd has a list of demonstration nominal accounts set up. You need to clear these nominal accounts from the system and set up your own structure of accounts. To do this, you need to clear down the data files (s14).

Select **(0)Central > (4)User Password Maintenance > (9)Cleardown Data Files**.

The screen will then be displayed as shown (s15). Select 'All Data', and click on **Cleardown**. A warning message will be displayed to prompt you that the action is not reversible. Click **Yes** and the process will then be complete.

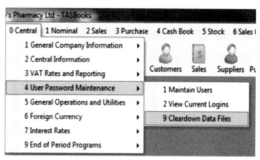

S14

S15

Setting up Daly's Pharmacy Ltd

You need to work through this section carefully to enter the company details of Daly's Pharmacy Ltd and the configuration settings. Each ledger within *TASBooks* needs certain options and default settings to work correctly.

Using the Company Configuration and *TASBooks* Configuration windows, you will need to enter VAT options, default nominal accounts, ageing periods and so on.

Please refer to the online Student Resources on www.gillmacmillan.ie for TASBooks Configuration. A backup file of Daly's Pharmacy Ltd is contained in your Student Resources. This contains the set-up of Daly's Pharmacy Ltd. Refer to section 5.3 to restore the backup file.

5·3 Files and Folders in *TASBooks*

Learning outcomes (Accounting Manual and Computerised 5N1348): 8 (part) and 11 (part)

In order to have more than one company running at the same time in *TASBooks*, your program needs to be a multi-company version. If it is a single-company version, then it will only be possible to have one company running at a time. In this instance, it would be necessary to clear down or delete the files of the first company to continue with the transactions of another company. The program used here for demonstration purposes is a multi-company version.

Delete a company from *TASBooks*

From the *TASBooks* Company Manager window, you can see two companies – Daly's Pharmacy Ltd (that you have set up) and a Demonstration Company (s1). To delete or remove the Demonstration Company, open the *TASBooks* Company Manager as shown. Select the Demonstration Company.

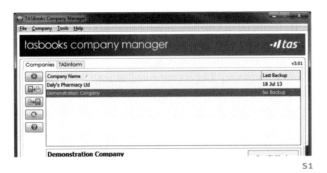

S1

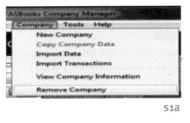

S1a

Click on **Company > Remove Company** from the menu, as displayed (1a). The screen will be displayed as shown (s2). Click **Next**. The window will be displayed as shown (s3). Check the box 'I understand that this process will remove all datafiles for this company and that I'm happy to continue'. Then click **Finish**. The company will then be successfully removed.

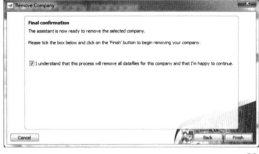

S2 S3

Backup a company in *TASBooks*

It is most important to take regular backups of your data files in case of loss of data on your computer. Backup storage can be on the hard drive of your computer, CD, DVD or memory key. In order to perform a backup, the company must be closed down and the *TASBooks* Company Manager window open. To take a backup of Daly's Pharmacy Ltd, open the *TASBooks* Company Manager window (s4). Select the company, if not already selected.

S4

Click on the backup icon on the left-hand side to start the backup. The screen will be displayed as shown (s5). Click on **Browse** to choose the location of your backup. Displayed is the C: drive on the computer. Click **Start** and the backup will be performed.

S5

Restore a company in *TASBooks*

You may need to restore files from a previous backup in a situation where you need the files on a different computer, or the existing files on your computer were damaged or deleted in error. In order to restore files, there must be a previous backup of the same files. Again, to restore files, you must exit *TASBooks* and open the *TASBooks* Company Manager window. To restore the files of Daly's Pharmacy Ltd, open the *TASBooks* Company Manager window and select the company, if not already selected.

Click on the Restore icon on the left-hand side to start the restore (s6). The screen will be displayed as shown (s7). Click **Browse** to choose the location of your last backup file that is to be restored. The C: drive on the computer was chosen as the last backup file that is now to be restored. Click **Next**.

After you click **Next**, the screen will be displayed as shown (s8). Select 'Restore all files', if not already selected and click **Next**.

s6

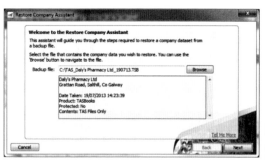

s7

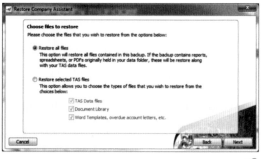

s8

The screen displayed may state that the company exists already (s9). If you restore, you will overwrite the files of Daly's Pharmacy Ltd, which in this instance is what you need to do. Select the check box accordingly. Click **Next**.

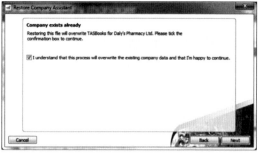

s9

S10

The screen will be displayed as shown (s10). Click **Restore** to confirm you want to restore the files.

The restore process will commence and the screen will inform you that the restore was successful (s11). Click **Close**.

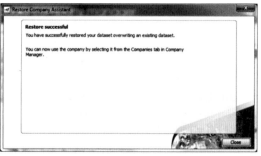

S11

Set up a new company in *TASBooks*

In order to set up a second company, your program needs to be a multi-company version. To set up a new company, select the 'Add Company' icon on the left-hand side (s12). The following text will be displayed as shown (s13).

S12

- **Create a new company from scratch** – This could be an option to use if you wish to set up a company from scratch where you intend to clear down the data files and set up the company configuration. It would also be acceptable to use this option and restore set-up files from a previous company that you have backed up.
- **Create a new company from a backup file** – As it suggests, use this option if you are using a previous backup file and you want to restore the files to a new company.
- **Transfer from a different TAS program** – Use this option if your backup file was from a previous version of *TASBooks*. It will restore the files to the present version.
- **Create a demonstration company** – Use this option if you want to restore the demonstration company already deleted previously.
-

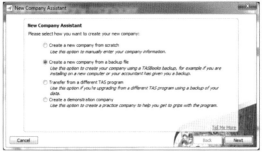

S13   S14

In this demonstration, a new company will be created from the backup file already created of Daly's Pharmacy Ltd. Select this option and click **Next**. The screen will be displayed as shown (s14). Browse for the backup folder, which was created on the C: drive, as shown. Click **Next**.

TASBooks will ask you to confirm the information to create a new company and click **Finish** (s15). A new company has been created successfully (s16). Click **Close**.

You will now have two companies in the *TASBooks* Company Manager (s17). The second company is the new company created.

S15

s16

s17

If you wish to start a new company, select the company and make the necessary changes to the name and all the company details. For example, open the new company and rename it 'Longville Ltd' in the Central menu.

Refresh a company list

After you make changes to the company name, the new name may not be in the *TASBooks* Company Manager window. If this is the case, click on the 'Refresh Company List' icon on the left-hand side of the company window. The new name, as displayed, Longville Ltd, will then appear in the *TASBooks* Company Manager (s18).

s18

Review assignment

Set up a new company in *TASBooks* for Watchworld Ltd, Main Street, Athlone, Co Westmeath. The telephone number is 094-12336 and the VAT registration number is IE1288572N. Use the same VAT codes as used for Daly's Pharmacy Ltd and the same defaults in the company configuration. *Note:* If you are not in a position to set up a company from scratch, use the backup file from Daly's Pharmacy Ltd set up and restore it to a new company. Change the details of the company as required.

5.4 Setting up Company Information in *TASBooks*

Learning outcomes (Accounting Manual and Computerised 5N1348): 8 (part)
Learning outcomes (Bookkeeping Manual and Computerised 5N1354): 8 (part)

Refer back to the source documents of Daly's Pharmacy Ltd on your Student Resources.

Load the company Daly's Pharmacy Ltd from the *TASBooks* Company Manager window.

Set financial year date

As the Daly's Pharmacy Ltd financial year runs from January to December, this needs to be confirmed as set up correctly.

Select **(0)Central > (2)Central Information > (1)Maintain Accounting Period Dates**.

The following screen will be displayed. Click on 'Period – 1' in the 'From' field and enter the date as '01/01/2013', if not already entered. When entering all dates in *TASBooks*, use a double-digit day and month. The year is

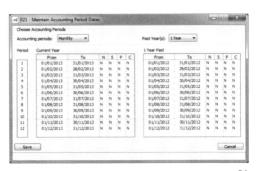

S1

expressed in full with four digits. Press the **Tab** key and all the dates are displayed (s1). Save the changes. Period 1 will represent January, Period 2 February, and so on, when printing reports.

Set up nominal accounts

The default nominal accounts have already been set up for this company. You need to add to this list to include other nominal accounts that are needed to process the records.

Select **(1)Nominal > (1)Nominal Account > (1)Maintain Chart of Accounts**.

The nominal accounts that you need to set up are:

1. Purchases
2. Wages
3. Light & Heat
4. Insurance
5. Motor expenses
6. Printing & Postage
7. Bank Charges
8. Capital.

Be conscious of the numbering and the type of account. Purchases are classified as Cost of Sales, as they will be reported in the Trading account and are part of the cost of sales. Wages, Light & Heat, Insurance, Motor expenses, Printing & Postage and Bank Charges are expenses and will be reported in the Profit and Loss account. Capital is classified as Owners Equity and is reported in the Balance Sheet. The numbering should follow that all Trading accounts are listed first, Profit and Loss account expenses are listed next. Fixed Assets, Current Assets, Current Liabilities are listed next as Balance Sheet items. The last listing should be Owners Equity as a Balance Sheet item.

Remember you cannot delete a nominal account once it has had transactions posted to it, even if the transactions are later deleted. The list of complete nominal accounts should look as shown (s2). There is flexibility in the numbering used, provided all the accounts are in the correct order.

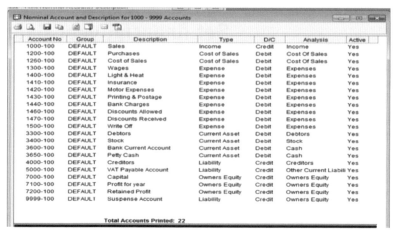

Account No	Group	Description	Type	D/C	Analysis	Active
1000-100	DEFAULT	Sales	Income	Credit	Income	Yes
1200-100	DEFAULT	Purchases	Cost of Sales	Debit	Cost Of Sales	Yes
1260-100	DEFAULT	Cost of Sales	Cost of Sales	Debit	Cost Of Sales	Yes
1300-100	DEFAULT	Wages	Expense	Debit	Expenses	Yes
1400-100	DEFAULT	Light & Heat	Expense	Debit	Expenses	Yes
1410-100	DEFAULT	Insurance	Expense	Debit	Expenses	Yes
1420-100	DEFAULT	Motor Expenses	Expense	Debit	Expenses	Yes
1430-100	DEFAULT	Printing & Postage	Expense	Debit	Expenses	Yes
1440-100	DEFAULT	Bank Charges	Expense	Debit	Expenses	Yes
1460-100	DEFAULT	Discounts Allowed	Expense	Debit	Expenses	Yes
1470-100	DEFAULT	Discounts Received	Expense	Debit	Expenses	Yes
1500-100	DEFAULT	Write Off	Expense	Debit	Expenses	Yes
3300-100	DEFAULT	Debtors	Current Asset	Debit	Debtors	Yes
3400-100	DEFAULT	Stock	Current Asset	Debit	Stock	Yes
3600-100	DEFAULT	Bank Current Account	Current Asset	Debit	Cash	Yes
3650-100	DEFAULT	Petty Cash	Current Asset	Debit	Cash	Yes
4000-100	DEFAULT	Creditors	Liability	Credit	Creditors	Yes
5000-100	DEFAULT	VAT Payable Account	Liability	Credit	Other Current Liabili	Yes
7000-100	DEFAULT	Capital	Owners Equity	Credit	Owners Equity	Yes
7100-100	DEFAULT	Profit for year	Owners Equity	Credit	Owners Equity	Yes
7200-100	DEFAULT	Retained Profit	Owners Equity	Credit	Owners Equity	Yes
9999-100	DEFAULT	Suspense Account	Liability	Credit	Owners Equity	Yes

Total Accounts Printed: 22

S2

Set up suppliers

To set up suppliers, select **(3)Purchase > (1)Suppliers > (1)Maintain Suppliers**. The suppliers that Daly's Pharmacy Ltd purchases goods from are:

- Alchemy Ltd
- United Drugs Ltd
- Stafford Lynch
- Electric Ireland.

Please refer to your source documents for the addresses for these suppliers.

S3

The supplier records hold specific information about each supplier, such as address, telephone number, contact name, credit limit and so on. You can add and edit information in the supplier record at any time. The 'Maintain Suppliers' screen is presented when accessing the menu (s3). It contains five sections displayed as tabs, but you can ignore much of this data. The data that you need to enter for suppliers would be: Supplier Code (use first 3 digits of name, if possible), supplier name and address. All of the other fields default to match the default settings in the configuration. After you enter the information for the first supplier, Alchemy Ltd, it should appear as shown. Click **Save**.

Set up the remaining suppliers: United Drugs Ltd, Stafford Lynch and Electric Ireland.

Set up customers

Customer records act in the same manner as supplier records and the set-up is similar. Select **(2)Sales > (1)Customers > (1)Maintain Customers**. The customers that you need to set up are:

- Mr James Mulcahy
- Ms Martha Downey
- Cash Sales.

Please refer to your source documents for their addresses.

Use codes such as the first three characters of the name. The only fields you need to set up are Code, Name and Address. Always use supplier and customer codes that can be remembered or accessed easily with the look-up function.

Set ledger dates

It is usual to record accounts on a monthly basis, recording one month and then moving onto the next month until the end of the accounting year. To do this, the ledger month end dates need to be set for each month that is being recorded. There are three ledger dates, namely nominal ledger, purchase ledger and sales ledger. These three dates are set to the end of the month that we are recording, which is the month of November for Daly's Pharmacy Ltd. All you need to change when entering the accounts is the *day* of the month. The month and the year will be correct.

Select **(0)Central > (9)End of Period Programs > (9)Change Ledger Date**. Click the tab for the ledger date you want to set, which will be all three tabs

s4

here (s4). Enter the month end date for November, taking note of double-digit day and month. Note that the cash book uses the same date as the nominal ledger. Select the option 'Set to today's date at start up' only if you want to change the ledger date to today's date every time *TASBooks* is opened. Select 'No' here as we want to keep November as the ledger dates. You can also change the ledger dates by double-clicking on the displayed dates in the bottom-right corner of the *TASBooks* window.

As the accounting year is January to December, note that November will be reported as Period 11 in all reports. When November accounts are completed, all three ledger dates would be set to 31 December to record the next month's accounts, which will be the last period of the accounting year, Period 12.

Review assignment

Open the company Watchworld Ltd that you have set up in *TASBooks* and carry out the following tasks:

1. Set the financial year to run from 1 January 2014 to 31 December 2014.
2. Set up the following nominal ledger accounts, using appropriate nominal codes. Ensure that you select the correct *type* for each account.
   a. Purchases
   b. Staff Salaries
   c. Insurance
   d. Repairs
   e. Postage & Stationery
   f. Telephone
   g. Capital.
3. Set up the following suppliers, using appropriate supplier codes:
   a. The Watchery Ltd, D'Olier Street, Dublin 1
   b. Time 2 Watches, Capel Street, Dublin 1
   c. Print Solutions, Kill Avenue, Ballymahon, Co Longford.
4. Set up the following customers, using appropriate customer codes:
   a. Livia Jewellers, Ballygar, Co Galway
   b. Timepiece Ltd, Hodson Bay, Athlone, Co Westmeath
   c. Sheehan's Ltd, Castle Street, Castlerea, Co Roscommon.
5. Set the Sales, Purchases and Nominal ledger dates to 31/03/2014.

5.5 Purchase Ledger in *TASBooks*

Learning outcomes (Accounting Manual and Computerised 5N1348): 9 (part)
Learning outcomes (Bookkeeping Manual and Computerised 5N1354): 8 (part)

The Purchase ledger is where you enter all your supplier details, where you can record invoices and credit notes that you have received outside the *TASBooks* system and where you enter all the money you pay your suppliers.

We will enter the purchase invoices and credit note of Daly's Pharmacy Ltd. *Refer to the source documents in your Student Resources.* Remember to press the **Tab** key to move from field to field.

Purchase invoices

Select **(3)Purchase > (2)Enter/Change Journals > (1)Enter/Change Supplier Invoices/Credit Journals**. Use this option to record invoices that you have received from your suppliers. You can also record stopped cheques, refunds and write-backs in this window.

A screen is displayed to enter the first purchase invoice from Alchemy Ltd (s1). Enter the following details:

* **Posting Number** – This field is automatically updated by *TASBooks* when you save the transaction, so make no entry here.
* **Date** – This displays the current purchase ledger date, which is set to 30 November, so make no entry here.
* **Type** – From the drop-down list, accept the default 'PL Invoice' which is what you are entering.
* **Def Dist** – You need not enter anything here.
* **Supplier Code** – Enter the required supplier code or press F2 and select the supplier code from the look-up list, and the name is entered automatically on selection of code.
* **Ref No** – Enter a reference for the invoice, which is the invoice number.

- **Date** – Enter the date of the invoice. You need only change the day, as the month and year are set by the ledger dates. The 'Exp Pay Date' is displayed automatically, accounting for the credit limit on payment of the invoice.
- **Desc** – This will default to 'Purchase Invoice'. You can overtype this with a description of your choice, but there is usually no need.
- **O/S Bal and Cr Rem** – This automatically displays the amount outstanding on invoices and no entries are made here.

As the invoice from Alchemy Ltd has multiple VAT rates, the following needs to be entered carefully:

- **Net** – Enter the Net amount of the invoice.
- **VAT code** – This will default to VAT Rate 1 as per the VAT set up. For multiple VAT rates, enter 'M' here for multiple rates.
- **VAT** – Enter the VAT amount, as on this occasion, *TASBooks* cannot automatically calculate the VAT amount due on multiple rates.
- **Total** – The Total amount will be calculated automatically.
- **Disc** – This is the amount of discount received from the supplier on the entry. No entry is made here.

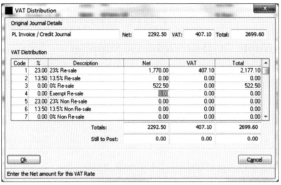

s2

A VAT Distribution screen will be displayed due to multiple rates of VAT (s2). This screen will only display when you select multiple rates of VAT to allow for the breakdown of the different VAT rates.

Complete the breakdown of VAT, inputting the Net at 23% Re-sale as per the invoice. The VAT amount will calculate automatically. Input the net amount at 0% Re-sale as per the invoice. The VAT amount will calculate automatically, which will be zero. When complete, click **OK** and you will be returned to the main purchase invoice screen.

The following fields are now completed as shown (s3):

- **Account/Dept Lines 1 and 2** – This part of the transaction will be completed for you showing the Creditors account and the VAT Payable account (if applicable). These are automatically completed as they are control accounts in the configuration set up. The double-entry completed for you is to *credit* the Creditors with the total value and *debit* the VAT account with the VAT amount.
- **Line 3** – Here you enter the nominal account you would like to post this transaction to or press **F2** and select the account from the look-up list. In this case the double-entry is to *debit* the Purchases account with the net value of the invoice. You can complete as many lines as necessary until the transaction is balanced and the total debits equal the total credits. If you make an entry for this supplier again, the nominal account that you

last used will automatically appear and if it is the correct account, you simply enter the net amount of the invoice in the debit column.

- **Description** – This depends on the setting chosen in TASBooks Configuration > Purchase Ledger > Purchase Journal Entry. Either the nominal description will be displayed, or if you have changed this setting, you can enter a description for each line of the transaction.
- **Debit/Credit** – Here you enter the net value of the invoice that relates to the purchases account you have selected.

If the transaction is balanced, the 'Still to Post' boxes will be 0.00.

To save the transaction, click **Save** or press the **Tab** key. When asked to save the entry, click **Yes**. The posting number is displayed in the bottom right corner of the window.

You now enter the second purchase invoice from United Drugs Ltd in the same way. This invoice also contains multiple VAT rates. To help, the VAT Distribution screen is displayed (s4).

s3

The third purchase invoice from Stafford Lynch has only one rate of VAT, which is 23% Re-sale. This is much simpler to enter, as you do not need multiple VAT rates. Here you can skip the Net and the VAT amount and enter only the Total amount of the invoice in the Total field. The VAT is defaulted to Rate 1, which is 23% Re-sale. This is the correct rate for this invoice. After entering the Total amount, *TASBooks* automatically calculates the Net and VAT amount from this. Alternatively, you can enter the Net amount, with VAT code 1 and *TASBooks* will calculate the VAT amount and the Total amount automatically. Remember to press the Tab key to see the result from field to field.

s4

The fourth purchase invoice is from Electric Ireland. Here, the VAT code is 6, which represents 13.5% Non Re-sale in the VAT set up. Again, you need only set the VAT code to 6 (use look-up for codes) and enter the Total of the invoice. *TASBooks* will then calculate the Net and VAT amount automatically. The double-entry for an electricity invoice is posted to the debit of the Light & Heat expense account, being the net amount.

Purchase credit notes

Select **(3)Purchase > (2)Enter/Change Journals > (2)Enter/Change Supplier Credit Notes/Debit Journals**. This is used for recording credit notes received from your suppliers. You can allocate any credit note entered to an invoice, when required, on a different menu at a later stage.

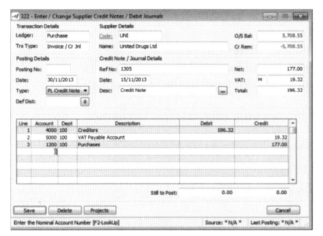

s5

The screen displayed (s5 is similar to the purchase invoice screen in layout. Due to similar screens, it is important to distinguish clearly between both, as credit notes have the opposite effect to the accounts as invoices. The fields in the screen are exactly the same as the purchase invoice screen.

The credit note for United Drugs Ltd contains multiple VAT rates. As a result, the Net amount, VAT code M and the VAT amount are entered in the fields. The VAT distribution is displayed due to the multiple rates of VAT. This is completed according to the figures in the credit note. The previous double-entry for a purchase credit note was to *debit* the Creditors with the total value, *credit* VAT with the VAT amount (both completed automatically by *TASBooks*). The corresponding entry is to *credit* the Purchases account with the net amount, because purchases for the company are reduced as goods are being returned to the supplier.

When you enter a credit note, it should be allocated. It must be matched against the relevant invoice. In this way, it is treated as part payment of the invoice and therefore it is allocated in the payments section of the purchase ledger. This credit note will be allocated later.

Purchase ledger reporting

Purchase daybook

As you complete purchase invoices and credit notes, the purchase daybook is automatically updated in the accounts. This can be viewed by selecting **(3)Purchase > (4)Purchase ledger Reports > (1)Print Purchase/ Cash Daybooks**. This report can also be assessed by clicking on the toolbar 'Purchases' (s6).

The Print Purchase/Cash Daybooks is displayed. The period number is defaulted to the ledger date. The Cash Daybook would report payments to suppliers, for which no entries have been entered yet. This box can be unchecked. Select the default print 'To Screen' to view the report without

s6

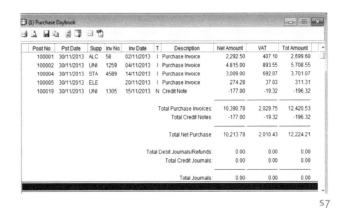

s7

printing. Use the down arrow to select 'To Printer' if you wish to print the report.

The Purchase Daybook report should look like the report shown (s7). You can also use the print icon in the top left-hand corner to print the report.

Aged creditors report

This summarises all the suppliers' ledger balances in one report. It is a very useful report to catch a glimpse of the creditors' balances in one page. It will total the amount owed to all suppliers at the bottom of the report. Select **(3)Purchase > (4)Purchase Ledger Reports > (2)Print Aged Creditors Report**.

The Print Aged Creditors Report is shown (s8). There is an option to display the supplier balances as 'Details' or 'Totals only'. 'Details' is selected here. The ageing option is by months, as set up in the configuration settings. Again, you can print to screen or to the printer with the option at the bottom of the screen. You can also use the print icon at the top left-hand corner of the report to print.

The report should look like that displayed (s9). This report is customised, as explained in section 5.1.

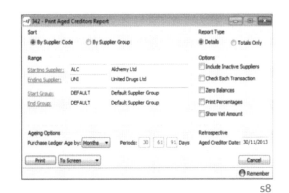

s8

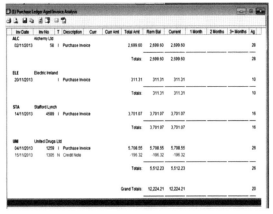

s9

S10

S11

Supplier account enquiry

This report is used to view the transactions in one particular supplier's account. Select **(3)Purchase > (1) Suppliers > (2)Supplier Account Enquiry**.

The supplier account enquiry for United Drugs Ltd is displayed (s10). Enter the supplier code in the Supplier Code field and press the **Tab** key. The screen shows the outstanding balance on the account in the bottom-right section.

The option at the bottom of the screen 'Open Items' displays only the invoices outstanding and payments/credits not allocated to the account. Use the drop-down menu to select 'All Items' to view all transactions in the account, including invoices that are paid in full. Here you enter a cut-off date to view all items dated back to the selected date.

Press the **Enter** key to accept the 'Print to Screen' option to report in more detail on the supplier. On the screen displayed (s11), if you wish to print the report, use the drop-down menu to select 'To Printer' above. Note that onscreen the credit note is displayed in red to indicate that it has not yet been allocated to an invoice. You can also use the print icon at the top left-hand corner of the report to print.

Purchase ledger payments

To keep all the entries in the purchase ledger together, the purchase ledger payments can now be entered at this stage. These are the payments to suppliers in Daly's Pharmacy Ltd. Other payments will be entered in the Cash Book later. There are two payments to suppliers in the records of Daly's Pharmacy Ltd. These are a payment to Alchemy Ltd and United Drugs Ltd. All money paid to suppliers needs to be entered in the Purchase ledger when the company is paying an invoice and is *not* entered in the Cash Book menu. This is sometimes confusing for students as payments to suppliers are entered in the Cash Book in manual accounts. Once entered, you can allocate the payment to a specific invoice so you can always see what is still outstanding. As well as allocating payments, you can also allocate credit notes and refunds here.

Select **(3)Purchase > (5)Payments on Account > (1)Enter/Allocate Purchase Ledger Payments**.

The window displayed shows the payment made to Alchemy Ltd (s12). Enter the following fields:

- **Bank** – Enter the bank account number where the payment is made from, in this case, the main bank current account, which is number 1 in the set-up of the bank accounts. You can type 1 in this field.
- **Date** – The date will display the current ledger date. There is no need to change this.
- **Code** – Enter the supplier code to whom the payment is made. Use the look-up function key (F2) for a list of supplier codes. The supplier name and the amount owed will automatically display.
- **Method** – The cheque will automatically display as the bank account was set up as a current account.
- **Cheque No** – You must enter the cheque number of the payment here.
- **Chq date** – Enter the date of the payment by changing the day only in this field.
- **Description** – The description 'PL Payment' will display automatically on pressing the **Tab** key. This can be changed if you wish.
- **Amount** – Enter the payment amount here.
- **Unalloc** – This will display the amount automatically, as the payment has not yet been allocated to the account.

On pressing the **Tab** key, the message 'Confirm to save this payment' will display. Press the Enter key or click **Yes** to save the payment.

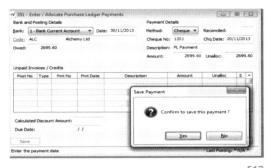

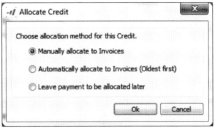

S12   S13

The 'Allocate Credit' message will display (s13). In the configuration settings, the allocation method was defaulted to a manual allocation. Accept this by pressing enter or clicking **OK**. This allows you to choose which invoices you want to allocate the payment to, or apply a discount, an underpayment or overpayment if required. Occasionally, you may enter a payment to a supplier without allocating it straightaway. In this instance, choose the option 'Leave payment to be allocated later'.

If you select 'Automatically allocate to Invoices (Oldest first)', *TASBooks* will do an automatic allocation. After you select manual allocation, the screen will display all the invoices outstanding in the supplier's account. In this case, there is only one invoice outstanding in the account of Alchemy Ltd. Select the invoice that you intend to allocate the payment against. Press the **Tab** key and follow the cursor at each tab press. You can see there is an option to include a discount in the 'Allocated Discount Amount' field on the bottom right-hand side of the screen. If there is a discount on the payment, enter the discount here. Also, there is an option to include part of the payment against the invoice in the 'Allocated Cash Amount' on the bottom right-hand side of the screen. This may arise where a payment pays part of two different invoices. Alternatively, double-click on your selection to allocate the payment if there is no discount. Note in the screen that the amount owed to Alchemy Ltd now displays a zero balance as the cheque pays the total value of the invoice. Also note that the Bank field is now displaying '0 – None (Existing Payment)', as you are now allocating that payment.

When you have finished the allocation, you will be asked if you want to save it. Save the allocation by clicking **Yes** or pressing the **Enter** key.

Enter the payment to United Drugs Ltd from the same menu as demonstrated for Alchemy Ltd and allocate the payment to the invoice outstanding in the account. You will notice that a message will display that the invoice is only partly paid. Accept this message by clicking **OK**.

Allocating existing purchase ledger credit notes and payments

Occasionally you may enter a payment to a supplier without allocating it straightaway, or you may have entered a credit note from a supplier, who you want to allocate to an invoice. In these circumstances you can allocate the

S14

payment or credit note using the same menu as in the previous Purchase Ledger Payments. The credit note entered in the account of United Drugs Ltd can now be allocated in this way. In the screen shown (s14), enter the following:

- **Bank** – From the Bank drop-down list choose 0 – None (Existing Payment). There is no payment being made here, but you are allocating an existing payment or credit. The menu is used to *enter* and/or *allocate* payments or credits.
- **Code** – Enter or select the appropriate supplier code of the supplier. The supplier's name and the amount owed will display automatically. The payment details section is greyed out, as this is not a payment. Press the **Tab** key and all unallocated payments and credits will display on the

screen. Here displayed is the credit note entered earlier that is now to be allocated.

Press the **Tab** key and you will be asked to choose the method of allocation. As previously, choose manual allocation. Press the **Tab** key when the invoice requiring allocation is selected. After the credit is allocated, the message 'Note: This invoice is only part-paid' is displayed. Click **OK** and the remaining balance on the invoice is reduced by the amount of the credit note. Accept the part-payment message and save the allocation.

If you print the Aged Creditors Report, you can see that the above two payments have been entered in the suppliers' accounts and the payments and credit note are allocated in full.

Unallocated Cash Report

If you are unsure whether there are outstanding payments or credit notes in the suppliers' accounts that remain unallocated, you can run an Unallocated Cash Report from the Purchases ledger. This gives a list of all unallocated items in the suppliers' accounts. Select **(3)Purchase > (4)Purchase Ledger Reports > (5)Print Unallocated Cash Report**.

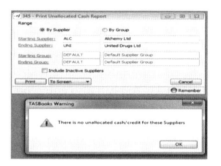

s15

The screen displayed shows that all payments and credits have been allocated, there is no unallocated cash/credit for the suppliers (s15).

Review assignment

Refer to the source documents on your Student Resources relating to Watchworld Ltd.

Open the company Watchworld Ltd, which you have set up in *TASBooks*, and perform the following tasks.

1. Using the source documents, enter the purchase invoices and credit note received from the suppliers.
2. Enter the purchase ledger payments and allocate to the invoices in each supplier's account.
3. Allocate the credit note to the supplier's account.
4. Print the following reports to either the printer or screen:
   a. Purchase Daybook
   b. Aged Creditors
   c. Supplier account enquiry for Time 2 Watches.

5.6 Sales Ledger in *TASBooks*

Learning outcomes (Accounting Manual and Computerised 5N1348): 9 (part)
Learning outcomes (Bookkeeping Manual and Computerised 5N1354): 8 (part)

The sales ledger is where you enter all your customer details, where you record invoices and credit notes that you have produced outside of *TASBooks* and where you enter all the money you have received from your customers.

Sales invoices

Use this option to record invoices that you do not want to print from *TASBooks*. You can also enter 'bounced' cheques, refunds and write-backs from this window. Select **(2)Sales > (2)Enter/Change Journals > (1)Enter/ Change Customer Invoices/Debit Journals**.

The window will show the first sales invoice of Daly's Pharmacy Ltd from the source documents in your Student Resources (s1). The screen details for entry are similar to purchase invoices, but, of course, cannot be confused with the purchases menu.

Enter the following details, as below, using the **Tab** key to move through the various fields:

- **Posting No** – This is automatically created when the transaction is saved. If you want to recall an existing transaction, enter the posting number here.
- **Date** – This displays the current sales ledger date, which is 30 November. There is no need to change this date.
- **Type** – Choose the default type 'SL Invoice', which should be already chosen.
- **Def Dist** – No need for any entry here.
- **(Customer) Code** – Enter the required customer code or press **F2** and select the customer code from the look-up list. The name will then be displayed automatically.
- **Ref No** – Enter the sales invoice number here.
- **Date** – Enter the date of the invoice. The Exp Pay Date will automatically display according to the payment terms in the customer configuration.
- **Desc** – This defaults to 'Sales Invoice'. You can overtype this with a description of your choice if you wish.

- **Project** – If applicable, enter a project code or press **F2** and select the project from the look-up list. There are no projects set up and there is no need for any entry here.
- **O/S Bal and Cr Rem** – This automatically displays the amount outstanding on the customer's account for information purposes.

As the invoice below has only one rate of VAT, the entry for the amounts is a simple process:

- **Net** – Enter the net amount of the invoice or leave blank and continue.
- **VAT (code)** – If the customer's VAT type in their record is set to Home, this defaults to VAT code 1, which is 23% Resale. This is the code required here.
- **VAT** – The VAT amount is calculated automatically when the net amount is entered.
- **Total** – The total amount is calculated automatically when the net amount is entered.

If you prefer, you can enter the Total, and the Net and VAT amounts are calculated automatically.

- **Account/Dept Lines 1 and 2** – This part of the transaction will be completed for you, showing the Debtors account and the VAT Payable account (if applicable). The double-entry is:
Debit: Debtors with the total value of the invoice
Credit: VAT with the VAT amount on the invoice. This is done automatically by *TASBooks*.
- **Line 3** – Enter the sales account you want to post this transaction to or press **F2** and select the account from the look-up list. Here there is a *credit* in the sales account with the net value of the invoice. You can complete as many lines as necessary until the transaction is balanced.
- **Description** – The description of the chosen nominal account appears automatically. If you would rather enter your own description, you can do so, but you need to switch this option on *TASBooks* Configuration (option 012) first.

S1

S2

- **Debit/Credit** – Enter the net value to be posted to the nominal code for the sales account.

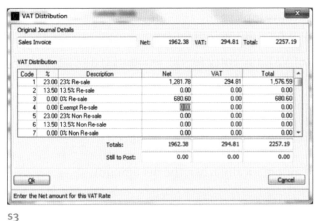

s3

When the transaction is balanced the Still to Post boxes will be 0.00.

To save the transaction, click **Save** or press **Tab** and when asked to save the entry click **Yes**. The posting number is displayed in the bottom-right corner of the window.

The second invoice is entered in the same manner. Multiple VAT rates are entered for the two different rates on this invoice (s2).

The VAT distribution screen distributes the VAT between the two rates (s3). Enter all other sales invoices in the same manner, taking note of multiple VAT rates.

Sales credit notes

Select (2)Sales > (2)Enter/Change Journals > (2)Enter/Change Customer Credit Notes/Credit Journals. This is used for recording credit notes you have sent to your customers. You can allocate any credit note entered to an invoice, when required, on a different menu at a later stage.

The screen will display as shown (s4), which is similar to the sales invoice screen in layout. Due to similar screens, it is important to distinguish clearly between both, as credit notes have the opposite effect in the accounts as invoices. The fields in the screen are similar to that described already. The credit note

s4

below for Martha Downey Ltd contains multiple VAT rates. As a result, the Net amount, VAT code M and the VAT amount are entered in the fields. Enter the VAT distribution on the VAT distribution screen as per the credit note. This credit note will be allocated later. The double-entry is:

Credit: Debtors with the total amount
Debit: VAT with the VAT amount, which is completed automatically.

The corresponding entry is a *debit* in the Sales account with the net amount, as shown.

Sales ledger reporting

Sales daybook

As you complete sales invoices and credit notes, the sales daybook is automatically updated in the accounts. This can be viewed by selecting **(2)Sales > (4)Sales Ledger Reports > (1)Print Sales/Cash Daybooks**. This report can also be assessed by clicking 'Sales' on the toolbar.

The Print Sales/Cash Daybooks box will display as shown (s5). The period number is defaulted to the ledger date. The Cash Daybook would report receipts from customers, for whom no entries have been entered yet. This box can be unchecked. Select the default print 'To Screen' to view the report without printing. Use the down-arrow to select 'To Printer' if you wish to print the report.

The Sales Daybook report should look like the report shown (s6). You can also use the print icon on the top left-hand corner of the report below to print the report.

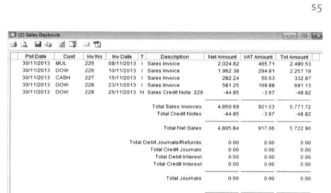

s5

s6

Aged debtors report

This summarises all the customers' ledger balances in one report. It is a very useful report to catch a glimpse of the customers' balances in one page. This can be used for credit control to collect outstanding balances in accounts. It will total the amount owed to all customers at the bottom of the report.

Select **(2)Sales > (4)Sales Ledger Reports > (2)Print Aged Debtors Report**.

The Print Aged Debtors Report is displayed (s7). There is an option to display the customer balances as Details or Totals Only. 'Details' is selected here. The ageing option is by months, as set up in the configuration settings. Again, you can print to screen or to the printer with the option at the bottom of the screen. You can also use the print icon at the top left-hand corner of the report to print.

s7

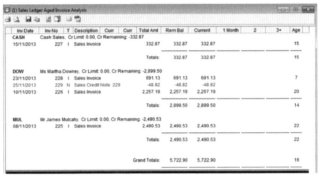

s8

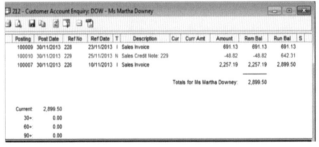

s9

The report should look as shown (s8). This report is customised, as explained in section 5.1.

Customer account enquiry

This gives you a complete picture of all activity with each of your customers. The Customer Account Enquiry is ideal for checking which invoices, receipts and the like have been processed and which are still outstanding. This report is used to view the transactions in one particular customer's account. Select **(2) Sales > (1)Customers > (2) Customer Account Enquiry**.

The customer account enquiry for Ms Martha Downey is displayed (s9). Enter the code in the Customer Code field and press the **Tab** key. The screen shows the outstanding balance on the account on the bottom right section.

The option at the bottom of the screen 'Open (Unpaid) Items' displays only the invoices outstanding and payments/credits not allocated to the account. Use the drop-down menu to select 'All Items' to view all transactions in the account, including invoices that are paid

s10

in full. Here you enter a cut-off date to view all items dated back to the selected date.

Press the Enter key to accept the print 'To Screen' option to report on the customer in more detail. The screen will display as shown (s10). If you wish to print the report, use the drop-down menu to select 'To Printer' above. Note that the credit note is displayed in red to indicate that it has not yet been allocated to an invoice. You can also use the print icon at the top left-hand corner of the report to print.

Sales ledger receipts

To keep all the entries in the sales ledger together, the receipts can now be entered at this stage. These are the sales ledger receipts from customers in Daly's Pharmacy Ltd. There are two receipts from customers in the business's records. These are: one receipt from Cash Sales and another from Ms Martha Downey. All receipts from customers are entered in the sales ledger and *not* the cash book. Once entered, you can allocate the receipt to a specific invoice so you can always see what is still outstanding. As well as allocating receipts you can also allocate credit notes and refunds here.

Select **(2)Sales > (5)Receipts > (1)Enter/Allocate Sales Ledger Receipts**. The screen will show the receipt from Cash Sales (s11). Enter the following fields:

- **Bank** – Enter the bank account number where the receipt is lodged, in this case, the main bank current account, which is number 1 in the set-up of the bank accounts. You can type '1' in this field.
- **Date** – The date will display the current ledger date. There is no need to change this.
- **Code** – Enter the customer code from whom the payment is received. Use the look-up function key (**F2**) for a list of customer codes if required. The customer name and the amount owed will automatically display.
- **Slip Ref** – You must enter the slip reference for this receipt here. Otherwise the receipt will not appear for the bank reconciliation later.
- **Cheque No** – There is no need to enter any cheque number here.
- **Chq date** – Enter the date of the receipt by changing the day only in this field.
- **Description** – The description 'SL Receipt' will display automatically on pressing the **Tab** key. This can be changed if you wish.
- **Amount** – Enter the amount of the receipt here.
- **Unalloc** – This will display the amount automatically, as the receipt has not yet been allocated to the account.

On pressing the **Tab** key, the message 'Confirm to save this receipt' will display. Press the **Enter** key or click **Yes** to save the receipt.

The 'Allocate Credit' message will display. In the configuration settings the allocation method was defaulted to a manual allocation. Accept this by pressing **Enter** or clicking **OK**. This allows you to choose which invoices you want to allocate the receipt to, or apply a discount, underpayment or overpayment if required. The method of allocation is identical to the purchases ledger described in section 5.5. After you choose manual allocation, the screen will display all the invoices outstanding in the customer's account. In this case, there is only one invoice outstanding in the account of 'Cash Sales'. Select the invoice that you intend to

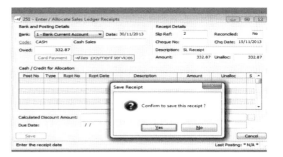

allocate the receipt against. Press the **Tab** key and follow the cursor at each tab press.

Similar to the purchases ledger, there is an option to include Discount in the Allocated Discount Amount field on the bottom right-hand side of the screen. If there is a discount on the receipt, enter it here. Also, there is an option to include part of the receipt against the invoice in the Allocated Cash Amount field. You can also double-click on your selection to allocate the receipt if there is no discount. The amount owed from Cash Sales now displays a zero balance and the Bank field is now displaying '0 – None (Existing Receipt)', as you are now allocating the receipt.

When you have finished the allocation, you will be asked if you wish to save it. Save the allocation by clicking **Yes** or pressing the **Enter** key.

Enter the receipt from Ms Martha Downey in the same menu as in s11 and allocate the receipt to the oldest invoice outstanding in the account.

Allocating existing sales ledger credit notes and receipts

You may occasionally enter a receipt from a customer without allocating it straightaway. This may arise where you are unsure of what invoice the receipt should be matched against. You may also enter a credit note for a customer that you then want to allocate to an invoice. In these circumstances you can allocate the existing receipt or credit note using the same menu as above. It is important to allocate receipts and credit notes against the correct invoices, so that your aged debtors report and customer statements give an accurate picture of what each customer owes.

The credit note sent to the customer, Ms Martha Downey, can now be allocated. In the screen shown, enter the following:

- **Bank** – From the Bank drop-down list choose '0 – None (Existing Receipt)'. There is no receipt here, but you are allocating an existing receipt or credit. The menu is used to *enter* and/or *allocate* receipts or credits.
- **Code** – Enter or select the appropriate customer code. The customer's name and the amount owed will be displayed automatically. The receipt details section is greyed out, as this is not a receipt. Press the **Tab** key and all unallocated receipts and credits will display on the screen. Here displayed is the credit note entered earlier that is now to be allocated.

Press the **Tab** key and you will be asked to choose the method of allocation. As previously, choose manual allocation. Press the **Tab** key when the invoice that requires the allocation is selected. After the credit is allocated, you will be asked to save the allocation. Note that the invoice is only partly paid and the remaining balance on the invoice is reduced by the amount of the credit note. Accept the part-payment message and save the allocation.

If you print the Aged Debtors Report, you can see that these two receipts have been entered in the customers' accounts and the receipts and credit note are allocated in full.

Unallocated cash report

Similar to the purchases ledger, if you are unsure whether there are outstanding receipts or credit notes in the customers' accounts that remain unallocated, you can run an Unallocated Cash Report from the sales ledger. This gives a list of all unallocated items in the customers' accounts.

Select (2)**Sales** > (4)**Sales Ledger Reports** > (5)**Print Unallocated Cash Report**. As all receipts and credits have been allocated, there is no unallocated cash/credit for the customers.

Customer statements

At the end of the month, once all invoices, credits and receipts have been entered in the customers' accounts, statements are sent to the customers. To maintain efficient credit control, it is important to keep your customers informed of what they owe. These can be printed at any time, but it is usual to send them to your customers as part of your regular credit control routine at the end of each month.

S12

Select (2)**Sales** > (4)**Sales Ledger Reports** > (3)**Print Statements**. The screen will display as shown (s12). Select whether you want to print the statements for a range of customers, by entering the Start Customer and End Customer in the appropriate fields. If you want to print the statements for all customers, leave the range as it appears by default. In the Ageing Options field, choose whether you want to show age by days or by months. If you choose 'Days', you can amend the period days if required. In the Print Options area, select how you want to generate the statements. In the Use Standard Stationery option, the name and details of the company are displayed automatically at the header of each statement. Alternatively, you can use a Microsoft Word template file created or you can email the statements to customers by selecting the appropriate options. Also select 'Include Ageing Breakdown', where the statements will display the ageing balances on each account. By selecting Print at the bottom left-hand corner of the screen, the statements will transfer directly to the printer.

Review assignment

Refer to the source documents in your Student Resources relating to Watchworld Ltd.
Open the company Watchworld Ltd that you have set up in *TASBooks* and perform the following tasks:

1. Enter the sales invoices and credit note sent to the customers from the source documents.
2. Enter the sales ledger receipts and allocate to the invoices in each customer account.
3. Allocate the credit note to the customer's account.
4. Print the following reports to either the printer or screen:
   a. Sales daybook
   b. Aged debtors report
   c. Customer account enquiry for Livia Jewellers.

5·7 Cash Book and Bank Reconciliation in *TASBooks*

Learning outcomes (Accounting Manual and Computerised 5N1348): 9 (part)
Learning outcomes (Bookkeeping Manual and Computerised 5N1354): 8 (part)

The cash book is used for all payments and receipts that are not identified with an appropriate customer or supplier, e.g. rent, rates, VAT. Payments to suppliers are recorded in the purchases ledger and receipts from customers are recorded in the sales ledger, where respective supplier and customer accounts are set up. You can use the cash book to record cash purchases and cash sales where you do not wish to set up supplier and customer accounts. For example, you can use the cash book if you are running a retail business such as a shop or restaurant, where customers pay at the point of sale and no invoice is raised. The cash book has the facility to record VAT on receipts and VAT on purchases. The cash book also contains the facility to reconcile your bank accounts.

Cash receipts lodged to bank

This menu is used for cash or cheques received that are lodged to the bank current account but do not relate to a customer account. Examples are: capital invested by the owner and lodged to the bank, rent received, and a loan received and lodged to the bank current account.

Select **(4)Cash Book > (2)Enter/Change Journals > (1)Enter/Change Cash Receipts/Sales**.

The capital invested and lodged to the bank in Daly's Pharmacy Ltd will be entered. The screen will display as shown (s1).

Enter the relevant details, using the **Tab** key to move through the options:

- **To Bank** – Select bank account number 1, being the current bank account the money is being lodged to.
- **Date** – Enter the date of the receipt.
- **Type** – Select 'Non-VAT Jnl' from the drop-down list as there is no VAT on the receipt. The type is defaulted to 'Home Receipt'. Home receipt will assume that there is VAT on the receipt. In the case of capital lodged, there

is no VAT here. Alternatively, you can leave the type as Home Receipt and use the VAT code 9, which is set up in the configuration as 'Outside Scope of VAT'. An alternative code for a non-VAT journal is O (alphabetic character). When you select the type as 'Non-VAT Jnl', you will notice that the VAT code and VAT amount field are greyed out. The other type options are:

- 'EC Receipt' – sales to EU countries
- 'Non-EC Rcpt' – sales to non-EU countries
- 'Inter-Bank' – cash transferred between bank accounts
- 'VAT Refund' – to record a refund of VAT from Revenue.

- **Slip No** – Enter the lodgement slip number for the receipt. You must enter a reference here for the receipt. Otherwise the receipt will not appear on the bank reconciliation. If you do not know the slip number you can enter it at a later date.
- **Desc** – Enter a specific description here. It is good practice to always enter a specific description so that it can be recognised in the bank account report.
- **Net Amt** – You can enter the receipt amount here if you wish or enter the amount in the Total Amt. The VAT is greyed out, as there is no VAT on this receipt.
- **VAT** – This is greyed out here. If there was VAT on the receipt, select the correct VAT code.
- **Total Amt** – The total amount will be entered automatically. You can skip the net amount and enter the amount in the total if you wish.

On pressing the **Tab** key, the double-entry needs to be completed, which is *debit* in the bank account and credit in the capital account.

- **Debit and Credit** – The nominal account for the bank account appears automatically with a *debit* amount. The VAT account would also appear with a *credit* of the VAT amount if there was VAT on the receipt. Enter the nominal account number for the receipt to be posted to (use F2 look-up) and enter the amount of the receipt in the credit column, as shown.

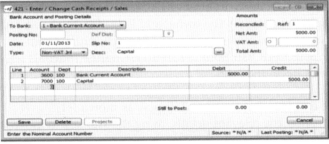

When the debits equal the credits, that is, the Still to Post is 0.00, save the receipt.

Cheque payments

There are many types of payment or cash purchases that do not relate to a supplier account. These include payments such as salaries, payments of VAT and PAYE to Revenue, repayments of directors' loans and insurance. Miscellaneous items such as bank charges are also entered using this option.

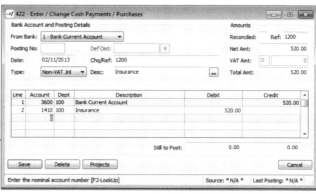

S2

To enter a cheque payment, select **(4)Cash Book > (2)Enter/ Change Journals > (2)Enter/ Change Cash Payments/Purchases**. The screen is displayed as shown (s2). The payment of insurance in Daly's Pharmacy Ltd will be entered here. Enter the following details in the fields below, using the **Tab** key to move through the options:

- **From Bank** – Choose the bank account number 1, which is the bank current account where the cheque is being paid from.
- **Date** – Enter the cheque date.
- **Type** – Select from the drop-down list the payment type 'Non-VAT Jnl'. The type is defaulted to 'Home Purch'. Home purchase will assume that there is VAT on the payment. In the case of insurance, there is no VAT on the payment. Alternatively, similar to a receipt above, you can leave the type as 'Home Purchase' and use the VAT code 9 or O (alphabetic character). When you select the type as 'Non-VAT Jnl', you will notice that the VAT code and VAT amount field are greyed out. The other type options are:
  - – 'EC Purch' – purchases from EU countries
  - – 'Non-EC Purch' – purchases from non-EU countries
  - – 'Inter-Bank'– cash transferred between bank accounts
  - – 'VAT Payment' – payment made for VAT to Revenue.
- **Chq/Ref** – Enter the cheque number or reference, which must be entered here.
- **Desc** – The description defaults to Cash Payment but enter a specific description for the payment here. It is good practice to always enter a description in the cash book ledger in order to identify the payments in the cash book report.
- **Net Amt** – You can enter the cheque amount here if you wish or enter the amount in the Total Amt. The VAT is greyed out, as there is no VAT on this payment.
- **VAT** – This is greyed out here. If there was VAT on the payment, select the correct VAT code.

- **Total Amt** – The total amount will be entered automatically. You can skip the net amount and enter the amount in the total if you wish.

On pressing the **Tab** key, the double-entry needs to be completed, which is credit in the bank account and debit in the insurance expense account.

- **Debit and Credit** – The nominal account for the bank account appears automatically with a *credit* amount. The VAT account would also appear with a *debit* of the VAT amount if there was VAT on the payment. Enter the nominal account number for the payment to be posted to (use **F2** look-up) and enter the amount of the cheque in the debit column. When the debits equal the credits, that is, the Still to Post is 0.00, save the payment.
    The second cheque payment is for payment of wages. The same menu is used. The double-entry is *credit* the bank account (displayed automatically) and select the Wages account for the *debit* entry.

Petty cash

Every business keeps a certain amount of cash on hand to pay for small purchase items. It may not be practical to write cheques for these. Money is withdrawn from the bank current account at regular intervals to have cash on hand for these items of expenditure.

Petty cash receipts

In the case of Daly's Pharmacy Ltd, the company withdrew €300 from the bank current account and lodged to the petty cash account. The petty cash is another 'bank account' in *TASBooks*. In setting up the bank accounts, the petty cash account was set up as bank account number 2. To enter a petty cash receipt, the same menu is used as for bank receipts covered earlier in this section.
    Select **(4)Cash Book > (2)Enter/Change Journals > (1)Enter/Change Cash Receipts/Sales**. The details in the fields would be as follows:

- **To Bank** – Select bank account number 2, being the petty cash account. As you are in the menu 'Cash Receipts', select the bank account that is 'receiving' the money.
- **Date** – Enter the date of the receipt.
- **Type** – Select 'Inter-Bank'. Money is being transferred from the current account to the petty cash account.
- **Slip No** – Enter the cheque number that was presented to the bank current account to receive the cash.
- **Desc** – This will automatically display as Inter-Bank Transfer, which will be self-explanatory in the bank reports.
- **Net Amt** – You can enter the receipt amount here if you wish or enter the amount in the Total Amt. The VAT is greyed out, as there is no VAT on this receipt.

- **Total Amt** – The total amount will be entered automatically. You can skip the Net amount and enter the amount in the total if you wish.
- On pressing the **Tab** key, a 'Choose a Bank Account' message box will display (s3). Click to choose the bank that is paying out the money, being '1 – Bank Current Account' and click **OK**.

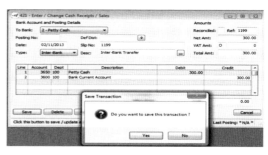

s3   s4

The double-entry will be completed automatically (s4). Here *TASBooks* will *debit* the petty cash account (receiving money in) and *credit* the bank current account (paying money out). Save the receipt.

Entering bank transfers

The above receipt into petty cash from the bank current account is termed a bank transfer.

This is used for recording:

- cash paid into the petty cash account
- payment of credit card balances, where the credit card account is set up as a bank account
- repayment of a bank loan, where a bank account for a bank loan has been set up.

The bank transfer can be recorded in both the cash receipts option and the cash payments option. For example, the receipt into petty cash recorded previously (in s3 and s4) could also be recorded as shown (s5).

Select **(4)Cash Book > (2)Enter/Change Journals > (2)Enter/Change Cash Payments/Purchases**.

From Bank – This is the '1 – Bank Current Account', being the bank account paying the money. All other details are similar to those described previously.

In the 'Choose a Bank Account' message box, you select the bank account that is

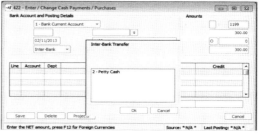

s5

receiving the money. This is the Petty Cash account. The double-entry is automatically completed by *TASBooks*, which is to *credit* the bank current account and *debit* the petty cash account.

Petty cash payments

These are payments for small items from the cash in the petty cash account. Usually, on each occasion where cash is needed from the petty cash, a voucher is completed listing the details of the purchase. The payments are entered in the same menu as that used for cheque payments.

Select **(4)Cash Book > (2)Enter/Change Journals > (2)Enter/Change Cash Payments/Purchases**. The petty cash payment for diesel in Daly's Pharmacy Ltd is entered as shown (s6)

- **From Bank** – Choose '2 – Petty Cash', which is the bank account the cash is being paid from.
- **Date** – Enter the cash payment date.
- **Type** – The type is defaulted to 'Home Purch'. Home purchase will assume that there is VAT on the payment. VAT can be claimed on diesel, so leave the selection as home purchase.
- **Chq/Ref** – Enter the voucher number.
- **Desc** – The description defaults to 'Cash Payment' but enter a specific description for the payment here.
- **Net Amt** – You can enter the net amount if you wish or enter the total amount.
- **VAT code and amount** – Diesel is a non-resale expense at 23% VAT. The VAT code set up in the 'maintain VAT rates' section is code 5. (Use the **F2** look-up for a list of codes.) The VAT amount is calculated automatically if the net amount is entered.
- **Total Amt** – The total amount will be entered automatically if the net amount is entered. You can skip the net amount and enter the amount in the Total Amt if you wish.
- On pressing the **Tab** key, the double-entry needs to be completed, which is a *credit* in the petty cash account with the total, a *debit* in the VAT account with the VAT and a *debit* in the motor expenses account with the net.
- **Debit and Credit** – The Nominal account for the petty cash appears automatically with a *credit* amount. The VAT account also appears with a *debit* of the VAT amount. Enter the nominal account number for Motor Expenses (use F2 look-up) and enter the net amount in the debit column, as below. When the debits equal the credits, that is, the Still to Post is 0.00, save the payment.

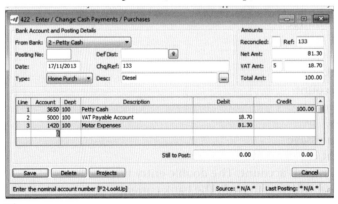

The second petty cash payment for stamps in Daly's Pharmacy Ltd is displayed. Note that this is a Non-VAT journal entry, as there is no VAT on stamps. This is posted to the Printing & Postage account as a *debit* entry.

s6

Cash book reports

There are a number of reports you can run to show information about your bank accounts.

Bank account enquiry

This shows all transactions posted to the bank account including payments and receipts posted through the purchase and sales ledger.

To view the Bank Account Enquiry report, select **(4)Cash Book > (1)Bank Accounts > (2)Bank Account Enquiry**.

In the Bank Account Enquiry screen, select the bank account that you need to report (s7). This is defaulted to '1 – Bank Current Account'. Choose the start and end period for which you wish to run the report. Select to include opening balance, if required. Choose print 'To Screen'.

s7

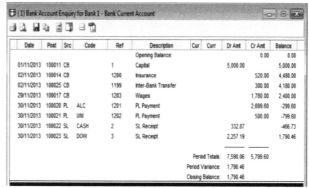

s8

The next screen shows the bank account of Daly's Pharmacy Ltd as it should appear after all entries are completed (s8). The debit entries are monies received into the bank account. The credit entries are cheque payments from the bank account. The report displays the closing balance in the bank account. The entries are listed according to the ledger date and not the order of posting. If you wish to print the report, choose print 'To Printer' at the bottom of the screen.

To run a Bank Account Enquiry on the petty cash account, use the same menu and choose bank account number '2 – Petty Cash'. The report should display as shown (s9).

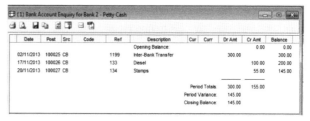

s9

Cash book payments and receipts report

This represents a manual cash book showing you money in and money out. Select **(4)Cash Book > (4)Reporting > (1)Print Cash Book Payments/ Receipts**. Alternatively, click on the toolbar 'Cash Daybook'.

The screen is displayed as shown (s10). You can choose to sort By Date (sorted in date order) or By Reference (sorted by Chq/Ref number). Choose the bank account from the Bank No. drop-down list. Select the options Receipts and/or Payments and select the starting and ending periods you wish to report. Choose print 'To Screen' to view the report.

The report is displayed in two separate reports. The cash receipts represent the debit side of a manual cash book. The Cash Payments represent the credit side of a manual cash book. This report does not display the closing balance in the bank account.

For the Petty Cash report, select '2 – Petty Cash' from the Bank No. drop-down menu.

S10

Bank reconciliation

Bank Statement

Irish Bank
Salthill, Galway

Your account name: Daly's Pharmacy Ltd

Current account

Account no: 19385298
Statement date: 30-Nov-13

Date	Transaction details	Payments out	Payments in	Balance
	Balance forward			0.00
1-Nov	Lodgement		5000.00	5,000.00
2-Nov	Cheque 1199	300.00		4,700.00
2-Nov	Cheque book Govt Duty	25.00		4,675.00
6-Nov	Cheque 1200	520.00		4,155.00
15-Nov	Lodgement		332.87	4,487.87
28-Nov	Cheque 1201	2699.60		1,788.27
29-Nov	Bank charges	25.63		1,762.64
30-Nov	James Mulcahy EFT		1000.00	2,762.64

Bank reconciliation is the process of matching the cash book transactions in the bank current account with the statement from the bank. It helps you pinpoint any incorrect entries or omissions in your *TASBooks* bank current account, or any incorrect withdrawals or deposits shown on your bank statement. You should reconcile your bank current account when you receive your bank statement. If you do this regularly, it will be easier to do. The bank reconciliation for Daly's Pharmacy Ltd will now be completed. Refer to the bank statement received by the company from the bank at 30 November, which is reproduced from section 1.4(1) as shown.

The steps to perform a bank reconciliation for Daly's Pharmacy Ltd are explained in steps 1 to 3 below.

Step 1: Check the bank statement balance

You will need to make sure the statement balance on the bank account is the same as the opening balance on your bank statement. If it is different, you will need to find out why. Select **(4)Cash Book > (3)Bank Account Programs > (2)Display Bank Account Balances**. The Display Bank Account Balances window displays as shown (s11). The statement balance for each bank account is displayed in the 'Stmt Bal' column. This shows a zero balance to match the bank statement of Daly's Pharmacy Ltd. As the balances match, there is no need to proceed with any adjustments here.

S11

Step 2: Ensure that paying-in slip numbers are allocated

You will also need to ensure that all receipts entered into your *TASBooks* have a paying-in slip number or reference. Receipts without paying-in slip numbers will not appear on the bank reconciliation window. To make the receipt side of bank-statement reconciliation easy, when you pay money into the bank, you can use the same paying-in slip number for each receipt if the money is lodged on the same day. This means that one paying-in slip number can relate to multiple receipts. Once paying-in slip numbers have been allocated to all your receipts, the bank-statement reconciliation option will simply list the paying-in slip numbers and the total value of the receipts that have been linked to each one. These totals should be the same as the amounts on the statement from your bank.

Select **(4)Cash Book > (3)Bank Account Programs > (1)Allocate/Change Paying-In Slip Numbers**. Choose the appropriate bank account from the drop-down list and click 'Display'. The window displays all the cash transactions that have not been allocated a paying-in slip number. In Daly's Pharmacy Ltd, a slip number was allocated to all receipts and displays this message accordingly.

If there are no slip numbers for receipts, enter the paying-in slip number or a reference for the first receipt and press the **Tab** key. The cursor is now in the Ref field of the second payment. If you want to allocate the same reference to all the receipts click 'Automatic' and click **Yes** to confirm. The reference is then automatically added to every transaction listed. If each receipt has a different reference, enter the reference required on each line. To save the records, click **Save**.

Step 3: Reconcile the bank statement

The bank reconciliation option has been designed to reflect a printed bank statement. It lists the items as withdrawals and deposits. It shows the previous statement balance brought forward (if relevant) and lists all unreconciled payments and receipts. As you select transactions for reconciliation, the figures are added or deducted, to give you a running balance. Your new statement balance is continuously calculated and when you have flagged all the relevant transactions and the total matches your new bank statement balance, you know you have finished with the page. There may be situations where the total does not match your bank statement balance, for example, if there is an incorrect transaction on your bank statement that you need to query with your bank. If this is the case, you can save the back reconciliation with this difference in figures.

S12

Select **(4)Cash Book > (3)Bank Account Programs > (3) Reconcile Cash/Bank Statement**. The Reconcile Bank Account window will appear (s12). From the drop-down list, choose the bank account you want to reconcile. Enter the ending date of the statement that you are going to reconcile. The statement ending date is used as a cut-off point. Here the date of the bank statement is 30 November. This means that any transactions entered with a posting date after the statement ending date will not be displayed in the reconciliation window.

Enter the starting balance, which should also be the same as the statement balance in the Display Bank Account Balances (see s11). You can overtype the starting balance with the correct one. If this is the first time you are reconciling this bank account, leave the starting balance as 0.00, which is correct here. The first transaction on the bank reconciliation window should be the opening balance. You need to reconcile the opening balance transaction first, even though this will not appear on your bank statement. Enter the ending balance of the statement. This is the balance you are aiming to reconcile your bank account to, which is €2,762.64, the final balance on the bank statement.

Enter this amount in the Ending Balance in the Reconcile Bank Account window (s13). To start the reconciliation, click **Next**.

S13

All unreconciled receipts and payments up to the chosen date are displayed as shown (s14). Each line represents either a withdrawal or a deposit to this bank account. They also show the Date, Type, Reference and Description. For withdrawals, the reference is usually the cheque number and, for direct debits or standing orders, use a reference of your choice. To reconcile an item that matches a transaction on your bank statement, double-click

S14

it. Think of this as 'ticking off' the items listed in the reconciliation window against the items on your statement. The bottom-left of the window displays a summary of the amounts you have marked as reconciled, broken down into deposits, withdrawals and the net activity. On the right-hand side, you will see the Opening Balance, Ending Balance and the Reconciled Balance (how much you have already checked off) and the Difference. When the Reconciled Balance is the same as the Ending Balance, that is, when you have matched off all of the entries on your bank statement,

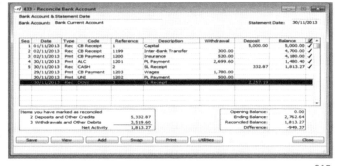

S15

your difference will be zero. If a transaction appears on your bank statement that has not been recorded in *TASBooks*, you can enter it without leaving the reconciliation window.

After ticking off the items that appear in the bank statement of Daly's Pharmacy Ltd, the window should appear as shown (s15).

All items appear in the bank statement, except for:

- Cheque number 1202 for €500
- Cheque number 1203 for €1,780
- SL receipt of €2,257.19.

There are also items on the bank statement that are not in the bank account of Daly's Pharmacy Ltd. These are:

- Cheque book govt duty of €25.00
- Bank charges of €25.63
- Receipt by EFT from James Mulcahy for €1,000.

To add a transaction shown on the bank statement that you were previously unaware of, click **Add**. A list of options appears. Select the relevant option and the appropriate entry window appears (s16).

From the previous lists of missing transactions, the options selected are:

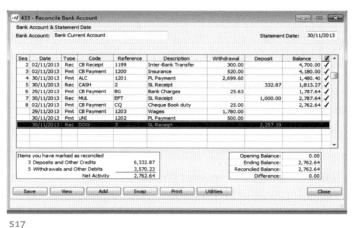

s16

- Cheque book govt duty: 'Enter Cash Payment'
- Bank charges: 'Enter Cash Payment'
  (*Note:* The 'Enter Bank Charges' option is not selected, as bank charges as a control account has not been set up in the *TASBooks* configuration. Make sure you have a nominal ledger for Bank Charges set up.)
- Receipt from James Mulcahy: 'Enter Receipt from Customer'.

When you select the options above, you are directed to the relevant menus. After entering the three transactions, they are then added to the reconciliation list (s17). To reconcile the new items, double-click each item. The running balances at the bottom of the screen are updated. If you entered the ending balance of your bank statement at the start, the ending balance and reconciled balance will show 0.00 when you have reconciled, or matched, all of the transactions on your bank statement. When you have finished, click **Save**.

You will be asked if you want to print a Cash Book Summary report. If you click **Yes**, the report will be displayed. This report shows the corrected balance in the bank account of €2,739.83.

S17

Completing the bank reconciliation

You can also print a Display Bank Account Balances report by selecting: **(4) Cash Book > (3)Bank Account Programs > (2)Display Bank Account Balances**. The Display Bank Account Balances window will appear, showing the updated bank balance and statement balance (s18). Double check that the statement balance matches that of the bank statement.

The revised bank account of Daly's Pharmacy Ltd in the menu option **(4)Cash Book > (1) Bank Accounts > (2)Bank Account Enquiry** is displayed

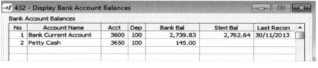

s18

showing the three items entered during reconciliation (s19).

You have now successfully completed the bank reconciliation for Daly's Pharmacy Ltd.

The bank reconciliation will run smoothly if there are no errors in the process and if it is performed on a regular basis. To make it easier, this should be done at least monthly or on receipt of each bank statement.

S19

If the reconciled balance does *not* match the ending balance, i.e. where the difference in the Reconcile Bank Account window does not display 0.00, you will be given three options (s20):

S20

1. 'Go back and finish reconciling the account.' Use this option if you want to complete the reconciliation. Match off any entries needed to get your reconciled balance to match your statement balance.
2. 'Ignore the difference and save reconciliation.' Use this option if you are happy to complete the reconciliation, but showing a difference between the reconciled balance and statement balance, for example, because there are entries on your bank statement that are under query and you cannot therefore match the balance on your statement.
3. 'Save the work I've done so far. I will come back and complete the reconciliation later.' Use this option if you want to pause the reconciliation and complete it later. For example, if you need to take a break or do some other work before you can finish the reconciliation. When you restart the bank reconciliation, you will then be asked if you want to continue where you left off or discard the unfinished reconciliation.

To continue, select the option you want, then click **OK**. You will then be asked if you want to print the Cash Book Summary Report.

Review assignments

Assignment 1

Refer to the source documents in your Student Resources relating to Watchworld Ltd.

Open the company Watchworld Ltd, which you have set up in *TASBooks* and perform the following tasks:

1. Enter the receipts into the current bank account and petty cash account.
2. Enter the cheque book payments into the current bank account.
3. Enter the petty cash payments into the petty cash account.
4. Print the following reports to either the printer or screen:
   a. Bank account enquiry for both current bank account and petty cash
   b. Cash Book payments and receipts report for both current bank account and petty cash.

Assignment 2

Refer to the bank statement received by Watchworld Ltd in section 1.4, assignment 1.

Prepare a bank reconciliation in *TASBooks* for Watchworld Ltd and enter in the accounts any transactions that are in the bank statement but not already entered in the accounts.

Check the bank statement balance using 'Display Bank Account Balances'. *Note:* You will need to set up a new nominal ledger account for Bank Charges before commencing.

5.8 Entering Opening Balances in *TASBooks*

Learning outcomes (Accounting Manual and Computerised 5N1348): 8 (part)
Learning outcomes (Bookkeeping Manual and Computerised 5N1354): 8 (part)

If your business has been trading before you began using *TASBooks*, you will need to enter the accounts of the business to date as opening balances, which are the current values on your various accounts. Even if you are starting a new business, there may be opening balances you need to add, e.g. your bank account balance, a loan that you took out to start up the business and so on. When you enter opening balances you should use the closing date of your previous accounting period. For example, if you are starting to use *TASBooks* for a new financial year starting 1 January 2014, enter the date of your opening balances as 31 December 2013.

Opening balances

To enter opening balances you will need the following information to hand:

- Closing Trial Balance as at the end of the period, where the accounts were completed using an accounting method other than *TASBooks*.
- A list of outstanding (unpaid) sales invoices, i.e. individual debtor balances.
- A list of outstanding (unpaid) supplier invoices, i.e. individual creditor balances.
- Closing bank statement balance.

The nominal ledger is used to enter opening balances from the Trial Balance that do not relate to customers, suppliers or the cash book/bank account. That is, all the accounts in the Trial Balance, but excluding debtors, creditors, bank and petty cash. These balances are entered in their respective ledgers.

To demonstrate the process of entering opening balances in *TASBooks*, the following details relate to Equipment Supplies Ltd. The accounts are completed up to 30 November 2014. The accounting year is from 1 January to 31 December 2014.

Business name	Equipment Supplies Ltd
Address	108 Abbott Street, Dublin 1
Telephone	01-872 3456
VAT reg. no.	IE 4567823H
Business activity	Sales and repair of office equipment

VAT is charged on sales at the standard rate of 23%. VAT is charged on repairs at the lower rate of 13.5%.

All of the above information should be entered in *TASBooks* Configuration, along with the VAT rates, bank accounts, accounting year and default accounts. You can set up this company from scratch, or alternatively, create a new company from the backup file of Daly's Pharmacy Ltd (fig.1).

TRIAL BALANCE of Equipment Supplies Ltd as at 30 November 2014

	Debit	Credit
Sales of goods		337,148
Repair Income		13,033
Opening Stock 1 Jan 2014	16,448	
Purchases	164,300	
Salaries	36,960	
Printing, Postage & Stationery	9,600	
Delivery Costs	690	
Telephone	1,842	
Light & Heat	1,790	
Rent	15,000	
Miscellaneous Expenses	123	
Bank Charges	247	
Furniture	34,500	
Office Equipment	29,000	
Bank	27,450	
Petty Cash	1,600	
Debtors	102,630	
Creditors		66,852
VAT Payable		2,656
Capital		22,491
	442,180	**442,180**

Note: VAT Payable equals VAT on Sales – €5,448 and VAT on Purchases – €2,792 (for the month of November 2014).

Debtors Balances as at 30 November 2014

NAME	ADDRESS	BALANCE
O'Sullivan's Office Centre	12 Patrick St, Navan, Co Meath	24,912.00
Cal Computing	16 Main St, Clifden, Co Galway	23,339.00
Earls Office Supplies	56 Mountain View, Athlone, Co Westmeath	37,479.00
Mr Joe Malone	Main Street, Trim, Co Meath	16,900.00
	TOTAL	**102,630.00**

Creditors Balances as at 30 November 2014

NAME	ADDRESS	BALANCE
Electric Ireland	Fleet St, Dublin 2	434.53
Eircom	Leopardstown, Co Dublin	508.32
Pentech Office Ltd	57 York Rd, Dun Laoghaire, Co Dublin	52,269.00
Tech Supplies Ltd	63 Landscape, Ballinteer, Dublin 16	13,640.15
	TOTAL	**66,852.00**

Figure 1

All the nominal accounts in the Trial Balance would need to be set up in *TASBooks*. Set up these nominal accounts, using the nominal codes, as shown (s1).

Before entering the balances in the Trial Balance, set all three ledger dates to 30 November 2014.

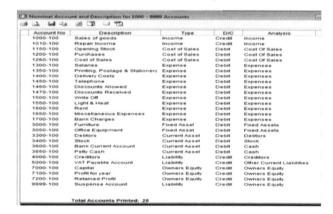

S1

Nominal opening balances

All of the nominal accounts in the Trial Balance in s1, excluding debtors, creditors, bank and petty cash, are entered through the nominal ledger in *TASBooks*.

Select **(1)Nominal > (2)Enter/Change Journals > (1)Enter/Change General Journals**. The screen will display as shown (s2). You do not need to enter a posting number. In the Description box, enter a description for this journal, e.g. 'Opening Balance'. Accept the date for this journal as 30 November 2014. Enter a reference for this journal. Tab into the grid and enter the first nominal account or press **F2** and select it from the list. Enter the debit or credit amount for the first opening balance. Continue through the grid, entering the opening

S2

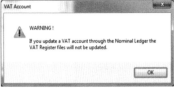

S3

balance for each of the nominal accounts on your Trial Balance, excluding the debtors, creditors, bank and petty cash balances. These four balances are not entered through the nominal ledger. The debits will not equal the credits due to debtors, creditors, bank and petty cash being omitted. The balancing value, that is, the difference between the debits and credits should be posted to the Suspense account – analysis code 9999. The main purpose of the suspense account is to hold the difference between debits and credits until all balances are fully entered. When you have finished, your debit and credit columns should show the same total value, since you have entered the balancing value to analysis code 9999.

Press **Tab** to save the opening balance journal and click **Save**. The entries are displayed as shown.

As you enter the nominal code for the VAT Payable account, a message will display (s3). As stated, VAT items are entered through the sales, purchases and cash book ledgers. VAT items should not be entered through the nominal ledger, as the central file and the VAT analysis report will not be updated. Accept the warning message in order to enter the opening balance in the VAT payable account.

Bank account opening balance

When you enter your bank account opening balances there are three things that you must look at:

- the closing balance of your last bank statement reconciliation
- all payments that have been made since the last statement was reconciled
- all receipts that have been paid in since the last statement was reconciled.

The main opening balance of your bank account will be the closing balance of your last bank statement. After you have entered this amount we recommend that you itemise each subsequent bank transaction so that when you come to reconcile your next bank statement, it will be a straightforward procedure.

To enter a positive opening balance (as in Equipment Supplies Ltd), select **(4)Cash Book > (2)Enter/Change Journals > (1)Enter/Change Cash Receipts/Sales** (s4).

To enter a negative opening balance, select **(4)Cash Book > (2)Enter/ Change Journals > (2) Enter/Change Cash Payments/Purchases**:

- **To Bank** – Choose the bank account from the drop-down list.

- **Date** – The date will be entered automatically as the last day of your previous accounting period, 30 November 2014.
- **Type** – Select 'Non-VAT Jnl', as there is no VAT element in the opening balance.
- **Slip No** – Enter a reference for transaction. This box must be completed for the transaction to appear in the bank reconciliation screen.
- **Desc** – Enter a description, such as 'Opening Balance'.
- **Net Amt** – Enter the amount of the opening balance.
- **Total Amt** – The total should calculate automatically.
- **Debits and Credits** – The nominal account number for this bank account will automatically appear. Enter the amount of the opening balance in the debit column. The opening balance should then be posted to the Suspense account – 9999 in the credit column to complete the double-entry.

s4

To save the details, click **Save**.

Once the opening balance has been entered you will need to enter all items in your bank account that are uncleared since you last reconciled the bank account as cash payments or cash receipts as appropriate. We will assume there are no unreconciled items for Equipment Supplies Ltd.

The petty cash balance also needs to be entered. The same menu used for the bank account is used here, where the 'To Bank' will display '2 – Petty Cash' (s5). The balancing credit entry will be posted to the suspense account.

s5

Suppliers' opening balances

When entering the opening balance for each of your suppliers, it is recommended that you itemise each transaction or invoice outstanding. Although this is initially more time consuming, it will give you an accurate picture of the history of each supplier account. It will also make it easier to select the correct invoices when entering and allocating your supplier payments in the future. The opening balances must be entered through the Purchase Ledger and individually to each supplier account. You cannot enter a supplier opening balance as a journal to the creditors account in the nominal ledger as this will not appear on your aged creditors report.

To enter supplier opening balances, select **(3)Purchase > (2)Enter/Change Journals > (1)Enter/Change Supplier Invoices/Credit Journals**.

To enter any outstanding credit notes, select **(3)Purchase > (2)Enter/ Change Journals > (2)Enter/Change Supplier Credit Notes/Credit Journals**.

This is the same menu you would use if you were entering purchase invoices from a supplier, but you are using this menu as a 'Credit Journal'. You are not entering purchase invoices. Enter the details for the opening balance of Electric Ireland, as shown (s6):

- **Date** – Use the last day of your previous accounting period as the posting date for every opening balance transaction, i.e. 30 November 2014, which will display automatically.
- **Type** – Select from the drop-down list 'Credit Journal', as you are entering a credit balance in the supplier's account.
- **Code** – Enter the code for Electric Ireland.
- **Ref No and Desc** – Enter an appropriate reference and description, e.g. 'Opening Balance'.
- **Net** – Enter the amount of the opening balance. The VAT is not displayed, as you are not entering any VAT element and the total will display automatically.

The creditors account will display automatically and enter the amount on the credit column. To balance the journal, enter account 9999, the Suspense account, and enter the amount on the debit column.

s6

Press **Tab** again, the Still to Post value will display 0.00.

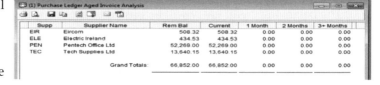

s7

To save the opening balance, click **Save**.

Enter the opening balances for the suppliers Eircom, Pentech Office Ltd and Tech Supplies Ltd from figure 1, posting the debit entry in each case to the Suspense account. When all opening balances have been entered, you can print an aged creditors report to view your entries (s7). The total of the creditors' balances equals the creditors balance in the Trial Balance.

To enter customers' opening balances

When entering the opening balance for each of your customers it is recommended, similar to suppliers, that you itemise each transaction.

Although it is initially more time consuming, this will give you an accurate picture of the history of each customer account. It will also make it easier to select the correct invoices when entering and allocating your customer receipts in the future. The opening balances must be entered through the sales ledger and individually to each customer account. You cannot enter an opening balance as a journal to the debtors account as this will not appear on your aged debtors report.

To enter customer opening balances, select **(2)Sales > (2) Enter/Change Journals > (1) Enter/Change Customer Invoices/Debit Journals**.

To enter any outstanding credit notes, select **(2)Sales > (2) Enter/Change Journals > (2) Enter/Change Customer Credit Notes/Credit Journals**.

This is the same menu you would use if you were entering sales invoices to customers, but you are using this menu as a 'Debit Journal'. You are not entering sales invoices. Enter the details for the opening balance of O'Sullivan's Office Centre (s8):

- **Date** – Use the last day of your previous accounting period as the posting date for every opening balance transaction, i.e. 30 November 2014, which will display automatically.
- **Type** – Select from the drop-down list 'Debit Journal', as you are entering a debit balance in the customer's account.
- **Code** – Enter the code for O'Sullivan's Office Centre.
- **Ref No and Desc** – Enter an appropriate reference and description, e.g. 'Opening Balance'.
- **Net** – Enter the amount of the opening balance. The VAT is not displayed, as you are not entering any VAT element and the total will display automatically.

The Debtors account will display automatically and enter the amount on the debit column. To balance the journal, enter account 9999, the Suspense account, and enter the amount on the credit column.

Press **Tab** again, the Still to Post value will display 0.00. To save the opening balance, click **Save**.

Enter the opening balances for the customers, Cal Computing, Earls Office Supplies and Mr Joe Malone from figure 1, posting the credit

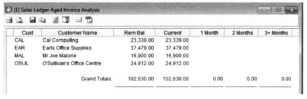

s9

entry in each case to the suspense account. When all opening balances have been entered, you can print an aged debtors report to view your entries (s9). The total of all the debtors'

Acc	Dept	Description	YTD Debit	YTD Credit
1000	100	Sales of goods		337,148.00
1010	100	Repair Income		13,033.00
1150	100	Opening Stock	16,448.00	
1200	100	Purchases	164,300.00	
1300	100	Salaries	36,960.00	
1350	100	Printing, Postage & Stationery	9,600.00	
1400	100	Delivery Costs	690.00	
1450	100	Telephone	1,842.00	
1550	100	Light & Heat	1,790.00	
1600	100	Rent	15,000.00	
1650	100	Miscellaneous Expenses	123.00	
1700	100	Bank Charges	247.00	
3000	100	Furniture	34,500.00	
3050	100	Office Equipment	29,000.00	
3300	100	Debtors	102,630.00	
3600	100	Bank Current Account	27,450.00	
3650	100	Petty Cash	1,600.00	
4000	100	Creditors		66,852.00
5000	100	VAT Payable Account		2,656.00
7000	100	Capital		22,491.00
			442,180.00	442,180.00

Trial Balance - Current Year (Periods: 11 - 11)

S10

balances equals the debtors balance in the Trial Balance.

You have now entered all the opening balances as at 30 November 2014 for Equipment Supplies Ltd. The suspense account is now cleared and the Trial Balance should display as shown (s10). To print the Trial Balance, select **(1)Nominal > (3)Reporting > (4)Print Trial Balance**. Print the Trial Balance by selecting print 'To Screen'.

TASBooks has now been set up for the company, where transactions for the month following (i.e. December) can now be entered in the ledgers.

5.9 Nominal Ledger and VAT Reporting in *TASBooks*

Learning outcomes (Accounting Manual and Computerised 5N1348): 9 (part) and 10 (part)
Learning outcomes (Bookkeeping Manual and Computerised 5N1354): 10 (part)

When you record transactions in *TASBooks* they are 'posted' to nominal ledger accounts, for example, the VAT account, debtors account, creditors account or expenses accounts. This posting is automatic when transactions are entered in the purchases ledger, sales ledger and cash book. For example, when you enter a sales invoice, the entry is entered in the sales ledger. The double-entry is:

Debit: Customer with the total of the invoice
Credit: VAT with the VAT amount
Credit: Sales with the net amount.

You will see the double-entry displayed in the posting of this entry and you will soon discover which accounts should be debited and credited. The debtors, VAT and sales account are updated in the nominal ledger after you save the above transaction. The Trial Balance is updated automatically with every posting, no matter what ledger you selected to enter transactions. Also the Profit and Loss account and Balance Sheet are updated with every posting from all ledgers.

The nominal ledger is used to enter transactions that do not fit into the normal operations of the sales and purchase ledger or the cash book. These are transactions that are *not* related to purchases, sales or the bank accounts. Examples include adjustments to the accounts, where you need to debit one nominal ledger account and credit another. Typical entries posted to the nominal ledger are:

- depreciation
- provision for bad debts
- accruals and prepayments
- accounting for stock.

The nominal ledger is used to set up all the accounts needed to enter transactions for a company.

The nominal ledger may also be used to make other adjustments at the end of the financial year, for example, to transfer amounts from one nominal ledger account to another where the amount was incorrectly posted to the incorrect nominal ledger account.

Print Trial Balance

Load the company Daly's Pharmacy Ltd.

You will use the nominal ledger many times during *TASBooks* to view the balances in each nominal ledger account by printing a Trial Balance. Since all the entries have debits equal to credits, having been entered through the purchases, sales and cash book ledgers, the Trial Balance will always balance. This does not mean that all the entries in the system were correct: entries could be omitted, incorrect amounts could be entered or the incorrect menu could be used.

To print a Trial Balance, select **(1)Nominal > (3)Reporting > (4)Print Trial Balance**. The Print Trial Balance screen is displayed as shown (s1). In Daly's Pharmacy Ltd the starting period and ending period would both be displayed as 11, being the month of November. This would be correct here, as there is only one month of accounts entered. But it is good practice to always set the starting period as 1 and ending period as 12 to cover the full accounting year. In this case, check the box to include opening balances. The Trial Balance needs to be *cumulative* to get the correct picture of the accounts from the beginning of the accounting year to the last period entered. You can tick the 'Remember' button at the bottom and *TASBooks* will remember your last selections for the report. Choose the destination for the report from the drop-down list and print.

The Trial Balance of Daly's Pharmacy Ltd is displayed as shown (s2). This report is customised.

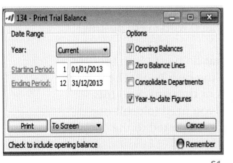

S1

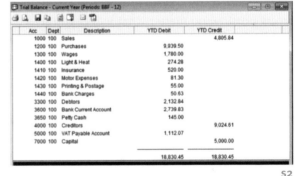

S2

Nominal ledger account enquiry

As explained above, all transactions, no matter what ledger they were posted in, are recorded in the nominal ledger accounts. This report enables you to view all the transactions posted to a nominal account for a selected period.

Select **(1)Nominal > (1)Nominal Account > (2)Nominal ledger Account Enquiry**. The nominal account for bank charges for Daly's Pharmacy Ltd is selected here (s3). Enter the following fields:

- **Number & Dept** – Enter the nominal code for the account.
- **From Period** – Enter the starting period for the report.
- **To Period** – Enter the ending period for the report.

As the bank charges are recorded for November only, these periods can remain at period 11. Check the box Include Opening Balance if you want to display the opening balance at the beginning of the period. Choose the destination for the report from the drop-down list and print.

The report for bank charges is displayed as shown (s4).

s3

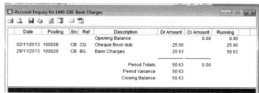

s4

Audit trail by nominal account

This reports on all transactions sorted by nominal account. Regardless of what the source was (purchase, sales, cash book or nominal, ledger), this option prints all transactions that were entered within the reporting period (s5).

Select **(1)Nominal > (3)Reporting > (2)Print Audit Trail by Nominal Account**.

Enter the starting and ending account that you want to report. Choose the starting and ending period and tick Opening Balance if this is what you want to display. Choose the destination for the report from the drop-down list and print.

This report is not displayed here due to the large amount of accounts in the report.

s5

Financial reports

The financial reports in line with all other reports in *TASBooks*, can be run for specific periods in your current financial year and up to four years past. The financial reports available in *TASBooks* are the Trial Balance, Profit and Loss and Balance Sheet. *Note*: If the Profit and Loss and Balance Sheet scripts are not set up in *TASBooks*, refer to your tutor on the details of how to set up financial statements scripts. The set-up of these scripts is outside the scope of your course.

Profit and Loss report

s6

This reports on whether or not the company is trading profitably. You can produce a Profit and Loss report for the current month, a range of consecutive months and for any prior financial year up to four years past.

Select **(1)Nominal > (4)Report Generator > (2)Print 4 Column Financial Statements**.

The Print 4 Column Financial Statements window will display (s6). Choose 'P&L A/C' from the Script drop-down list. The description automatically appears as 'Profit and Loss Account'. Choose the relevant financial year in column 1 and enter the relevant starting and ending period for the report. The column title automatically completes with the year. Ignore the Include BBF box as this does not apply to the Profit and Loss. The Profit and Loss account refers to one year only and there are no balances brought forward from previous years. Choose the destination for the report from the drop-down list and print.

The Profit and Loss account for Daly's Pharmacy Ltd is displayed as shown (s7). Note that it shows a net loss, as closing stock has not yet been entered in the accounts.

s7

Balance Sheet

The Balance Sheet shows the assets and liabilities of the business. The profit (or loss) from the Profit and Loss report needs to be transferred to the Balance Sheet and added to (subtracted from) the retained profit of the business (s8).

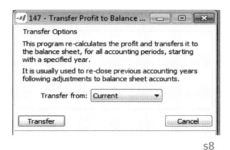

s8

s9

s10

To transfer the profit (or loss) to the Balance Sheet, select **(1)Nominal > (4)Report Generator > (7) Transfer Profit to Balance Sheet**. Click on 'Transfer' and the process will complete.

If there are any adjustments to the Profit and Loss account, this process needs to be completed for the revised profit or loss to be updated in the Balance Sheet.

To print the Balance Sheet, select **(1)Nominal > (4)Report Generator > (2)Print 4 Column Financial Statements**.

Choose 'BAL' from the Script drop-down list (s9). The description automatically appears as 'Balance Sheet'. Choose the relevant financial year in column 1 and enter the relevant starting and ending period for the report. The column title automatically shows the year selected. Select Include BBF as the Balance Sheet should include bought-forward balances from previous financial years. Choose the destination for the report from the drop-down list and print.

The Balance Sheet for Daly's Pharmacy Ltd is displayed as shown (s10). Note that the net loss is transferred to the retained profit of the company.

Adjustments to final accounts – entering nominal journals

Nominal, or general, journals are ledger transactions that do not fit into the normal operations of the sales and purchase ledger or the cash book. Items such as accruals, prepayments and depreciation are typical nominal ledger journals. Everything related to VAT is entered through the sales ledger, purchase ledger or cash book. Remember that if you journal from within the nominal ledger, *TASBooks* has no means of finding out whether the transaction has a VAT element.

To enter a nominal journal

A journal entry moves money from one nominal account to another. Every journal consists of credit and debit values so that every credit must have a debit and vice versa. This does not mean that for every single debit item you must post a single credit item. You can post several debits but one balancing credit, and vice versa. As long as the net difference between your postings is always zero, that is, the total value of credits equals the total value of debits, you can post the journal. It is important to adhere to strict double-entry bookkeeping principles, when recording journals.

Select **(1)Nominal > (2)Enter/Change Journals > (1)Enter/Change General Journals**.

S11

The Enter/Change General Journals window is displayed as shown (s11). We will enter the closing stock figure for Daly's Pharmacy Ltd. We will assume that 30 November is the end of the Daly's Pharmacy accounting year, as final accounts are normally prepared at the end of the accounting year. We will also assume that the business has no opening stock and that the closing stock at 30 November is valued at €8,000.

Note: A new nominal account will need to be set up in the nominal ledger before you can enter this journal. The account is: **'Closing Stock'** – Use code 1250 and the type is Cost of Sales.

This nominal account represents the closing stock for the trading account. The Enter/Change General Journals menu is displayed as shown.

- **Posting No** – This is the posting number, which is generated automatically by *TASBooks*. You leave this blank.
- **Description** – Enter a description for the journal. Here you can enter 'Stock'.
- **Ref No** – Enter a reference for the journal. You can enter 'Closing Stock'.
- **Date** – Enter the date you want to use for the journal or accept the date automatically displayed as 30 November.
- **Def Dist** – If you want to use the same selection of nominal accounts again, you can create a Default Distribution. Enter a code for the Distribution and click **Yes** to create a default distribution message. When you save this journal the nominal accounts you have used will be saved. You can use this list of nominal accounts for another journal by clicking the up-arrow and selecting the required code from the list. Here you can leave this blank.
- **Account** – Enter the nominal accounts the journal is to be posted to. Here is where you enter the double-entry for closing stock, which is:

Debit: Closing Stock (Current Asset – Balance Sheet)
Credit: Closing Stock (Trading account).

Press **F2** to select the account from the look-up list and choose the appropriate accounts, as shown. The description displays the nominal account description.

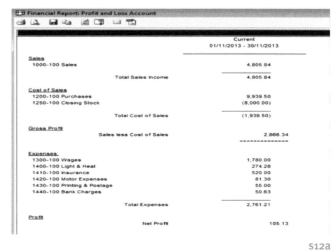

S12a

- **Debit/Credit** – Enter the amount to be debited/credited against each nominal account. When the value in the debit and credit columns balance, the Still to Post box will show 0.00 in both columns. To save the journal, click **Save**.

If you now transfer the profit to the Balance Sheet and reprint the Profit and Loss account and Balance Sheet for Daly's Pharmacy Ltd, the reports should display as shown (s12a and b).

Note the effect the closing stock has on the Profit and Loss account and Balance Sheet.

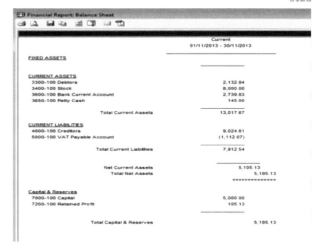

S12b

Other nominal ledger adjustments

Other adjustments to final accounts include:

- Depreciation
- Provision for bad debts
- Accruals and prepayments.

To enter these adjustments in *TASBooks*, select the same menu as in s11, that is, **(1)Nominal > (2)Enter/Change Journals > (1)Enter/Change General Journals**. Note that nominal accounts would need to be set up before entering these adjustments. The screen shown is displayed *as examples* of the above adjustments (s13). They do not form

S13

part of the accounts of Daly's Pharmacy Ltd. The account description has been edited to demonstrate clearly the accounts that require the double-entry. Also note that a range of double-entries can be entered in the same menu as long as the Still to Post displays 0.00.

- **Depreciation of fixed assets:** Nominal accounts need to be present for Depreciation Expense (Profit and Loss account) and Accumulated Depreciation of fixed assets (Balance Sheet). The double-entry is:

  Debit: Depreciation Expense account (Profit and Loss account), increasing the expenses and reducing the net profit in the Profit and Loss account
  Credit: Accumulated Depreciation of fixed assets (Balance Sheet), reducing the net book value of fixed assets in the Balance Sheet.

- **Create provision for bad debts:** Nominal accounts need to be present for Provision for Bad Debts Expense (Profit and Loss account) and Provision for Bad Debts (current asset in Balance Sheet), which will reduce the debtors figure in the Balance Sheet. The double-entry is:

  Debit: Provision for Bad Debts Expense (Profit and Loss account), increasing the expenses and reducing the net profit in the Profit and Loss account
  Credit: Provision for Bad Debts (current asset in Balance Sheet), reducing the debtors figure in the Balance Sheet.

- **Accruals:** If there are expenses accrued at the end of the year, a nominal account for accruals (current liability in Balance Sheet) would need to be set up. The double-entry is:

  Debit: Expense account (Profit and Loss account), increasing the expenses and reducing the net profit in the Profit and Loss account
  Credit: Accruals account (current liability in Balance Sheet).

- **Prepayments:** If expenses are paid in advance at the end of the year, a prepayments account (current asset in Balance Sheet) would need to be set up. The double-entry is:

  Debit: Prepayments account (current asset in Balance Sheet)
  Credit: Expense account (Profit and Loss account), reducing the expenses and increasing the net profit in the Profit and Loss account.

All of the nominal adjustments that you perform in the nominal ledger will automatically have an effect on the Profit and Loss account and the Balance Sheet of the company.

VAT returns

Load the company Daly's Pharmacy Ltd.

Before running the VAT return it is important to set the VAT period that applies to your company, which is how often you need to file a VAT return. To do this select **(0)Central > (1)General Company Information > (1)Company Configuration**. Select VAT > Scheme Selection. In Daly's Pharmacy Ltd, VAT is returned every two months. Every business that is registered for VAT needs to file a VAT return with the Revenue Commissioners.

S14

To view the entries for the VAT return for Daly's Pharmacy Ltd, open the VAT Return Manager. To open the VAT Return Manager, select **(0)Central > (3)VAT Rates and Reporting > (3)VAT Return Manager**.

The VAT Return Assistant is displayed as shown (s14). You can use the VAT Return Assistant to add a new VAT return, or view details of an existing return. Enter the ending month date for the VAT return. For Daly's Pharmacy Ltd, enter December 2013. *Note*: The entries in the accounts are only for November 2013, but VAT would normally be returned on a two-month basis, i.e. November/ December 2013. Click **Finish**.

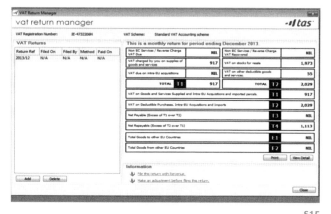

S15

Using the VAT Return Manager you can calculate your VAT returns, view details of existing returns and even record payments to the Revenue Commissioners (s15). You can see at a glance when a VAT return was filed, who filed the return and whether it has been paid to the Revenue Commissioners. The following options are available in the VAT Return Manager:

- **Add** – When you add a VAT return, it calculates for your chosen period and the VAT Return Manager displays the VAT form.
- **File this Return with Revenue** – Once you have checked the VAT return and you are ready to send it to the Revenue Commissioners, you need to file it. When you file a return you will be given the option to file it online or print and file it manually.
- **View detail** – This allows you to view more detail of an existing VAT return. Once a VAT return has been added and/or filed it appears in the VAT Return Manager window and can be viewed at any time.
- **Delete** – If you add a VAT return in error, or have subsequently entered transactions that you want to include in a return you have not yet filed, you can delete and add it again.

- **Make an adjustment before filing this return** – You can enter adjustments to VAT returns which do not affect the underlying transactions that make up the return. You should only do this with caution as the adjustments will not be reflected in the other ledgers.

As seen on the screen shown, VAT on sales for Daly's Pharmacy Ltd is €917 (T1) and VAT on purchases is €2,029 (T2). This represents VAT repayable of €1,113 (T4). These entries would be entered in the VAT3 form in the appropriate boxes.

Once you are satisfied with the results, print the details of the return if required by clicking **Print**. Close the VAT Return Manager by clicking **Close**. File the VAT return by filing online or completing a VAT3 form with the Revenue Commissioners. *A sample VAT3 return is in your Student Resources.*

Review assignments

Assignment 1

Open *TASBooks* and load the company Equipment Supplies Ltd. The opening Trial Balance at 30 November should already be entered. Use the source documents contained in your Student Resources and enter the transactions for December 2014. Remember to set the three ledger dates to 31 December 2014. You may need to set up additional supplier, customer and nominal ledger accounts.

Assignment 2

Open *TASBooks* and load the company Equipment Supplies Ltd. Perform the following tasks:

Task 1

The customer, O'Sullivan's Office Centre has gone into liquidation and the balance outstanding in the account is to be written off as a bad debt. Enter this transaction in the appropriate ledger. *Note*: The company is entitled to claim a refund of VAT for a specific bad debt write-off, which is 23% for this customer.

Task 2

1. Enter the following nominal ledger adjustments (noting that you may need to set up appropriate nominal ledger accounts):
    a. The closing stock at 31 December 2014 is valued at €5,640.
    b. There is stock of stationery on hand valued at €672.
    c. There are salaries outstanding of €410 at the end of the year.

d. The company wishes to create a provision for bad debts equal to 2% of the debtors balance at the end of the year.

e. Depreciation is to be provided on the furniture at 20% per annum straight-line and on the office equipment at 10% per annum straight-line.

f. Rent of €15,000 in the accounts is for period 1, January 2014 to 31 March 2015.

2. Transfer the profit to the Balance Sheet as at period 12, 31 December 2014.

3. Print the Trial Balance, Profit and Loss account and Balance Sheet for the starting period 1 to ending period 12 to screen or printer.

4. Print a nominal ledger account enquiry for printing, postage and stationery.

5. Run the VAT Return manager and prepare a VAT return for November/December 2014. *A sample VAT3 return is in your Student Resources.*

Assignment 3

Load the Company Watchworld Ltd and open the VAT Return Manager. Run the VAT return for March 2014. You may have to enter the ending month for the period containing the transactions as April 2014, as VAT is normally returned every two months, which is March/April 2014. Complete the VAT3 return for March 2014 only. *A sample VAT3 return is in your Student Resources.*

Part 6

Sage 50 Accounts

6.1 Using *Sage 50* Accounts

Learning outcomes (Accounting Manual and Computerised 5N1348): 11 (part)

The *Sage 50* Accounts software used throughout this section is the 2013 version 19.00.

Exploring your desktop

Before you start entering company details in *Sage 50* Accounts, there are some notes that you should be aware of before you start. When you run *Sage 50* Accounts, the desktop window is displayed. Use the desktop to run all the facilities available.

The first step in familiarising yourself with *Sage 50* Accounts is to see how the desktop window works.

Menus

S1

To select a program, the menu option is mainly used (s1). The main menus that you will be using are the File menu and Modules menu.

File menu

This is used to open, close, backup and restore company data. It will also be used to perform file maintenance tasks and exit the software.

Modules menu

This is the main menu to access items such as customers, suppliers, bank and nominal ledger (s2).

The **Customers** module deals with activities needed to manage your customer records, such as entering sales invoices, credit notes and receipts from customers, creating customers and printing customer reports.

S2

The **Suppliers** module deals with activities needed to manage your suppliers, such as recording purchase invoices, credit notes and payments to suppliers, creating suppliers and printing supplier reports.

The **Company** module accesses the nominal ledger, which lists your nominal ledger accounts that are set up. The collective term for these nominal ledger accounts is the Chart of Accounts (COA). This module also provides access to the Financials module, where the Profit and Loss account and Balance Sheet are generated.

The **Bank** module deals with all the banking activities such as creating, editing and deleting bank accounts. It is also used for bank reconciliation. It is also used to make bank payments to include supplier payments and bank receipts to include customer receipts.

The **Nominal Ledger** module displays the same information as the Company module.

Settings menu

s3

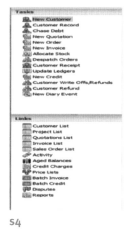

s4

This is used to open the company configuration editor to enter details such as the VAT rates. It is also used to enter company details, set up customer and supplier defaults, set the financial year and change the program date.

The **navigation bar** on the left-hand side of the window is the easiest way to access the features in your software as well as the services offered by *Sage* (s3). By selecting from the navigation bar, you are opening the Modules described above.

The **Tasks and Links pane** above the navigation bar provides easy access to the activities and information in each area (s4). For example, in the Customers module, the Tasks pane may include: New Customer, New Quotation, New Sales Order, and so on. The Links pane may include Project List, Invoice List, and so on.

Change view/View selector

Use the Change view/View selector to change what is displayed in the work area (s5). The options available depend on which module you are working in, but typically they might include the following:

- *Process map* – showing the workflow associated with the selected module
- *Ledger window* – showing a list of items appropriate to the selected module

s5

- *Dashboard window* – showing key information for the selected module
- *Diary* – showing due dates, reminders and scheduled tasks, as well as general notes.

To make a selection, click the Change View button shown in the top right-hand corner of the work area and then select the option you require from the drop-down list displayed.

Process maps provide a diagrammatic representation of the workflow associated with a particular navigation group. Each of the blocks displayed represents a function available within *Sage 50* Accounts. To access one of these, click on the appropriate icon. Process maps are available for the following modules:

- customers
- suppliers.

To view a process map window, select the appropriate option from the view selector.

Dashboard windows are used in *Sage 50* Accounts as a quick way of providing you with useful information, in relation to the module you are currently working in. The information displayed is up to date at the time the dashboard is first displayed. If you have the window displayed for any length of time, you can click on the $\mathbf{C}$ icon to refresh it. Dashboards are available for all modules, except Diary and Bank. To view a dashboard window, select the appropriate option from the view selector.

Entering data

To enter data, you can use the mouse by clicking into the box where you want to enter data and then type. To move from one box to another, use the **Tab** key to move to the next box. The following keyboard keys can be used when entering data:

- ESC – to exit the menu without saving
- TAB – to move to the next box to enter data
- SHIFT + TAB – to move back to the previous box
- END – to move the cursor to the last character of the last word in the box
- HOME – to move the cursor to the start of the box
- CTRL + Right Arrow – to move the cursor to the first character of the next word in the field
- CTRL + Left Arrow – to move the cursor to the first character of the previous word in the field.

To insert a row within a data entry table, the **Insert Row** option shifts the row in which the insertion point is located (and all of the following rows) down one place, thus creating an empty row in the table. Pressing **F7** also inserts a row.

To delete a row within a data entry table, the **Delete Row** option deletes the row in which the insertion point is located. The row that is deleted is removed from the table. Pressing **F8** also deletes a row.

The **Drop-down box** provides a list of valid entries from which you can select. To show the list of possible selections choose the down-pointing arrow. Click on the selection you require. For example, you can choose the Default Tax Code from the Customer Record's Defaults tab (s6).

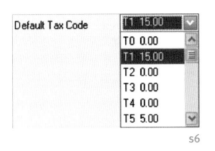

s6

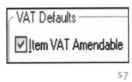

s7

s8

Check boxes let you select one or more from a range of actions (s7). To select or deselect a check box, either position the mouse on the required check box and left-click, or use the **Tab** or arrow keys to move to the check box required, then press the **Spacebar**.

All date text boxes have a **Calendar** button attached. When you choose this button a calendar appears, from which you can select the required date (s8).

A **Calculator** button is attached to many numeric data-entry boxes. Choose this button to display a mini calculator to help you enter any numeric values.

Wizards

Wizards are particularly designed to assist you in completing complicated procedures. For example, use the Bank Transfer wizard to help you transfer money from one bank or debit/credit card account to another. A wizard takes you through a procedure step by step, while prompting you to enter the relevant information. You can even return to items to alter mistakes or incorrect information previously entered. Once you have started a wizard, use the Next, Back and Finish Command buttons to control your progress. Clicking **Next** moves you to the next window of the wizard; clicking the **Back** button returns you to the previous window for error corrections. Once all the necessary data has been entered, the Finish button will activate. Click **Finish** to exit.

The following are some wizards that you may use in *Sage 50* Accounts:

* ActiveSetup wizard – to set up a new company
* New Customer wizard – to set up a new customer
* New Supplier wizard – to set up a new supplier

- New Bank Account wizard – to set up a new bank account
- Nominal Record wizard – to set up a new nominal ledger account
- Payments and receipts wizard – to record payments and receipts.

Toolbars

Toolbars can be used to access various tasks in *Sage 50* Accounts. For example, in the Customers module toolbar, where Customers is selected in the Change view window, you can use the toolbar to create a new customer, view an existing customer account, enter a sales invoice and access customer reports (s9).

s9

Each module has its own set of toolbars to allow quick access to common tasks.

Function keys

You can use function keys to access a number of important features if you prefer to use the keyboard. The following are a list of the shortcut keys:

- F1 opens online help.
- F2 opens the system calculator, which you can use to do mathematical calculations and, if needed, paste the result back into a data field.
- F3 displays the Edit Item Line window when entering invoice details.
- F4 displays the calendar, calculator or finder-search list if the selected text box has any of these special buttons attached. Also, if you select a drop-down list box, pressing F4 displays the list.
- F5 calls the currency calculator when the cursor is in a numeric box. This also calls the Spell Checker, when pressed while the cursor is in a text box.
- F6 is the duplicate cell command in the Edit menu.
- Shift+F6 copies the line above but also increment numbers by 1.
- F7 is the insert row command in the Edit menu.
- F8 is the delete row command in the Edit menu.
- F9 is the 'calculate net' command button. This function should be particularly remembered when you start entering invoices.
- F11 launches the Windows control panel.
- F12 launches the Report Designer.

Other keyboard shortcuts are:

- CTRL + key numbers 1–9 opens a module from the stack bar. As you open modules, you will notice that they remain open as tabs at the bottom of your screen. The module's position in the stack bar relates to the number you choose. For example, if Suppliers takes the second position in the stack bar, use CTRL + 2 to open that module.

- CTRL + TAB moves from the shortcut bar to the right pane.
- CTRL + 0 moves from the right pane to the shortcut bar.
- CTRL + ALT + Q closes all tabs in the right pane.
- Up-arrow or Down-arrow moves items up or down in the left or right pane.
- ENTER starts a selected feature in the left pane.
- Right arrow or Left arrow moves to next icon or command.

Menu shortcut keys

Menu shortcut keys are indicated in the menus and windows by an underlined letter.

To use the shortcuts press the Alt key on your keyboard and, while keeping the key pressed, press the key corresponding to the underlined letter shown in the menu. As an example, press Alt and F on your keyboard to open the File menu; then, keeping the Alt key pressed, press B on your keyboard to open the Backup window (s10).

S10

Customising the company

It would be useful to amend the company's name to include your own name or initials, especially if working in a classroom situation. This will help in the identification of printouts if other students are printing from the same printer. To do this, select **Settings** > **Company Preferences**. In the Details tab, amend the name of the company to include your own name and click **OK**.

Security and access

User and passwords

The default user code for *Sage 50* Accounts is **manager**, with no password. The user has all privileges and can use all the menus and run all the reports. While in a classroom situation, you can leave the password entry box blank, it is recommended that you enter a password to protect the confidentiality of the accounts in a working environment.

To enter a password, select **Settings** > **Change Password**. The Password Entry window is displayed. Enter your new password. The password is not case-sensitive, can be up to ten characters long and can include spaces and numbers. Enter your new password again to confirm details. To save your new password, click **OK**.

Access rights

Use access rights to control who can access your software and what changes they can make to your accounting information. You can set up access rights for individuals with or without password protection. You can also:

- *Copy access rights.* This is very useful if you have set someone up with restricted access to certain options and windows, and you want to impose the same access to another.
- *Block user access.* You can block access to any of the main areas in the software such as customers, nominal ledger or bank.
- *Limit user activity.* You can limit what an individual can do within the main areas of the software. For example, you can provide someone with access to the Bank module but prevent them from doing certain activities such as making payments.
- *Delete access rights.* This is particularly important when an individual leaves the company.

First, make sure that the Access Rights facility is available. To do this, select **Settings > Company Preferences**. Open the Parameters tab. Check the box 'Access Rights' and click OK.

When the Access Rights facility is enabled, select **Settings > Access Rights**. To create a new user, click **New** (s11). This facility includes:

S11

- **Logon Name:** Each person logging onto the software must have a logon name. The name can use upper or lower case characters, spaces or numbers, and you can use up to 30 characters.
- **Password:** A password for logging onto the software is optional but does provide extra security. The password can be up to 10 characters long and can include spaces and numbers. The individual can manage their own password from Settings > Change Password. If they forget their password the manager can reset it for them.
- **Full Access:** This is the starting point to opening up or limiting access to the software. You can choose between full access or no access. This depends on how much or how little access an individual should have. If you want to give an individual unlimited access to all or most areas of the software, select this option. Then, if needed, fine-tune access to specific areas and features. (See Fine-tune user access rights below).
- **No Access:** This blocks access to all parts of the software. If you want to limit access to most areas of the software, select this option. Then fine-tune access to specific areas and features.

Fine-tune user access rights

After setting up a user, the name will be displayed in the User Access Rights list. Select the user and click on Details. The Access Details – Logon Name box lists the main software areas that can have access rights attached. To see the features and activities within each area, select and double-click an area to expand the folder. To adjust access to the main areas of the software, click on Modules (s12).

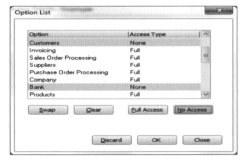

S12   S13

   The Option List displays the main areas in the software where access rights can be applied and indicates the user's access rights to each option (s13). This can be full, none or partial. Partial access means the user has access to specific areas within the option. For example, a user can have access to the Invoicing area of the software but no access to invoicing reports. To give the individual unlimited access to an option or most of an option, select the option then click on Full Access. Otherwise, click on No Access. If needed, fine-tune access to the option using 'Dialogs' in the Access Details box. Click **OK** to save the details.

Exiting *Sage 50* Accounts

At the end of your session, to exit the program, select **File > Exit**. Alternatively, click on the **X** at the top right-hand of the screen. You will be prompted if you wish to take a backup of your files.

   In order to demonstrate how the menus in *Sage 50* Accounts are used, the previously completed manual accounts of Daly's Pharmacy Ltd will now be applied throughout the remainder of section 6.

Installing *Sage* *50* Accounts and Creating a New Company

Learning outcomes (Accounting Manual and Computerised 5N1348): 8 (part)
Learning outcomes (Bookkeeping Manual and Computerised 5N1354): 8 (part)

Follow the installation instructions to install *Sage 50* Accounts software on your computer, if not already installed.

After installation, select the program from your desktop. The Software Registration window will be displayed (s1). Enter the Serial Number and Activation Key supplied with the licence. This information will be supplied by your college or the holder of the licence agreement.

S1

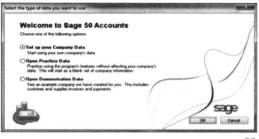

S2

Click Continue and the software will be registered. The screen will display as shown (s2). Choose the option 'Set up your Company Data' and click **OK**. *Sage 50* Accounts has a demonstration company set up, but it is preferable to create a company from scratch. In this way, you can set up your own structure of nominal ledger accounts.

You will be presented with the 'ActiveSetup' screens that follow. Select 'Set-up a new company' and click **Next** (s3).

s3

s4

We will set up the company 'Daly's Pharmacy Ltd', which you completed on a manual basis in Part 1. In the Network Sharing panel (2), uncheck the box 'Share this folder for all users' and click **Next** (s4).

In the Company Details panel (3), enter the name and address of Daly's Pharmacy Ltd and click **Next** (s5).

s5

s6

In the Business Type panel (4), select 'Limited Company' and click **Next** (s6).

In the Financial Year panel (5), enter the month start as 'January' and the year start '2013' and click **Next** (s7).

In the VAT panel (6), enter Yes for VAT registered, enter the VAT registration number, select 'Standard VAT' as the VAT scheme and enter the standard rate of VAT as 23%. Click **Next** (s8). *Note:* Refer to Part 1 on explanation of Standard VAT/Invoice Basis of VAT.

In the Currency panel (7), select the currency as 'Euro' and click **Next**.

In the Manager Password panel (8), the default login user name for *Sage 50* Accounts is 'Manager'. We will also set the password as 'Manager'. Enter this and click **Next**.

s7

s8

In the Confirm Details panel (9), review your set-up information for Daly's Pharmacy Ltd and click **Create**.

You have now created a company for Daly's Pharmacy Ltd. You will now be asked to Log on to Daly's Pharmacy Ltd. Enter the password 'Manager' and click **OK** (s9).

A 'Customise your company' screen will be displayed. There is no need to customise the company at this stage, as we are setting up Daly's Pharmacy Ltd from scratch. Click **Close**.

A 'Welcome to Sage 50 Accounts' window will be displayed. You can close the welcome page and the Customer Process is defaulted as the home page.

s9

Chart of Accounts

The Chart of Accounts (COA) is the collective term for every nominal account you use to record the financial activity of your business. The values on these nominal accounts are used to generate your day-to-day business reports. Of particular interest are your financial reports, i.e. the Profit and Loss account and Balance Sheet. Some nominal accounts record your income and expenditure and are used in your Profit and Loss report, while others record your assets and liabilities and are used in your Balance Sheet report. To generate a financial report, *Sage 50* Accounts uses a COA layout. The layout controls what is included in a report. We will be setting up our own layout for COA.

As stated, you are creating Daly's Pharmacy Ltd from scratch. At this time in *Sage 50* Accounts, a list of demonstration nominal accounts is set up. You will need to clear these nominal accounts from the system and set up your own COA structure.

To view these nominal accounts, select **Modules > Nominal Ledger** (s10 and s10a).

Change the Layout to 'List' to display a list of the nominal accounts that are present. Most of these nominal accounts you are unlikely to use, so it is preferable to clear these down and create your own set of nominal accounts. It is possible to add new nominal accounts at any time and you can personalise the names to make them more meaningful to you.

s10

There are numerous nominal accounts present, which were installed with *Sage 50* Accounts. These need to be deleted to create our own COA. Some of these accounts are Control accounts. These are the accounts needed by *Sage 50* Accounts in order for the system to work. *(Note: These Control accounts cannot be deleted.)*

To clear down the data files in order to create our own COA, select **File > Maintenance**. The message will display as shown (s11). Click **Yes** to close all open windows. This message will display on every occasion that the File menu is selected.

s10a

S11

S12

S13

S14

The File maintenance window will open as shown (s12). Select 'Rebuild'.

Uncheck all the boxes and check the box 'I wish to create my own nominal structure' (s13). Click **OK**. It will ask if you are sure you want to rebuild your data files? Click **Yes**. It will then prompt you to enter the date in which your financial year is to start. Enter the start month January and the year 2013.

After rebuilding the data files, all the nominal ledger accounts have been deleted, excluding the Control accounts, which are displayed as shown (s14). *Please refer to the online student resources on www.gillmacmillan.ie for the set-up of the COA configuration. If you are not in a position to set up the COA of Daly's Pharmacy Ltd at this time, please restore the company's backup file, which is contained in your Student Resources.*

6.3 Files and Folders in *Sage 50* Accounts

Learning outcomes (Accounting Manual and Computerised 5N1348): 8 (part) and 11 (part)

In order to have more than one company running at the same time in *Sage 50* Accounts, your program needs to be a multi-company version. If it is a single-company version, then it will only be possible to have one company running at a time. In this instance, it would be necessary to clear down or delete the files of the first company to continue with the transactions of another company. The program that is used for demonstration purposes here is a multi-company version.

Set up a new company in *Sage 50* Accounts

In order to set up a second company, your program needs to be a multi-company version. To set up a new company, open the first company, e.g. Daly's Pharmacy Ltd. Select **File > New > Company**. The ActiveSetup window is displayed (s1).

The following options are available:

- **Set up a new company** – if you want to create a company from scratch where you intend to clear down the data files and set up your own structure of Chart of Accounts (COA), as in section 6.2.
- **Use an existing company stored on your network** – if you are upgrading the software and want to use a company you have already installed on your PC or network. This option connects to the company data making it ready to use in your new installation of *Sage 50* Accounts.
- **Restore data from a backup file** – if, as the option suggests, you are using a previous backup file and want to restore the files to a new company.

Here, use the option 'Set-up a new company', as shown onscreen. Name this company 'Longville Ltd'. Follow the onscreen instructions by

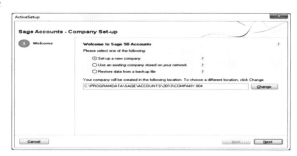

s2

clicking **Next**. Set the financial year start as January 2013, set the standard rate of VAT at 23%. Click **Create** at the end of the wizard. Your new company will then be created.

When you exit *Sage 50* Accounts and re-open from your desktop, you will be presented with a window displaying two companies (s2). Select the company you wish to open from the Select Company window.

Backup a company in *Sage 50* Accounts

It is most important to take regular backups of your data files in case of a loss of data on your computer. Backup storage can be on the hard drive of your computer, CD, DVD or memory key. In order to perform a backup, the company must be open in *Sage 50* Accounts. To take a backup of Daly's

s3

Pharmacy Ltd, open the company from the Select Company window. Select **File > Backup**. A confirm message asks 'Would you like to check your data before you run the backup'? If you select Yes, your data will be checked to report no problems on data files. Close the message and the backup window will be displayed (s3).

Click on 'Browse' to choose the location of your backup. Displayed onscreen is the C: drive on the computer. Click **OK** and the backup will be performed.

Restore a company in *Sage 50* Accounts

You may need to restore files from a previous backup in a situation where you need the files on a different computer or if the existing files on your computer were damaged or deleted in error. In order to restore files, there must be a previous backup of the same files. To restore files, you must open the company where you want the files to be restored to in *Sage 50* Accounts.

To restore the files of Daly's Pharmacy Ltd to Longville Ltd, the files of Daly's Pharmacy Ltd must be backed up, as previously shown. To do this, open the company Longville Ltd. Click on **File > Restore**. The Restore window is displayed (s4). Click on 'Browse' to choose the location of the backup file. The file chosen is the previous backup file of Daly's Pharmacy Ltd located on the C: drive of the computer. This will restore the files of Daly's Pharmacy Ltd to the company Longville Ltd. Click **OK**.

A Confirm message will display to warn that any data in the current company will be overwritten (s5). Click on **Yes** and restore will be completed. You now have two companies that are identical in their set up.

s4

s5

Delete a company from *Sage 50* Accounts

To delete a company in *Sage 50* Accounts, the company to be deleted must not be open. Instead, another company (that is not to be deleted) must be open. If you have two

s6

companies, you can switch from one company to another quite easily by selecting **File > Open > Open Company Data**. We will delete the company created, called 'Longville Ltd', from *Sage 50* Accounts. To do this, open the company Daly's Pharmacy Ltd in *Sage 50* Accounts. Then click on **File > Delete Company**. A Delete Company window will display, listing all the other companies that are set up (s6). Select Longville Ltd and click **OK**. A warning message will ask you if you wish to delete the company. Click on **Yes** and the company will be deleted.

Review assignment

Set up a new company in *Sage 50* Accounts for Watchworld Ltd, Main Street, Athlone, Co. Westmeath. The telephone number is 094-12336 and the VAT registration number is IE1288572N. Use the same VAT codes as described earlier in the section and the same defaults in the company settings. *Note*: If you are not in a position to set up a new company from scratch, use the backup file from Daly's Pharmacy Ltd and restore it to a new company. Change the details of the company as required.

6.4 Setting Up Company Information in *Sage 50* Accounts

Learning outcomes (Accounting Manual and Computerised 5N1348): 8 (part)
Learning outcomes (Bookkeeping Manual and Computerised 5N1354): 8 (part)

Please refer back to the source documents of Daly's Pharmacy Ltd in your Student Resources. Alternatively, restore the company from the backup file in your Student Resources.

You have the set-up of Daly's Pharmacy Ltd complete as described in section 6.2. You can now set up the ledger accounts, customers and suppliers needed to process the transactions.

Setting up company information

Financial year date

S1

As the Daly's Pharmacy Ltd financial year runs from January to December, this needs to be confirmed as set up correctly.

Select **Settings** > **Financial Year**. The Financial Year screen is displayed (s1). Confirm that the start month is January and the year is 2013. This setting was performed when you set up the company.

Nominal accounts

The control accounts have already been set up for this company. You need to add to this list to include other nominal accounts that are needed to process the records.

Select **Modules** > **Nominal Ledger**. Change the layout to 'List' view, if not already selected. This will display the accounts as you create them. Click on

the toolbar 'New Nominal' to open the wizard to create a new account (s2).

The nominal accounts to create, including their account 'Type', are:

- Purchases – Cost of Sales
- Wages – Overheads
- Light & Heat – Overheads
- Insurance – Overheads
- Motor Expenses – Overheads
- Printing & Postage – Overheads
- Bank Charges – Overheads
- Capital – Capital & Reserves

S2

For the creation of the Purchases account, enter the Name and use the down arrow to select the Type. The Category will display automatically, as the Chart of Accounts (COA) has been set up previously. The N/C number assigned to this account will display automatically as 5000, being the first number set up in the High/Low box in the COA. Click **Next**.

On the screen displayed (s3), accept the selection 'No, there is no opening balance to enter' and click on **Create.** The nominal account has been set up. *Note:* You may need to go back to the Supplier Defaults to enter Purchases – 5000, as the default account for posting invoices and credit notes.

Create the remaining nominal accounts, making sure that you select the correct Type. You cannot delete a nominal account once it has transactions posted to it. The list of complete accounts should look as shown (s4). They are listed in the order of their numbering, with the Balance Sheet accounts listed first followed by the Profit and Loss accounts.

S3

N/C	Name
1100	Debtors Control Account
1103	Prepayments
1200	Bank Current Account
1201	Petty Cash
2100	Creditors Control Account
2109	Accruals
2200	VAT on Sales
2201	VAT on Purchases
2202	VAT Liability
2204	Manual Adjustments
3000	Capital
3200	Profit and Loss Account
4000	Sales
4009	Discounts Allowed
4400	Credit Charges (Late Payments)
5000	Purchases
5009	Discounts Received
7000	Wages
7001	Light & Heat
7002	Insurance
7003	Motor Expenses
7004	Printing & Postage
7005	Bank Charges
7906	Exchange Rate Variance
8100	Bad Debt Write Off
9998	Suspense Account
9999	Mispostings Account

S4

Suppliers

To set up suppliers, select **Modules > Suppliers**. Change the view to 'Suppliers' if not already selected. This will display the suppliers as you create them. Click on the toolbar 'New Supplier' to open the wizard to create a new supplier.

The suppliers that Daly's Pharmacy Ltd purchases goods from are:

- Alchemy Ltd
- United Drugs Ltd

- Stafford Lynch
- Electric Ireland.

Note: Please refer to the source documents for the addresses of these suppliers.

Supplier accounts hold all the information you need when dealing with your suppliers. They hold basic details, such as the address and VAT number, but are also essential for keeping track of your suppliers when you want to

know what you have purchased or what you owe. Each supplier needs a unique reference code (use the first three digits of the name, if possible). These codes need to be chosen carefully as they cannot be changed once any activity has been applied to the account. You have already saved time recording transactions for a supplier by setting options in their account, known as defaults. For example, you have set credit limits, the VAT code and the nominal account that transactions

s5

should be posted to. The New Supplier wizard is opened for the first supplier, Alchemy Ltd (s5).

In the **Supplier Details**, enter the name of the supplier and overtype the supplier code (A/C Ref) to display the first three digits of the name. Enter the address and click on **Next**. Proceed as follows according to the New Supplier screen:

1. **Contact Details** – There is no need to enter any information. Click **Next**.
2. **Supplier Defaults** – This has the nominal code 5000 already set up as the nominal account (Purchases), where all purchase invoices and credit notes should be posted. The Tax Code (VAT) displays T1 23% as the default VAT code for purchases. Accept this information and click **Next**.
3. **Credit Details** – This has the default set-up of €10,000 credit limit. The payment due period is 60 days and the Terms Agreed box has been checked. Accept this information and click **Next**.
4. **Bank Address** – There is no need to enter any information. Click **Next**.
5. **Bank Account** – There is no need to enter any information. Click **Next**.
6. **Opening Balance** – Accept the selected option, 'No, there is no opening balance to enter'.

Click **Create** and the supplier is set up.

Set up the suppliers United Drugs Ltd and Stafford Lynch with the same defaults. For the supplier Electric Ireland, change the default nominal code in the Supplier Defaults to the

s6

Light & Heat account. This account should be represented by the nominal code 7001. Use the drop-down list box to select. All purchase invoices from Electric Ireland should be posted to this account rather than the Purchases account. The default Tax (VAT) Code should be T6, which is 13.5% Non-Resale (s6). Use the drop-down list box to select.

Customers

To set up customers, select **Modules > Customers**. Change the view to 'Customers' if not already selected. This will display the customers as you create them. Click on the toolbar 'New Customer' to open the wizard to create a new customer.

The customers that Daly's Pharmacy Ltd sells goods to are:

- Mr James Mulcahy
- Ms Martha Downey
- Cash Sales.

Note: Please refer to the source documents for the addresses of these customers.

Customer accounts are essential for keeping track of your customers to determine what you sold to them and what they owe the company. Each customer has a separate account that is unique to them and holds contact details, sales invoices and receipts. Each customer needs a unique reference code (use the first three digits of the name, if possible). These codes need careful planning as they cannot be changed once an activity has been applied to the account. You have already saved time recording transactions for a customer by setting options in their account, known as defaults. For example, you have set credit limits, the VAT code and the nominal account that transactions should be posted to.

s7

The New Customer wizard is opened for the first customer, Mr James Mulcahy (s7).

In the **Customer Details**, enter the name of the customer and overtype the customer code (A/C Ref) to display the first three digits of the name. Enter the address and click **Next**.

Proceed as follows on the New Customer screen:

- **Contact Details** – There is no need to enter any information. Click **Next**.
- **Customer Defaults** – This has the nominal code 4000 already set up as the nominal account (Sales), where all sales invoices and credit notes should

be posted. The Tax Code (VAT) displays T1 23% as the default VAT code for sales. Accept this information and click **Next**.

- **Credit Details** – This has the default set up of €10,000 credit limit, payment due days of 60 days and the Terms Agreed box has been checked. Accept this information and click **Next**.
- **Bank Address** – There is no need to enter any information. Click **Next**.
- **Bank Account** – There is no need to enter any information. Click **Next**.
- **Opening Balance** – Accept the selected option, 'No, there is no opening balance to enter'.

Click Create and the customer is set up. Now set up the customers Ms Martha Downey and Cash Sales with the same defaults.

Ledger dates

It is usual to record transactions on a monthly basis, recording one month and then moving onto the next month until the end of the accounting year. To do this, the ledger or program date needs to be set for each month that is being recorded. The *Sage 50* Accounts date is based on your computer's system date, which is set in the Windows control panel. As you record your transactions, the program date is displayed as the transaction date, although another date can be entered at that point.

s8

To change your program date, select **Settings > Change Program Date**. The Confirm window will close any windows that are open. Click **Yes** here. The Change Program Date window is displayed (s8). As we will be entering the transactions for Daly's Pharmacy Ltd for the month of November, set the date to 30/11/2013. Use the calendar to select the date and click **OK**. When entering transactions for November, all you need to change is the *day* of the month. The month and the year will be correct.

When you close and then re-open *Sage 50* Accounts, the program date resets to your computer's system date. You must remember to reset the program date to the correct month date for entering transactions. When November accounts are completed, the program date is set to 31 December to record the next month's accounts, which will be the last period of the accounting year.

Review assignment

Open the company Watchworld Ltd that you set up in *Sage 50* Accounts and carry out the following tasks:

1. Set the financial year to run from 1 January 2014 to 31 December 2014.
2. Set up the following nominal ledger accounts, using the *correct account Type and correct account Category*:

a. Purchases
b. Staff Salaries
c. Insurance
d. Repairs
e. Postage & Stationery
f. Telephone
g. Capital.
3 Set up the following suppliers, using appropriate supplier codes:
a. The Watchery Ltd, D'Olier Street, Dublin 1
b. Time 2 Watches, Capel Street, Dublin 1
c. Print Solutions, Kill Avenue, Ballymahon, Co Longford. Set the default nominal code to Postage & Stationery with the default VAT code T5 for 23% Non-Resale.
4. Set up the following customers, using appropriate customer codes:
a. Livia Jewellers, Ballygar, Co Galway
b. Timepiece Ltd, Hodson Bay, Athlone, Co Westmeath
c. Sheehan's Ltd, Castle Street, Castlerea, Co Roscommon.
5. Set the Program date to 31/03/2014. These dates will have to be reset later after exiting the company.

6.5 Purchase Ledger in *Sage 50* Accounts

Learning outcomes (Accounting Manual and Computerised 5N1348): 9 (part)
Learning outcomes (Bookkeeping Manual and Computerised 5N1354): 8 (part)

The Supplier module is where you enter all your supplier details, where you can record invoices and credit notes that you have received outside the *Sage 50* Accounts system and where you enter all the money you pay your suppliers.

We will now enter the purchase invoices and credit note of Daly's Pharmacy Ltd. *Refer to the source documents in your Student Resources.* Remember to press the **Tab** key to move from field to field.

Purchase invoices

Select **Modules > Suppliers**. If not already selected, use the view 'Supplier Process' by selecting from the drop-down list at the top right-hand corner of your screen (Change View). Select the icon Batch Invoice. You can also access this icon from the toolbar if you have selected 'Suppliers' in the Change View drop-down list.

The amount of detail you enter is up to you, but it is sufficient to enter only one line per invoice, if there is only one VAT rate. If there is more than one VAT rate, as in the screen displayed, you must enter each invoice item separately with each breakdown of VAT (s1). Here, give each line of the same invoice the same supplier account code, reference and date. These are then grouped together and listed, as for the items that make up a single invoice.

The screen is displayed to enter the first purchase invoice from Alchemy Ltd. Enter the following details, using the **Tab** key to move from field to field.

- **A/C** – Use the drop-down arrow to select the supplier code for Alchemy Ltd or type the code if known.
- **Date** – The date should display as the program date, 30/11/2013. Enter the date of this invoice by typing the day. The month and the year are set by the program date.
- **Ref** – Enter a reference for the invoice, which is the invoice number.
- **Ex. Ref** – This is an additional reference (but does not apply here).
- **N/C** – The nominal ledger account, 5000 Purchases, is defaulted here, which is the Purchases account where the debit entry will be posted to.

This was the default account set up for Alchemy Ltd. *Sage 50* Accounts will automatically complete the double-entry of this purchase invoice, which will be:

Debit: Purchases account with the net value of the invoice.

Debit: VAT on Purchases account with the VAT on the invoice.

Credit: Creditors with the total value of the invoice.

- **Dept, Project Ref, Cost Code** and **Details** – There is no need to enter any information.
- **Net** – You can enter the net value of the invoice here at the first rate of VAT at 23%.
- **T/C** – Select the VAT code for this part of the invoice by using the drop-down arrow. Here it is T1, which is the default VAT code.
- **VAT** – The VAT amount will be entered automatically once the VAT code is selected.

Alternatively, rather than entering the net amount in the Net column, enter the Total amount (Net plus VAT) in the Net column and press the function key **F9**, the Calculate Net command button. You can also click the 'Calc. Net' button at the bottom of the window. This will convert the Total amount to the Net amount. It is sometimes easier to see the total on a purchase invoice rather than the net amount.

Enter the second line of this invoice to represent the goods purchased at 13.5% VAT, using the same A/C, Date and Ref. Both lines of this invoice will then be grouped together and listed, as the items that make up a single invoice. The grand total of the invoice is displayed at the top right-hand side of the window.

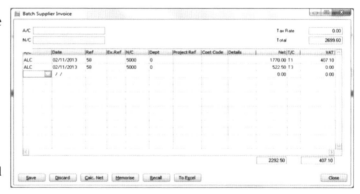

Once your entries are complete, click **Save**. The details are posted to update the nominal ledger and the relevant supplier's details.

You now enter the second purchase invoice from United Drugs Ltd in the same way as above. This invoice also contains multiple VAT rates, so the details need to be entered in two lines as displayed.

The third purchase invoice from Stafford Lynch has only one VAT rate, which is 23% Resale. This is much simpler to enter, as the details are entered on one line.

The fourth purchase invoice is from Electric Ireland. Here, the N/C is posted to 7001 Light & Heat expense account; the VAT code is T6, which represents 13.5% Non-Resale. These defaults for Electric Ireland were put in place when you set up this supplier. The double-entry for an electricity invoice is:

S1

Debit: Light & Heat expense account with the net value of the invoice.
Debit: VAT on Purchases account with the VAT on the invoice.
Credit: Creditors with the total value of the invoice.

Once all your entries are complete, click **Save**. The details are posted to update the Nominal Ledger and the relevant supplier's details. Click **Close** to exit the window.

Purchase credit notes

Select **Modules > Suppliers**. If you are in the view 'Supplier Process', from the drop-down list at the top right-hand corner of your screen (Change View), in the Links pane on the left-hand side, you select Batch Credit. You can also access this icon from the toolbar if you have selected 'Suppliers' in the Change View drop-down list.

Batch
Credit

The amount of detail you enter per each purchase credit note is up to you, but it is sufficient to enter one line per credit note if there is only one VAT rate on the credit note. If there is more than one VAT rate, as with purchase invoices above, you must enter each credit item with each breakdown of VAT separately. Here give each line of the same credit note the same supplier account code, reference and date, as these are then grouped together and listed, as the items that make up a single credit note.

The Batch Supplier Credit screen displayed is similar to the Batch Invoice screen in layout (s3). Due to the similar screens, it is important to distinguish clearly between both, as credit notes have the opposite effect as invoices to the accounts. Credit notes entries are displayed in red to make the distinction easier. The fields in the screen are exactly the same as the Batch Invoice screen.

Links
- Supplier List
- Product List
- Purchase Order List
- Activity
- Aged Balances
- Price List
- Batch Invoice
- Batch Credit
- Disputes
- Reports

S2

Batch Supplier Credit

A/C United Drugs Ltd   Tax Rate   0.00
N/C Purchases   Total   196.32

A/C	Date	Credit No	Ex.Ref	N/C	Dept	Project Ref	Cost Code	Details		Net	T/C	VAT
UNI	15/11/2013	1305		5000	0					84.00	T1	19.32
UNI	15/11/2013	1305		5000	0					93.00	T3	0.00

S3

The credit note for United Drugs Ltd contains multiple VAT rates. As a result, there is a need to enter separate lines for each rate. The N/C account is also Purchases 5000, where the credit note contains a double-entry as follows:

Debit: Creditors with the total value of the invoice, reducing the creditor's balance.
Credit: Purchases account with the net value of the invoice, reducing purchases for the period.
Credit: VAT on Purchases account with the VAT on the invoice, reducing the VAT on purchases.

Once all your entries are complete, click **Save**. The details are posted to update the nominal ledger and the relevant supplier's details. Click **Close** to exit the window.

Purchase ledger reporting

Purchases daybook

As you complete purchase invoices and credit notes, the purchases daybook is automatically updated in the accounts. This can be viewed by generating a supplier report.

Select **Modules > Suppliers**. If you are in the view 'Supplier Process', from the drop-down list at the top right-hand corner of your screen (Change View), in the Links pane on the left-hand side, select Reports (s4). You can also access this icon from the toolbar if you have selected 'Suppliers' in the Change View drop-down list.

Reports

The Supplier reports browser will appear (s5). Most reports and documents are managed by the Report browser. It is designed to help with the generation and distribution of reports. Locate and select the type of report you want from the folders in the left-hand side of the browser. Here selected is 'Day books'. There are numerous reports to choose from, as listed here. From the Report browser toolbar, select the action you want to take, e.g. preview, print, export, export to Excel or email. In the report browser, Supplier Invoices are separate from Supplier Credits.

The screen displayed has selected **Day Books: Supplier Invoices (Summary)**. Note the icons at the top of the report browser:

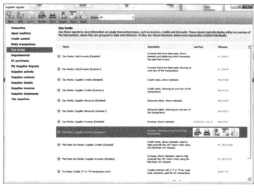

s4

s5

- **New** – creates a new layout for a report or document using the Report wizard to guide you through the process. This opens the Report Designer where layouts are set up.
- **Edit** – changes an existing layout. Again this is done in the Report Designer.
- **Delete** – removes an obsolete layout.
- **Preview** – displays onscreen exactly how a document will appear once printed. If you are satisfied with the look of the report, you can send it directly to the printer by choosing Print.
- **Print** – generates the report and sends it to your default printer.
- **Export** – saves documents to file, perhaps to print at a future date. Storing documents on disk is useful if you want to use the data in the document in another application, such as a word processor or spreadsheet. When you run a report or layout to a file, the Save As window appears.

- **Excel** – displays the report in Microsoft Excel, once you have entered the criteria.
- **Email** – sends any document you want to generate directly to email, provided you are using Microsoft Outlook or an Internet email service such as Google Mail.

Depending on the selected report, the Criteria window may appear (s9). Use the Criteria to limit the number of transactions present in the report. If you leave the Preview value as 0, all transactions are listed. To generate the report, click **OK**.

The Purchases Daybook listing supplier invoices is generated (s6).

In order to view the credit note entered, select Day Books: Supplier Credits (Detailed or Summary) from the same report browser (s7).

You can use the Print icon at the top of the report if you wish to print the report in print preview.

Time: 18:26:47

Day Books: Supplier Invoices (Summary)

| Date From: | 01/01/1980 | Supplier From: | |
| Date To: | 31/12/2019 | Supplier To: | ZZZZZZZ |

| Transaction From: | 1 |
| Transaction To: | 99,999,999 |

Tran No.	Item	Type	Date	A/C Ref	Inv Ref	Details	Net Amount	Tax Amount	Gross Amount
1	2	PI	02/11/2013	ALC	58		2,292.50	407.10	2,699.60
3	2	PI	04/11/2013	UNI	1259		4,815.00	893.55	5,708.55
5	1	PI	18/11/2013	STA	4589		3,009.00	692.07	3,701.07
6	1	PI	20/11/2013	ELE			274.28	37.03	311.31
						Totals	10,390.78	2,029.75	12,420.53

s6

Time: 18:30:46

Day Books: Supplier Credits (Summary)

| Date From: | 01/01/1980 | Supplier From: | |
| Date To: | 31/12/2019 | Supplier To: | ZZZZZZZ |

| Transaction From: | 1 |
| Transaction To: | 99,999,999 |

Tran No.	Item	Type	Date	A/C Ref	Inv Ref	Details	Net Amount	Tax Amount	Gross Amount
7	2	PC	15/11/2013	UNI	1305		177.00	19.32	196.32
						Totals	177.00	19.32	196.32

s7

Aged creditors report

This summarises all the suppliers' ledger balances in one report. It is a very useful report to catch a glimpse of the creditors' balances in one page. It will total the amount owed to all suppliers at the bottom of the report. In the Supplier report browser, select Aged Creditors from the left-hand side and select Aged Creditors Analysis (Contacts) from the main window.

Depending on the selected report, the Criteria window may appear. Use the Criteria to limit the number of transactions present in the report. If you leave the Preview value as 0, all transactions are listed. To generate the report (s8), click **OK**.

You can use the Print icon at the top of the report if you wish to print the report in print preview.

Time: 18:49:16

Aged Creditors Analysis (Contacts)

Report Date:	30/11/2013	Supplier From:	
Include future transactions:	No	Supplier To:	ZZZZZZZ
Exclude Later Payments:	No		

** NOTE: All report values are shown in Base Currency, unless otherwise indicated **

A/C	Name & Contact	Credit Limit	Turnover	Balance	Future	Current	Period 1	Period 2	Period 3	Older
ALC	Alchemy Ltd	€ 10,000.00	2,292.50	2,699.60	0.00	2,699.60	0.00	0.00	0.00	0.00
ELE	Electric Ireland	€ 10,000.00	274.28	311.31	0.00	311.31	0.00	0.00	0.00	0.00
STA	Stafford Lynch	€ 10,000.00	3,009.00	3,701.07	0.00	3,701.07	0.00	0.00	0.00	0.00
UNI	United Drugs Ltd	€ 10,000.00	4,638.00	5,512.23	0.00	5,512.23	0.00	0.00	0.00	0.00
	Totals:		10,213.78	12,224.21	0.00	12,224.21	0.00	0.00	0.00	0.00

s8

Alternatively, to view the aged creditors report, select the icon Aged Balances from the toolbar if you are in the 'Suppliers' view. To include all suppliers, they must be selected from the supplier window. To select all suppliers at once, clear all selections by clicking 'Clear' at the bottom of the window and then click 'Swap' at the bottom of the window. You can also access the Aged Balances from the Links pane if you are in the 'Supplier Process' view.

Supplier account enquiry

This report is used to view the transactions in one particular supplier's account. In the Supplier report browser, select Supplier activity from the left-hand side and select Supplier Activity (Summary) from the main window.

The Criteria window appears (s9). Run a report for the supplier United Drugs Ltd. In the Supplier Ref, using the drop-down box, select 'Is' to limit to one supplier only in the report and select the code for United Drugs Ltd in the drop-down box, as shown. To generate the report, click **OK** (s10).

You can use the Print icon at the top of the report if you wish to print the report in print preview.

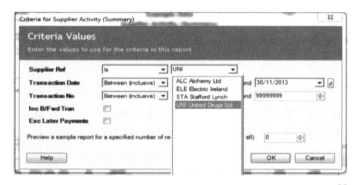

s9

s10

Supplier account enquiry – alternative method

As an alternative method to view the activity in a supplier's account, select **Modules > Suppliers**. If you are using the view 'Supplier Process', select Supplier Record from the Tasks pane on the left-hand side (s11). If you are using the view 'Suppliers' in the Change View drop-down list, select the Supplier Record from the toolbar or double-click into the supplier's name on the list displayed.

In the A/C Details tab, enter the supplier's code from the drop-down list. We will use the supplier, Electric Ireland. Click on the Activity tab to view the account details of the supplier. This is a great way to view the history of trading between you and your supplier. It also displays your credit limit with them and the balance owed, as well as the total amount you have paid and

S11

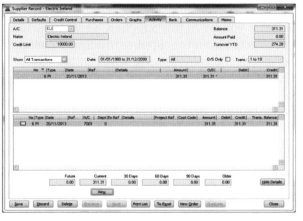

S12

the expenditure for the year. A summary of dealings you have had with the supplier are displayed in a list (s12). Each line in the list represents a transaction such as an invoice or payment.

Purchase ledger payments

To keep all the entries in the Purchase ledger together, the purchase ledger payments can now be entered at this stage. These are the payments to suppliers in Daly's Pharmacy Ltd. Other payments will be entered later. There are two payments to suppliers in the records of Daly's Pharmacy Ltd. These are payments to Alchemy Ltd and United Drugs Ltd.

S13

Select **Modules > Suppliers**. Use the view 'Supplier Process', if not already selected, by selecting from the drop-down list at the top right-hand corner of your screen (Change View). Select the icon Supplier Payment (s13). You can also access this menu from Tasks on the left-hand side of the screen if you have selected 'Suppliers' in the Change View drop-down list.

You can also access this menu from the Bank Module, by selecting Supplier Payment from the toolbar.

The Supplier Payment window is displayed (s14). It also displays the name of the selected bank account, defaulted to Ref 1200 Bank Current Account. This is the bank from which the payment will be made. Enter the information for the payment to Alchemy Ltd, as follows.

- **Payee** – Select the supplier you want to pay using the drop-down list. All items that the supplier has invoiced the company (but are not paid), as well as payments made and credit notes, appear automatically in the table.
- **Date** – The date will display the program date. Enter the date of the payment. The month and the year should be correct.
- **Cheque No** – Enter the cheque number or other reference number.
- **€** – Enter the amount of the payment here. If you do enter an amount, to allocate the payment to the invoices in the table, click Automatic. The money is allocated to the items in the order displayed in the table. You can choose to record any money left over after allocation as a payment on account.
- **Payment €** – If you do not want the payment to be automatically allocated, for each invoiced you want to pay in the table, enter the

amount to be paid in its
Payment box. You can part pay
an invoice or pay it off in full,
but you cannot allocate more
than the full value of the item.
Alternatively, if you are paying
an invoice in full, click on the
item's Payment box then click
'**Pay in Full**'. The amount
needed to pay the invoice in full
is then entered automatically for
you. Continue allocating money
in this way until all the money

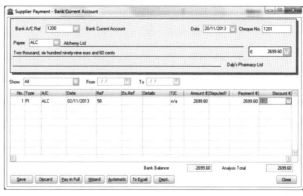

S14

you entered in the cheque amount box is used up. The payment has now
been allocated to the invoices in the supplier's account.

- **Discount €** – If you have been given any discount against an invoice item,
  enter the discount amount, not the percentage amount, in the discount
  box. The analysis box decreases by the amount of any discount values
  entered. This may mean that you can allocate more of the amount you
  entered in the cheque amount box against further invoice items.

To save your payment details, click **Save**, or to start again, click **Discard**. To exit
from the Supplier Payment window without saving the details, click **Close**.
Note: You can also click **Wizard** at the bottom of this window to guide you
through the process of recording a payment to the supplier.

   Enter the payment to United Drugs in the same way as previously and
allocate the payment to the invoice outstanding in the account.

Allocating existing purchase ledger credit notes and payments

Occasionally you may enter a payment to a supplier without allocating it
straightaway, or you have entered a credit note from a supplier that you want
to allocate to an invoice. In these circumstances you can allocate the payment
or credit note using the Supplier Payment, as previously. The credit note
entered in the account of United
Drugs Ltd can now be allocated in
this way. Select Supplier
Payment and the
supplier payment
window is displayed
(s15). In this window, payments
on account are shown with a
transaction type code of PA and
have a description of 'Payment on
Account'. Invoices are shown with
a type code of PI, credit notes are
shown with a type code of PC.

S15

- **Payee** – Enter the supplier account code in the Payee box. All outstanding items are then displayed in the invoice table, along with any payments on account and unallocated credit notes received.
- **Date** – The date will display the program date, which is acceptable for allocating credit notes.
- **Cheque No** – Leave blank.
- **€** – Leave blank. You are not entering a payment, but you are allocating an existing credit.
- **Payment €** – select the credit note and enter the amount of the credit note in the payment box. If you want to pick up the full amount, you can click 'Pay in Full'. As you pick up credit notes the € box displays the amount that you can allocate against the invoice items as a negative number. Allocate the picked-up amount by entering the value in the payment box against the invoice; use the 'Pay in Full' button if appropriate. You can only save the transaction when the € box returns to zero, showing that the amount you picked up has been fully allocated.

To save your allocation, click **Save**.

If you preview a supplier activity report for United Drugs Ltd, you can see that the payment has been entered and the credit note has been allocated in full (s16).

Time: 21:08:10			**Supplier Activity (Summary)**					
Date From: 01/01/1980					Supplier From: UNI			
Date To: 30/11/2013					Supplier To: UNI			
Inc b/fwd transaction: No					Transaction From: 1			
Exc later payment: No					Transaction To: 99,999,999			
** NOTE: All report values are shown in Base Currency, unless otherwise indicated **								
A/C: UNI	Name: United Drugs Ltd			Contact:		Tel:		
No	Items	Type	Date	Ref	Details	Value	O/S	Debit	Credit
3	2	PI	04/11/2013	1259		5,708.55p	5,012.23		5,708.55
7	2	PC	15/11/2013	1305		196.32	0.00	196.32	
10	1	PP	21/11/2013	1202	Purchase Payment	500.00	0.00	500.00	
					Totals:	5,012.23	5,012.23	696.32	5,708.55
Amount Outstanding:	5,012.23							
Amount paid this period	500.00							
Credit Limit €	10,000.00							

s16

Review assignment

Refer to the source documents in your Student Resources relating to Watchworld Ltd.
Open the company Watchworld Ltd, which you set up in *Sage 50* Accounts, and perform the following tasks:

1. Enter the purchase invoices and credit note received from the suppliers from the source documents.
2. Enter the purchase ledger payments and allocate to the invoices in each supplier account.
3. Allocate the credit note to the supplier's account.
4. Print the following reports to either the printer or screen:
   a. Daybooks: Supplier Invoices (Summary)
   b. Daybooks: Supplier Credits (Summary)
   c. Aged Creditors Analysis Report (Contacts)
   d. Supplier Activity (Summary) for Time 2 Watches.

6.6 Sales Ledger in *Sage 50* Accounts

Learning outcomes (Accounting Manual and Computerised 5N1348): 9 (part)
Learning outcomes (Bookkeeping Manual and Computerised 5N1354): 8 (part)

The Customer module is where you enter all your customer details, where you record invoices and credit notes that you have produced outside of *Sage 50* Accounts and where you enter all the money you have received from your customers.

Refer to the sales invoices of Daly's Pharmacy Ltd in your Student Resources.

Sales invoices

Select **Modules > Customers**. Use the view 'Customer Process', if not already selected, by selecting from the drop-down list at the top right-hand corner of your screen (Change View). Select the icon Batch Invoice. You can also access this icon from the toolbar if you have selected 'Customers' in the Change View drop-down list.The Batch Invoice icon is used to enter all sales invoices you have produced manually and sent to your customers. There is no printed sales invoice produced. It is recommended that you enter one line per invoice if there is only one VAT rate on the invoice. If there is more than one VAT rate, you must enter each invoice item with each breakdown of VAT separately. Here give each line of the same invoice the same customer account code, reference and date, as these are then grouped together and listed, as the items that make up a single invoice. *Note:* You should only log invoices here that have not been generated by the Invoicing option; otherwise the items are invoiced twice in your customer records.

The first sales invoice of Daly's Pharmacy Ltd sent to James Mulcahy is entered as shown (s1). There is only one rate of VAT on this invoice and can be entered in one line. Enter the following details, using the **Tab** key to move from field to field.

- **A/C** – Use the drop-down arrow to select the customer code for James Mulcahy or type the code if known.
- **Date** – The date should display as the program date, 30/11/2013. Enter the date of this invoice by typing the day. The month and the year are set by the program date.

- **Ref** – Enter a reference for the invoice, which is the invoice number.
- **Ex. Ref** – This is an additional reference, but does not apply here.
- **N/C** – The nominal ledger account, 4000 Sales, is defaulted here, which is the Sales account where the credit entry will be posted to. This was the default account set up for all customers. *Sage 50* Accounts will automatically complete the double-entry of this sales invoice. The double-entry will be:
  Debit: Debtors with the total value of the invoice.
  Credit: VAT on Sales account with the VAT on the invoice.
  Credit: Sales with the net value of the invoice.
- **Dept, Project Ref, Details** – There is no need to enter any information.
- **Net** – You can enter the net value of the invoice here at VAT 23%.
- **T/C** – Select the VAT code for the invoice by using the drop-down arrow. Here it is T1, which is the default VAT code.
- **VAT** – The VAT amount will be entered automatically once the VAT code is selected.

S1

S2

Alternatively, rather than entering the net amount in the Net column, enter the Total amount (Net plus VAT) and press the function key **F9**, the 'calculate net command' button. You can also click the 'Calc. Net' button at the bottom of the window. This will convert the Total amount to the Net amount. It is sometimes easier to see the total on a sales invoice rather than the net.

Once your entries are complete, click **Save**. The details are posted to update the nominal ledger and the relevant customer's details.

The second invoice to Martha Downey is entered in the same manner, but enter each invoice item corresponding to each VAT rate on two separate lines, as displayed (s2).

Enter the remaining two sales invoices, noting the multiple VAT rates.

Sales credit notes

Select **Modules > Customers**. If you are in the view 'Customer Process', select Batch Credit from the drop-down list at the top right-hand corner of your screen (Change View), in the Links pane on the left-hand side. You can also access this icon from the toolbar if you have selected 'Customers' in the Change View drop-down list.

Batch Credit

It is sufficient to enter one line per credit note, if there is only one VAT rate on the credit note. If there is more than one VAT rate, as with sales invoices above, you must enter each credit item with each breakdown of VAT separately. Here, give each line of the same credit note the same customer account code, reference and date, as these are then grouped together and listed, as the items that make up a single credit note. *Note*: You should only log credit notes here that have not been generated by the Invoicing option; otherwise the items are credited twice in your customer records.

The screen will display as shown, which is similar to the Batch Invoice screen in layout (s4). Due to similar screens, it is important to distinguish clearly between both, as credit notes have the opposite effect to the accounts as invoices.

Credit notes entries are displayed in red to make the distinction easier. The fields in the screen are exactly the same as the Batch Invoice screen. The credit note below sent to Martha Downey contains multiple VAT rates. As a result, there is a need to enter separate lines for each VAT rate. The N/C account is also Sales 4000, where the credit note contains a double-entry as follows:

Debit: VAT on Sales with the VAT amount, reducing the VAT on sales for the period.
Debit: Sales account with the net value of the credit note, reducing sales for the period.
Credit: Debtors with the total amount of the credit note, reducing the amount owed from the debtor.

Once the entries are complete, click **Save**. The details are posted to update the nominal ledger and the customer's details. Click **Close** to exit the window.

Sales ledger reporting

Sales daybook

As you complete sales invoices and credit notes, the sales daybook is automatically updated in the accounts. This can be viewed by generating a customer report.

Select **Modules > Customers**. If you are in the view 'Customer Process', select Reports from the drop-down list at the top right-hand corner of your screen (Change View), in the Links pane on the left-hand side (s5). You can also access this icon from the toolbar if you have selected 'Customers' in the Change View drop-down list.

The Customer Reports browser appears (s6). Most reports and documents are managed by the Report browser. It is designed to help with

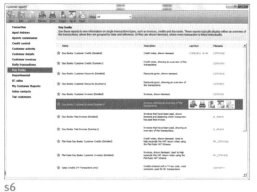

s6

the generation and distribution of reports. Locate and select the type of report you want from the folders in the left-hand side of the report browser. Here selected is Day books. There are numerous reports to choose from, as listed here. From the reports browser toolbar, select the action you want to take, e.g. preview, print, export, export to Excel or email. In the report browser, Customer Invoices are separate from Customer Credits. Here, **Day Books: Customer Invoices (Summary)** is selected.

Depending on the selected report, the Criteria window may appear. Use the Criteria to limit the number of transactions present in the report. If you leave the Preview value as 0, all transactions are listed. To generate the report, click **OK**.

The Sales Day Book listing customer invoices is generated (s7).

To view the credit note entered, select Day Books: Customer Credits (Detailed) or (Summary) from the same reports browser (s8).

You can use the Print icon at the top if you wish to print the report.

Time: 17:08:26

Day Books: Customer Invoices (Summary)

Date From:	01/01/1980							
Date To:	31/12/2019					Customer From:		
						Customer To:	ZZZZZZZ	

Transaction From: 1
Transaction To: 99,999,999

Tran No.	Items	Tp	Date	A/C Ref	Inv Ref	Details	Net Amount	Tax Amount	Gross Amount
11	1	SI	08/11/2013	MUL	225		2,024.82	465.71	2,490.53
12	2	SI	10/11/2013	DOW	226		1,962.38	294.81	2,257.19
14	2	SI	15/11/2013	CASH	227		282.24	50.63	332.87
16	2	SI	23/11/2013	DOW	228		581.25	109.88	691.13
						Totals:	4,850.69	921.03	5,771.72

s7

Time: 17:13:34

Day Books: Customer Credits (Summary)

Date From:	01/01/1980							
Date To:	31/12/2019					Customer From:		
						Customer To:	ZZZZZZZ	

Transaction From: 1
Transaction To: 99,999,999

Tran	Items	Tp	Date	A/C Ref	Inv Ref	Details	Net Amount	Tax Amount	Gross Amount
18	2	SC	25/11/2013	DOW	229		44.85	3.97	48.82
						Totals:	44.85	3.97	48.82

s8

Aged debtors report

This summarises all the customers' ledger balances in one report. It is a very useful report to catch a glimpse of the debtors' balances in one page for credit control purposes. It will total the amount owed by all customers at the bottom of the report. In the Customer reports browser, select Aged Debtors from the left-hand side and select Aged Debtors Analysis (Contacts) from the main window.

Depending on the selected report, the Criteria window may appear. Use the Criteria to limit the number of transactions present in the report. If you leave the Preview value as 0, all transactions are listed. To generate the report (s9), click **OK**.

You can use the Print icon at the top of the report if you wish to print the report.

Alternatively, to view the aged debtors report, select the icon Aged Balances from the toolbar if you are in the 'Customers' view. To include all customers, they must be selected from the customer window. To select all customers at once, clear all selections by clicking 'Clear' at the bottom of the window and then click 'Swap' at the bottom of the window. You can also access the Aged Balances from the Links pane if you are in the 'Customer Process' view.

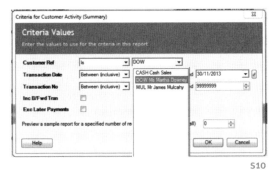

Aged Debtors Analysis (Contacts)

Time: 17:20:49

Report Date:	30/11/2013					Customer From:			
Include future transactions:	No					Customer To:	ZZZZZZZ		
Exclude later payments:	No								

** NOTE: All report values are shown in Base Currency, unless otherwise indicated **

A/C	Name	Credit Limit	Turnover	Balance	Future	Current	Period 1	Period 2	Period 3	Older
CASH	Cash Sales	€ 10,000.00	282.24	332.87	0.00	332.87	0.00	0.00	0.00	0.00
DOW	Ms Martha Downey	€ 10,000.00	2,498.78	2,899.50	0.00	2,899.50	0.00	0.00	0.00	0.00
MUL	Mr James Mulcahy	€ 10,000.00	2,024.82	2,490.53	0.00	2,490.53	0.00	0.00	0.00	0.00
	Totals:		4,805.84	5,722.90	0.00	5,722.90	0.00	0.00	0.00	0.00

S9

Customer account enquiry

This report views the transactions in one particular customer's account. In the Customer reports browser, select Customer activity from the left-hand side and select Customer Activity (Summary) from the main window.

The criteria window appears (s10). Run a report for the customer Martha Downey. In the Customer Ref, using the drop-down box, select 'Is' to limit to one customer only. Select the code for Martha Downey in the drop-down box, as shown. To generate the report, click **OK** (s11).

To print, use the Print icon at the top of the report.

Criteria for Customer Activity (Summary)

Criteria Values

Enter the values to use for the criteria in this report

Customer Ref	Is	DOW
Transaction Date	Between (inclusive)	CASH Cash Sales / 30/11/2013
Transaction No	Between (inclusive)	DOW Ms Martha Downey / MUL Mr James Mulcahy / 99999999
Inc B/F wd Tran	☐	
Exc Later Payments	☐	

Preview a sample report for a specified number of re ... (all) 0

Help   OK   Cancel

S10

Time: 17:31:23   **Customer Activity (Summary)**

Date From:	01/01/1980				Customer From:	DOW
Date To:	30/11/2013				Customer To:	DOW
Inc b/fwd transaction:	No				Transaction From:	1
Exc later payment:	No				Transaction To:	99,999,999

** NOTE: All report values are shown in Base Currency, unless otherwise indicated **

A/C: DOW	Name:	Ms Martha Downey			Contact:		Tel:		
No	Items	Type	Date	Ref	Details	Value	O/S	Debit	Credit
12	2	SI	10/11/2013	226		2,257.19 *	2,257.19	2,257.19	
16	2	SI	23/11/2013	228		691.13 *	691.13	691.13	
18	2	SC	25/11/2013	229		48.82 *	-48.82		48.82
						2,899.50	2,899.50	2,948.32	48.82

Amount Outstanding	2,899.50
Amount Paid this period	0.00
Credit Limit €	10,000.00

S11

Customer account enquiry – alternative method

An alternative method to view the activity in a customer's account is explained below.

Select **Modules > Customers**. If you are using the view 'Customer Process', select Customer Record from the Tasks pane on the left-hand side (s12). If you are using the view 'Customers' in the Change View drop-down list, select the Customer Record from the toolbar or double-click into the customer's name on the list displayed.

In the A/C Details tab, enter the customer's code from the drop-down list. Click on the Activity tab to view the account details of the customer (s13).

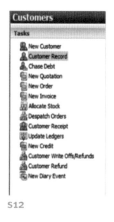

S12

S13

This is a great way to view the history of trading between you and your customer. It also displays the credit limit given and the balance owed, as well as the total amount you have received and the sales income for the year. A summary of dealings you have had with the customer are displayed in a list. Each line in the list represents a transaction such as an invoice or receipt. The bottom part of the preview pane lists the breakdown of the invoice selected in the top section.

Sales ledger receipts

S14

To keep all the entries in the Sales ledger together, the sales ledger receipts can now be entered at this stage. These are the receipts from customers in Daly's Pharmacy Ltd. There are two receipts from customers, i.e. Cash Sales and Ms Martha Downey.

Select **Modules > Customers**. Use the view 'Customer Process', if not already selected, from the drop-down list at the top right-hand corner of your screen (Change View). Select the icon Customer Receipt (s14). You can also access this menu from Tasks on the left-hand side of the screen if you have selected 'Customers' in the Change View drop-down list.

You can also access this menu from the Bank module, by selecting Customer Receipt from the toolbar.

The Customer Receipt window is displayed (s15). It also displays the name of the selected bank account, defaulted to Ref 1200 Bank Current Account. This is the bank where the receipt will be lodged. Enter the information for the receipt from Martha Downey, as shown.

- **Account** – Select the customer using the drop-down list. All items in the customer's account, which are not paid, as well as receipts and credit notes appear automatically in the table.
- **Date** – The date will display the program date. Enter the date of the receipt. The month and the year should be correct.

- **Amount** – Enter the amount of the receipt here.
- **Reference** – Enter the lodgement slip number or other reference number.
- **Receipt €** – If you do not want the receipt to be automatically allocated, for each invoice that is paid by the customer in the table, enter the amount received in its Receipt box. You can accept part-payment or payment in full, but you cannot allocate more than the full value of the item. Alternatively, if you are receiving payment for an invoice in full, click on the item's Receipt box, then click 'Pay in Full'. The amount needed to pay the invoice in full is then entered automatically for you. Continue allocating money in this way until all the money you entered in the amount box is used up. The receipt has now been allocated to the invoices in the customer's account.
- **Discount €** – If you have given any discount against an invoice item, then enter the discount amount, not the percentage amount, in the discount box. The analysis box decreases by the amount of any discount values entered. This may mean that you can allocate more of the amount you entered in the payment amount box against further invoice items.

You can use the Wizard at the bottom of the window to guide you through the process of recording a receipt from a customer. To save, click **Save**.

Enter the receipt from Cash Sales in the same window as previously. Here you do not need to enter the amount; select the customer, enter the receipt date and reference number and simply click 'Pay in Full', as this customer is paying the balance owed in full.

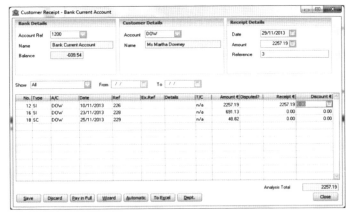

s15

Allocating existing sales ledger credit notes and receipts

You may occasionally enter a receipt from a customer without allocating it straightaway. This may arise where you are unsure of what invoice the receipt should be matched against. You may also enter a credit note for a customer that you then want to allocate to an invoice. In these circumstances, you can allocate the existing receipt or credit note using the Customer Receipt, as previously shown. It is important to allocate receipts and credit notes against the correct invoices, so that your aged debtors report and customer statements give an accurate picture of what each customer owes. The credit note sent to the customer, Ms Martha Downey, can now be allocated. Select Customer Receipt and the customer receipt window is displayed (s16). In this window, payments on account are shown with a transaction type code of SA and have a description of 'Payment on Account'. Invoices are shown with type code of SI, credit notes are shown with a type code of SC. Enter the following details to allocate the credit note to the invoice with reference number 228:

S16

- **Account** – Select the customer by using the drop-down list. All unpaid items in the customer's account, as well as receipts and credit notes, appear automatically in the table.
- **Date** – The date will display the program date.
- **Amount** – Leave blank. You are not entering a receipt, but allocating an existing credit note.
- **Reference** – Leave blank.
- **Receipt €** – Select the credit note and enter the amount in the Receipt box. If you want to pick up the full amount, you can click 'Pay in Full'. As you pick up credit notes the Amount box displays the amount that you can allocate against the invoice items as a negative number. Allocate the picked up amount by entering the value in the Receipt box against the invoice; use the Pay in Full button if appropriate. You can only save the transaction when the Amount box returns to zero, showing that the amount you picked up has been fully allocated.

To save the allocation, click Save. You can also use the Wizard at the bottom of the window to guide you through the process.

If you preview a customer activity report for Martha Downey, you can see that the receipt has been entered and the credit note has been allocated in full (s17).

Time: 19:07:58				**Customer Activity (Summary)**					
Date From:	01/01/1980				Customer From:	DOW			
Date To:	30/11/2013				Customer To:	DOW			
Inc b/fwd transaction:	No				Transaction From:	1			
Exc later payment:	No				Transaction To:	99,999,999			

** NOTE: All report values are shown in Base Currency, unless otherwise indicated **

A/C: DOW	Name:	Ms Martha Downey			Contact:		Tel:		
No	**Items**	**Type**	**Date**	**Ref**	**Details**	**Value**	**O/S**	**Debit**	**Credit**
12	2	SI	10/11/2013	226		2,257.19	0.00	2,257.19	
16	2	SI	23/11/2013	228		691.13 p	642.31	691.13	
18	2	SC	25/11/2013	229		48.82	0.00		48.82
21	1	SR	29/11/2013	3	Sales Receipt	2,257.19	0.00		2,257.19
						642.31	642.31	2,948.32	2,306.01

Amount Outstanding	642.31
Amount Paid this period	2,257.19
Credit Limit €	10,000.00

S17

Customer statements

At the end of the month, once all invoices, credits and receipts have been entered in the customers' accounts, statements are sent to the customers. It is important to keep your customers informed of what they owe in order to maintain efficient credit control and also to gently remind them that their payments are due. These can be printed at any time, but it is usual to send them to your customers as part of your regular credit control routine at the end of each month. Select **Modules > Customers**. If not already selected, use the view 'Customers' from the drop-down list at the top right-hand corner of your screen (Change View). From the Customers window, choose the customers required by selecting each one and click the Statements icon from the toolbar. To select all customers at once, clear all selections by clicking 'Clear' at the bottom of the window and then click 'Swap' at the bottom of the window.

Statements

The Layouts browser appears, listing the layouts that can be used to generate statements. Select Layouts from the left-hand side pane and from the list, select the statement layout you want to use. There are numerous layouts, some showing all transactions in a customer's account, others showing outstanding invoices in the account only. If you wish, you can choose a layout with a remittance slip as part of the statement.

Depending on the selected layout, the Criteria window may appear for you to enter your date range. All aged balance transactions are aged to the program date. In the Transaction Date, enter the date range required. All customer transactions falling on or within these dates are included in the statements. Select the 'Exc Later Payments' check-box if you want to exclude any future sales receipts and sales payments on account from your statement. This gives you the flexibility to run retrospective statements – i.e. to include or exclude invoices – depending on the payment date. Click **OK** to generate the statement.

The Preview window is displayed after generating the statements. Click **Print** to print the customer statements.

Review assignment

Refer to the source documents in your Student Resources relating to Watchworld Ltd.
Open the company Watchworld Ltd that you have set up in *Sage 50* Accounts and perform the following tasks:

1. Enter the sales invoices and credit note sent to the customers from the source documents.
2. Enter the sales ledger receipts and allocate to the invoices in each customer account.
3. Allocate the credit note to the customer's account.
4. Print the following reports to either the printer or screen:
   a. Daybooks: Customer Invoices (Summary)
   b. Daybooks: Customer Credits (Summary)
   c. Aged Debtors Analysis Report (Contacts)
   d. Customer Activity (Summary) for Livia Jewellers.

6.7 Cash Book and Bank Reconciliation in *Sage 50* Accounts

Learning outcomes (Accounting Manual and Computerised 5N1348): 9 (part)
Learning outcomes (Bookkeeping Manual and Computerised 5N1354): 8 (part)

To access the Bank module, select **Modules > Bank**. This module is used for cash and cheques received that are lodged to the bank current account or petty cash account, and for payments made from these bank accounts. This module is also used to perform a bank reconciliation. Supplier payments and customer receipts can also be recorded from this module by selecting the respective icon from the toolbar.

Cash receipts lodged to bank

We have already entered receipts from customers through the Customers module. They could also be entered through the Bank module, using Customer Receipts from the toolbar. To enter other receipts, such as capital invested by the owner and lodged to bank, rent received or a loan received, Bank Receipts from the toolbar must be used. The Bank Receipts window would also be used for cash sales where you do not wish to set up individual customer accounts, e.g. a retail business such as a shop or restaurant, where customers pay at the point of sale and no invoice is raised.

Bank Receipts

The capital invested and lodged to the bank in Daly's Pharmacy Ltd will be entered here. From the Bank module, select Bank Receipts from the toolbar. The Bank Receipts window is displayed (s1). Enter the following to record the capital invested by Daly's Pharmacy Ltd, using the **Tab** key to move from field to field:

- **Bank** – Choose 1200, being the current bank account if not already selected.
- **Date** – The program date will be displayed. Enter the date of the receipt by changing the day only.

- **Ref** – Enter the lodgement slip number for this receipt.
- **N/C** – Enter the nominal account for capital where the double-entry will be posted to. Use the drop-down list to select 'Capital'. *Sage 50* Accounts will update the nominal ledger by posting the double-entry as follows:
  Debit: Bank Current account
  Credit: Capital account.
- **Dept, Project Ref** – You can leave these fields blank.
- **Details** – Enter a description for the receipt here. This is good practice, as the receipt can be recognised in the bank account report.
- **Net** – Enter the receipt amount here.
- **T/C** – Enter the VAT code here by using the drop-down box. This is a non-VAT journal and the rate set to represent outside the scope of VAT is T9.
- **Tax** – This will display as 0.00 when T9 is selected as the VAT code.

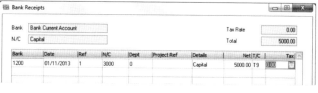

S1

Click on **Save** and the nominal ledger accounts are updated. Click on **Close** to exit the window.

Cheque payments

From the Bank module, select Bank Payments from the toolbar. This window is used to record payments such as salaries, payments of PAYE and insurance. It is not used to record payments to suppliers. (Use Supplier Payments in this case.) The Bank Payments window is displayed. Enter the insurance paid by Daly's Pharmacy Ltd as displayed (s2):

- **Bank** – Choose 1200, being the current bank account if not already selected.
- **Date** – The program date will be displayed. Enter the date of the payment by changing the day only.
- **Ref** – Enter the cheque number.
- **N/C** – Enter the nominal account for insurance where the double-entry will be posted to. Use the drop-down list to select insurance. *Sage 50* Accounts will update the nominal ledger by posting the double-entry as follows:
  Debit: Insurance
  Credit: Bank Current account.
- **Dept, Project Ref, Cost Code** – You can leave these fields blank.

S2

- **Details** – Enter a description for the payment here. This is good practice, as the payment can be recognised in the bank account report.
- **Net** – Enter the payment amount here.
- **T/C** – Enter the VAT code here by using the drop-down box. This is a non-VAT journal and the rate set to represent outside the scope of VAT is T9.
- **Tax** – This will display as 0.00 when T9 is selected as the VAT code.

The second cheque payment is for payment of wages. The same window is used and you can enter both payments there if you wish. Enter the details for wages, as displayed, using the date, reference and nominal code for wages from the drop-down box.

Click on **Save** and click on **Close** to exit the window.

Petty cash

Every business keeps a certain amount of cash on hand to pay for small purchase items. It may not be practical to write cheques for these items. Money is withdrawn from the bank current account at regular intervals to have cash on hand for these items of expenditure.

Petty cash receipts

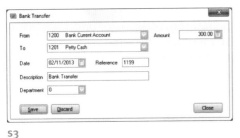

s3

In order to have cash on hand for petty cash purchases, the business must withdraw money from the bank current account and store as petty cash. In the case of Daly's Pharmacy Ltd, the company withdrew €300 from the bank current account and lodged it to the Petty Cash account. The petty cash is another 'bank account' in *Sage 50* Accounts. To enter a petty cash receipt, where money is being transferred from the bank current account to the petty cash account, from the Bank module, select Bank Transfer. The Bank Transfer window is displayed (s3). Enter the following:

- **From** – Enter '1200 Bank Current Account', where the money is being transferred from.
- **To** – Enter 'Petty Cash Account', where the money is being transferred to.
- **Date** – Displays the program date. Enter the date of the transfer.
- **Reference** – Enter the cheque number.
- **Description** – Will automatically display as 'Bank Transfer'.
- **Department** – No need to enter anything here.
- **Amount** – Enter the amount of money that is being transferred from the bank current account to the Petty Cash account. After you click **Save**, the nominal ledger will be automatically updated, as follows:
  Debit: Petty Cash account
  Credit: Bank Current account.

The Bank Transfer window would also be used to record:

*   payment of credit card balances, where the credit card account is set up as a bank account
*   repayment of a bank loan, where a bank account for a bank loan has been set up.

If you need to record receipts into petty cash where the amount is not transferred from a bank account, select Bank Receipts from the toolbar in the Bank module.

Petty cash payments

These are payments for small items from the Petty Cash account. Usually, where cash is needed from the petty cash, a voucher is completed listing the details of the small purchase. These payments are entered in the Bank Payments window; the same as that used for cheque payments. From the Bank module, select Bank Payments. The petty cash payment for diesel in Daly's Pharmacy Ltd is entered as shown (s4):

*   **Bank** – Choose 1201, being the Petty Cash account, if not already selected.
*   **Date** – The program date will be displayed. Enter the date of the payment by changing the day only.
*   **Ref** – Enter the voucher number.
*   **N/C** – Enter the nominal account for motor expenses where the double-entry will be posted to. Use the drop-down list to select.
*   **Dept, Project Ref, Cost Code** – You can leave these fields blank.
*   **Details** – Enter a description for the payment here. This is good practice, as the payment can be recognised in the bank account report.
*   **Net** – Enter the net payment amount here. If it is difficult to determine the net amount, enter the total amount here, select the VAT code and click on 'Calc. Net'. This will convert the total entered in the net column to the net amount.
*   **T/C** – Enter the VAT code here by using the drop-down box. The code is T5 to represent 23% Non-Resale.
*   **Tax** – This will display the VAT amount automatically.

Sage 50 Accounts will update the nominal ledger by posting the double-entry as follows:

Debit: Motor Expenses account with the net value of the payment.
Debit: VAT on Purchases account with the VAT amount.
Credit: Petty Cash account with the total value of the payment.

The second petty cash payment for stamps in Daly's Pharmacy Ltd is displayed below. Note that this is a non-VAT journal entry and the VAT code is T9. The net is posted to the Printing & Postage account as a debit entry. As

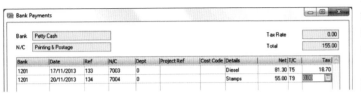

s4

with all payments, you can use the same window to enter multiple payments as shown.

Save the entries when all payments have been recorded and close the window.

Cash book reports

Bank record report

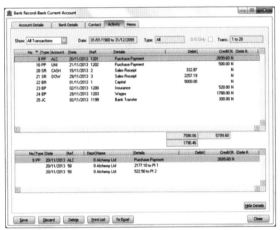

s5

s6

From the Bank module, select Bank Record from the toolbar. In the Account Details tab, enter the bank account in the A/C Ref box that you wish to report. Click on the Activity tab to view all transactions in the selected bank account. If you click on Show Details at the bottom of the report, it displays a second pane showing the details of the item selected on the first pane (s5).

The petty cash record report is displayed as shown (s6).

Alternatively, to run bank reports, select Reports from the toolbar in the Bank module or click Reports in the Links pane. The report browser window is displayed. Locate and select the report you want from the folders. Depending on which report you select, the criteria window may appear. Use the criteria to limit the number of transactions present in the report or leave the preview value as 0 and all transactions are listed. To generate the report, click **OK**.

This report browser window will be useful when you perform a bank reconciliation.

Bank reconciliation

Bank reconciliation is the process of matching the cash book transactions in the bank current account with the statement from the bank. It helps you pinpoint any incorrect entries or omissions in your *Sage 50* Accounts bank current account, or any incorrect withdrawals or deposits shown on your bank statement. You should reconcile your bank current account when you receive your bank statement. If you do this regularly, it will make the task easier.

The bank reconciliation for Daly's Pharmacy Ltd will be completed as shown. Refer to the Bank statement received by the company from the bank at 30 November, reproduced here from section 1.4(1).

Bank Statement

Irish Bank
Salthill, Galway

Your account name: Daly's Pharmacy Ltd

Current account

Account no: 19385298
Statement date: 30-Nov-13

Date	Transaction details	Payments out	Payments in	Balance
	Balance forward			0.00
1-Nov	Lodgement		5000.00	5,000.00
2-Nov	Cheque 1199	300.00		4,700.00
2-Nov	Cheque book Govt Duty	25.00		4,675.00
6-Nov	Cheque 1200	520.00		4,155.00
15-Nov	Lodgement		332.87	4,487.87
28-Nov	Cheque 1201	2699.60		1,788.27
29-Nov	Bank charges	25.63		1,762.64
30-Nov	James Mulcahy EFT		1000.00	2,762.64

Performing a bank reconciliation

The steps to perform a bank reconciliation for Daly's Pharmacy Ltd are given below.

Step 1

Open the Bank module and choose the bank account to be reconciled from the list displayed. In this case, it is the Bank Current Account.

Step 2

From the Tasks pane, click Reconcile or select Reconcile from the toolbar (s7). The Statement Summary window appears.

Step 3

Use the Statement Summary window to record information shown on your bank statement (s8).

View the Statement Summary window entry details, as follows:

s7

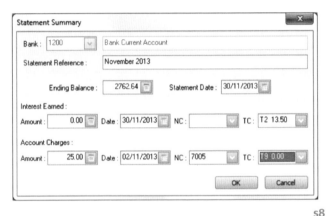

- **Statement Reference** – Enter a statement reference. This entry box is a mandatory entry and is recorded on the Bank Reconciliation PDF, when it is created during reconciliation. *Note:* The PDF is

s8

only created if the Create Bank Reconciliation PDF check box has been selected in your Bank Defaults settings. The Statement Reference entry box is automatically populated with a suggested reference that has a specific structure. For example, 1200 2013-01-11 01 representing Bank 1200, Year 2013, Month 01, Day 11 and a number; in this case, 01 represents the first statement reference entered. However, you can enter any reference you like, e.g. your bank statement reference or the month end of your bank statement. 'November 2013' is entered in the Statement Summary shown.
- **Ending Balance** – The amount the bank account is in credit, or perhaps overdrawn, is shown, according to your *Sage 50* Accounts record. Here, this figure reads €1,790.46. Enter the ending balance shown on your bank statement, which is €2,762.64. If your account is overdrawn, place a minus (–) at the beginning of the value to record a negative amount.
- **Statement Date** – The current program date should display. You can change this date to the date on your bank statement so that only those transactions up to and including the date are available for reconciliation. Here the bank statement date is also 30 November 2013.
- **Interest Earned** – If your bank statement shows interest earned, enter the amount. From the drop-down list select a nominal code you want to post the interest to. Select a tax code that you use for VAT exempt transactions. There is no interest earned on the Bank statement for Daly's Pharmacy Ltd.

- **Account Charges** – If any bank charges appear on your statement, enter an amount for charges. The amount is committed to the bank account when reconciliation is complete and appears as a bank payment. This amount is added to the reconciliation as a fixed amount, which cannot be split into separate charges. Enter the date the charges were applied to your account. From the drop-down list, select a nominal account you want to post the charge to. Select a tax code that you use for VAT-exempt transactions.
- Here is entered €25.00 for cheque book duty on 2 November. It is posted to the Bank Charges account with VAT code T9. The Bank charges of €25.63 are not entered, as we can only enter one group of charges. We will enter the bank charges later. See below for the cheque book duty of €25.00 entered.

When you have entered your statement information, click **OK**.

Step 4

The Bank Reconciliation window *before reconciliation* is displayed below, showing the selected account name at the top of the window (s9).

- Transactions up to and including the statement (end) date are displayed. All unreconciled transactions, up to and including the statement (end) date, are listed in the top half of the Bank Reconciliation window – the Unmatched Items section. An opening balance appears in the lower area of the window – the Matched Against section.
- If this is the first time the bank account is to be reconciled, the account's opening balance appears; otherwise, the reconciled balance from the previous reconciliation appears. It is displayed for information purposes only; it cannot be removed or changed.

s9

- The height of the upper and lower sections can be adjusted by dragging the horizontal splitter bar up or down, as required. The columns displayed in both panes are completely configurable – that is, right-click on a column header cell and select the columns to be displayed from the menu that appears.
- Any account charges or interest earned that have been recorded using the Statement Summary window appear in the Matched Against area of the window. They cannot be moved into the Unmatched Items area. To remove them click Edit, then set the charge/interest amount to zero on

the displayed Statement Summary window. Click **OK** and continue to confirm this action by clicking **OK** when prompted.

Step 5

Work through your bank statement, one line at a time. Match a transaction on your bank statement to a transaction in the Unmatched Items area. Select the item to be matched, then click Match or double-click on the item. The item is removed from the top Unmatched pane and appears in the lower Matched pane. To reverse transactions that you have matched in error, from the Matched Against pane, either double-click each transaction or select the relevant transactions then click Unmatch.

Step 6

As you move transactions the Matched Balance and Difference values in the Totals section change automatically. Similarly, the Payments and Receipts sub-totals change automatically as you match items in the unmatched section. The Book Balance – i.e. balance at statement end date – changes only when the adjustments or reconciliation changes are made. Transactions are positioned in the lower Matched Against pane in the order of which they are moved into the area. Any transaction within this area that is associated with a negative bank balance appears in red. To move a transaction from the lower Matched Against pane to the Unmatched upper pane, left-click on the transaction, then click Unmatch.

Step 7

The following items should now be reconciled with the bank statement:

- 01 Nov – Lodgement, €5,000
- 02 Nov – Cheque, 1199 €300
- 06 Nov – Cheque, 1200 €520
- 15 Nov – Lodgement, €332.87
- 28 Nov – Cheque, 1201 €2699.60.

These items have been matched and now appear in the Matched Items window. The unmatched transactions that do not appear on the bank statement are:

- Cheque number 1202, €500
- Cheque number 1203, €1,780
- SL Receipt, €2,257.19.

These items remain as Unmatched on the top window. There are items on the bank statement that are not in the bank account of Daly's Pharmacy

Ltd. The cheque book item Govt Duty of €25.00 is already entered. These two remaining items are:

- Bank charges, €25.63.
- Receipt by EFT from James Mulcahy, €1,000.

To add a transaction shown on the bank statement that you not were previously unaware of, such as the last two items above, click Adjust. An Adjustment window displays (s10). Select the relevant option and the appropriate entry window appears.

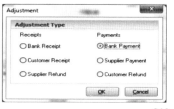

S10

For the missing transactions, the options selected are:

- Bank charges – Select Bank Payment. Click **OK** and the Bank Payments module is opened. Enter the details, using the nominal account for Bank charges and VAT code T9. Save the transaction and close. The adjustment is displayed in the Matched area of the window.
- Receipt from James Mulcahy – Click Adjust again and select Customer Receipt from the Adjustment window. Click **OK**.

  The Customer Receipt window is displayed. Enter the details of the receipt and allocate the money against the invoice on the account. Save the transaction and close the window.

You have now completed the bank reconciliation. The Difference displayed is 0.00 and the matched balance equals the statement balance (s11).

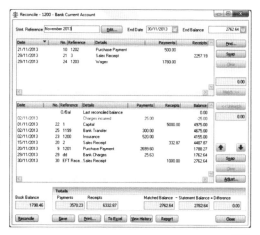

S11

To change the order of transactions in the Matched area, select a transaction and then click the up and down arrows to reposition the transaction within the list. Once you are satisfied you have completed the reconciliation – that is, all transactions are selected, the Matched Balance equals the Statement Balance and the Difference is zero, click Reconcile.

While the account is being reconciled a progress indicator is displayed. Once complete the Reconcile window closes.

Bank reconciliation reports

Bank record enquiry

Run a Bank Record enquiry by double-clicking on the Bank Current account or selecting Bank Record from the toolbar. The Bank Record window opens.

Bank Record

Click on the Activity tab and you will notice that reconciled transactions are displayed as R in the bank column and those that are not reconciled are marked as N. These transactions do not appear for reconciliation again. Click on the Memo tab and a history of the reconciliation is generated as a PDF report. It takes the statement reference as its title for easy identification. The book balance of €2,739.83 is the corrected bank balance in the bank account. This balance does not include transactions dated after the reconciliation date.

Bank reports

Click on Reports on the toolbar or from the Links pane. There are many reports to choose from on the left-hand side of the browser window. If you choose the Reconciled and Unreconciled transactions report, it will display every detail of your reconciliation (s12). The reconciled total equals the end balance on the bank statement. The bank balance at the bottom of the report equals the actual balance in the bank account.

Time: 01:55:49   **Bank Statement - Reconciled and Unreconciled**

Date From : 01/01/1980
Date To : 30/11/2013
** NOTE: All values shown on this report are shown in the Bank Account's operating Currency **

Bank Code : 1200   Bank Name : Bank Current Account

Reconciled Transactions

No	Type	Date	Ref	Details	Debit	Credit	Balance	Running Bal.
22	BR	01/11/2013	1	Capital	5,000.00		5,000.00	5,000.00
23	BP	02/11/2013	1200	Insurance		520.00	4,480.00	4,480.00
25	JC	02/11/2013	1199	Bank Transfer		300.00	4,180.00	4,180.00
31	BP	02/11/2013		Charges incurred		25.00	4,155.00	4,155.00
20	SR	15/11/2013	2	Sales Receipt	332.87		4,487.87	4,487.87
9	PP	20/11/2013	1201	Purchase Payment		2,699.60	1,788.27	1,788.27
29	BP	29/11/2013	dd	Bank Charges		25.63	1,762.64	1,762.64
30	SR	30/11/2013	EFT	Sales Receipt	1,000.00		2,762.64	2,762.64
				Reconciled Total :	**6,332.87**	**3,570.23**	**2,762.64**	

Unreconciled Transactions

No	Type	Date	Ref	Details	Debit	Credit	Balance	Running Bal.
10	PP	21/11/2013	1202	Purchase Payment		500.00	-500.00	2,262.64
21	SR	29/11/2013	3	Sales Receipt	2,257.19		1,757.19	4,519.83
24	BP	29/11/2013	1203	Wages		1,780.00	-22.81	2,739.83
				Non-Reconciled Total :	**2,257.19**	**2,280.00**	**-22.81**	
				Bank Balance :	**8,590.06**	**5,850.23**	**2,739.83**	

S12

Non-matching balances

If the Matched and Statement balances are not equal, you can choose to:

- *Put the bank reconciliation on hold.* Remember, you can put the process on hold and return to finish the bank reconciliation later. Any transactions you add to rectify the problem are made available for reconciliation, provided their date does not exceed the reconciliation's Statement (End) Date. To put the bank reconciliation on hold, click **Save**, then **OK** when prompted to do so. *Do not* click Reconcile.
- *Investigate and rectify the problem.* Use the Nominal Activity Report to investigate the problem. This report lists all the transactions that have been made to and from the bank, both reconciled and unreconciled. To do this, select **Modules > Nominal Ledger**. From the Links pane, click **Nominal Ledger > Reports > Nominal Activity Reports** and select Nominal Activity. Select the criteria for the bank account you are reconciling.
- *Save the reconciliation with a known discrepancy.* The bank reconciliation is saved as usual. However, the next time you reconcile the bank account the opening balance displayed for the bank is likely to be in doubt.

- *Enter an adjustment.* This is done to adjust the Matched Balance with the Statement balance.

To return to a saved reconciliation at any time, open the Bank module, select the bank account to be reconciled then click **Reconcile**. From the Previous Statement window, click **Use Saved** to open the previously saved reconciliation. To discard the previously saved statement and start again, click **Discard Saved**.

Review assignments

Assignment 1

Refer to the source documents in your Student Resources relating to Watchworld Ltd.
   Open the company Watchworld Ltd, which you set up in *Sage 50* Accounts, and perform the following tasks.

1. Enter the receipts into the current bank account and the Petty Cash account.
2. Enter the cheque book payments into the current bank account.
3. Enter the petty cash payments into the petty cash account.
4. Print the following reports to either the printer or screen:
   a. Bank Record report for both current bank account and petty cash
   b. Bank Statement report – Reconciled and Unreconciled.

Assignment 2

Refer to the Bank Statement received by Watchworld Ltd in section 1.4, assignment 1.
   Prepare a bank reconciliation in *Sage 50* Accounts for Watchworld Ltd and enter in the accounts any transactions that are in the bank statement but not already entered in the accounts. *Note:* You will need to set up a new nominal ledger account for Bank Charges before commencing.
   Reprint the Bank statement report – Reconciled and Unreconciled.

6.8 Entering Opening Balances in *Sage 50* Accounts

Learning outcomes (Accounting Manual and Computerised 5N1348): 8 (part)
Learning outcomes (Bookkeeping Manual and Computerised 5N1354): 8 (part)

If your business had been trading before you began using *Sage 50* Accounts, it is likely that you will have accounts to date that need to be entered. These accounts are entered into *Sage 50* Accounts as opening balances, which are the current values on your various accounts.

Even if you are starting a new business, there may be opening balances you need to add, e.g. your bank account balance, a start-up loan. When you enter opening balances you should use the closing date of your previous accounting period. For example, if you are starting to use *Sage 50* Accounts for a new financial year starting 1 January 2014, enter the date of your opening balances as 31 December 2013.

To enter opening balances you will need the following information to hand:

- Closing Trial Balance as at the end of the period, where the accounts were completed using an accounting method other than *Sage 50* Accounts.
- A list of outstanding (unpaid) sales invoices, i.e. individual debtor balances.
- A list of outstanding (unpaid) supplier invoices, i.e. individual creditor balances.
- Closing bank statement balance.

To demonstrate the process of entering opening balances in *Sage 50* Accounts, the following details relate to the company Equipment Supplies Ltd. The accounts are completed up to 30 November 2014. The accounting year is from 1 January to 31 December 2014.

Business name	Equipment Supplies Ltd
Address	108 Middle Abbey Street, Dublin 1
Telephone	01- 872 3456
VAT reg. no.	IE 4567823H
Business activity	Sales and repair of office equipment

VAT is charged on sales at the standard rate of 23% and on repairs at the lower rate of 13.5%.

All of the above information should be entered in *Sage 50* Accounts Configuration, along with the VAT rates, bank accounts, accounting year and defaults. You can set up this company from scratch, or alternatively, create a new company from the backup file of Daly's Pharmacy Ltd (fig. 1).

TRIAL BALANCE of Equipment Supplies Ltd as at 30 November 2014

	Debit	Credit
Sales of goods		337,148
Repair Income		13,033
Opening Stock 1 Jan 2014	16,448	
Purchases	164,300	
Salaries	36,960	
Printing, Postage & Stationery	9,600	
Delivery Costs	690	
Telephone	1,842	
Light & Heat	1,790	
Rent	15,000	
Miscellaneous Expenses	123	
Bank Charges	247	
Furniture	34,500	
Office Equipment	29,000	
Bank	27,450	
Petty Cash	1,600	
Debtors	102,630	
Creditors		66,852
VAT Payable		2,656
Capital		22,491
	442,180	442,180

Note: VAT Payable equals VAT on Sales −€5,448 and VAT on Purchases −€2,792 (for the month of Nov 2014)

Debtors Balances as at 30 November 2014

NAME	ADDRESS	BALANCE
O'Sullivan's Office Centre	12 Patrick St, Navan, Co Meath	24,912.00
Cal Computing	16 Main St, Clifden, Co Galway	23,339.00
Earls Office Supplies	56 Mountain View, Athlone, Co Westmeath	37,479.00
Mr Joe Malone	Main Street, Trim, Co Meath	16,900.00
	TOTAL	**102,630.00**

\ Creditors Balances as at 30 November 2014		
NAME	ADDRESS	BALANCE
Electric Ireland	Fleet St, Dublin 2	434.53
Eircom	Leopardstown, Co Dublin	508.32
Pentech Office Ltd	57 York Rd, Dun Laoghaire, Co Dublin	52,269.00
Tech Supplies Ltd	63 Landscape, Ballinteer, Dublin 16	13,640.15
	TOTAL	**66,852.00**

Figure 1

If you have taken a backup of Daly's Pharmacy Ltd, you could restore this backup to a 'new' company, i.e. Equipment Supplies Ltd, before entering any transactions in the accounts. Otherwise, you need to create a completely new company and set up the structure of the Chart of Accounts (COA). This would be good practice at this point.

Methods for entering opening balances

There are two methods for entering opening balances:

- **Method 1**: Set up the opening balances in the accounts as you create each nominal account, customer account, supplier account and bank account.
- **Method 2**: Use the Opening Balances window. Some users prefer this method as it brings together all the tasks needed to enter opening balances in one place. Here you can see at a glance how far on you are with entering balances. Mark tasks as complete and create customer and supplier records as you proceed through the process.

Method 1: Set up opening balances in the accounts

Firstly, we will use **Method 1** above and enter opening balances as accounts are created. The steps are set out below.

1. Set up Nominal accounts with opening balances

You need to set up new nominal accounts for all the accounts in the Trial Balance above, *except for*:

- Sales of goods
- Bank current account
- Debtors
- Creditors
- VAT Payable.

These accounts are already set up as they form part of the control accounts. *Exclude the Petty Cash account* as this will be set up in the Bank module.

To set up the first nominal account, Repair Income, open the Nominal or Company module and select New Nominal from the toolbar. *Note*: Ensure that the program date is set to 30/11/2014 for the entering of all opening balances.

The New Nominal window will open (s1). Enter the following:

- **Enter Details** – The repair Income account is set up with the Type: Sales and Category: Sales. It will automatically be assigned the N/C, 4001. Click Next.
- **Opening Balance** – Select the option: 'Yes, I wish to enter an opening balance.' The opening balance details are displayed as shown. Enter the opening balance for the Repair Income account as a credit balance.

Click on **Create** and the account is set up.

As you have entered a credit value of €13,033 in the Repair Income account, *Sage 50* Accounts automatically holds the corresponding debit entry in the Suspense account. The main purpose of the Suspense account is to hold the difference between debits and credits until all balances are fully entered. When you have completed all opening balances, your debit and credit columns should show the same total value as per the Trial Balance. The Suspense account will then be cleared showing a nil balance.

You can see the values entered in the Suspense account in the Nominal ledger window.

Set up the nominal accounts below in the same manner, entering the opening

S1

balances from the Trial Balance on the appropriate side. Do not yet enter the Debtors, Creditors, VAT Payable, Bank or Petty Cash account balances yet. These will be entered later.

Enter the following Nominal account balances as shown (fig. 2). The Repair Income has already been entered.

NOMINAL ACCOUNTS	TYPE	CATEGORY	DEBIT	CREDIT
Repair Income	Sales	Sales		13,033.00
Opening Stock	Cost of Sales	Opening Stock	16,448.00	
Purchases	Cost of Sales	Purchases	164,300.00	
Salaries	Overheads	Overheads	36,960.00	
Printing, Postage & Stationery	Overheads	Overheads	9,600.00	
Delivery Costs	Overheads	Overheads	690.00	
Telephone	Overheads	Overheads	1,842.00	
Light & Heat	Overheads	Overheads	1,790.00	
Rent	Overheads	Overheads	15,000.00	
Miscellaneous Expenses	Overheads	Overheads	123.00	
Bank Charges	Overheads	Overheads	247.00	
Furniture	Fixed Assets	Fixed Assets	34,500.00	
Office Equipment	Fixed Assets	Fixed Assets	29,000.00	
Capital	Capital & Reserves	Capital & Reserves		22,491.00
Total balances entered:			310,500.00	35,524.00

Suspense account should show a Credit balance of €274,976

Figure 2

2. Enter Sales account opening balance

The Sales account is already created, with a nominal code of 4000. It is a control account and was not deleted. We will use this account to enter the opening balance of Sales of Goods €337,148

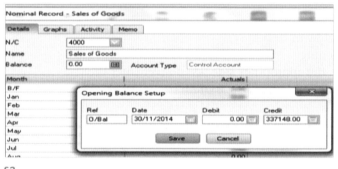

S2

Double-click on the Sales account in the Nominal Record window (s2). Edit the name to appropriately read 'Sales of Goods'. Click on the Balance field and the Opening Balance Setup will display. You will be asked to save the name. On the Credit column, enter the value of the opening balance for the Sales of Goods. Save the entry and close the Nominal Record.

As you save the Sales record, the corresponding debit entry will be posted automatically to the Suspense account.

3. Enter VAT account opening balance

Sage 50 Accounts has separate accounts for VAT on Sales and VAT on Purchases. Enter the opening balances into each account in the same manner as the Sales of Goods account above, by double-clicking on VAT on Sales in the Nominal module. Enter the VAT on Sales as a credit balance (s3).

Double-click on the VAT on Purchases and enter the amount of €2,792 as a debit balance.

4. Enter Bank Current account opening balance

You can enter the Bank Current account opening balance from the Nominal module if you wish (s4). Use the same method as above for the Sales of Goods. Double-click on the Bank account and enter the opening balance in the Debit column.

Alternatively, to enter the Bank Current account opening balance, use the Bank module and double-click on the Bank account. Click on Current Balance and the Opening Balance Setup window is displayed (s5). Enter the balance as a Receipt, (Debit balance). *Note*: Do not enter the opening balance twice by using both methods.

5. Enter Petty Cash opening balance

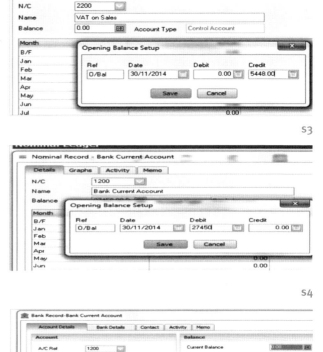

If the Petty Cash account is not set up, you can enter the opening balance when creating a new Bank account. Open the Bank module and select New Bank from the toolbar. The New Bank window is displayed.

- **Account Name (1)** – Enter Petty Cash. The Reference will be 1201. Select Account type: Cash Account. Check the box for 'No bank reconciliation. Skip the Account Details (2), Bank Details (3) and Contact Details (4), as there is no need to enter anything here.
- **Opening Balance (5)** – Select Money in Account to denote a debit balance. Enter the balance, €1,600, in the Amount EUR € field.
- Click **Create** and the Petty Cash account is created with the opening balance. The credit entry will be posted to the Suspense account.

6. Enter Suppliers opening balance

The opening balance of the Creditors in the Trial Balance needs to be entered into each individual supplier's account. When entering the opening balance for each of your suppliers, it is recommended that you itemise each transaction or invoice outstanding. Although this process is initially more time-consuming, it will give you an accurate picture of the history of each supplier's account. It will also make it easier to select the correct invoices when entering and allocating your supplier payments in the future.

The opening balances must be entered through the Suppliers module and individually to each supplier's account. You cannot enter a supplier's opening balance as a journal to the creditors account in the Nominal module as this will not appear on your Aged Creditors report.

As new supplier accounts need to be created, you can enter the opening balance at the same time when creating a new supplier record. Set up new suppliers by opening the Suppliers module and selecting New Supplier from the toolbar. The New Supplier window is opened. Enter the following for Electric Ireland:

- **Supplier Details (1)** – Enter the name Electric Ireland. Use A/C Ref: 'ELE' as the code. Enter the address.
- **Contact Details (2)** – No entry is required here.
- **Supplier Defaults (3)** – Select the nominal code for Light & Heat where the nominal postings will be entered for Electric Ireland. Select the Tax (VAT) Code T6 as 13.5% Non-Resale.
- **Credit Details (4)** – Accept the credit terms as set up in the Supplier Default settings.
- **Bank Address (5) and Bank Account (6)** – No entry is required here.
- **Opening Balance (7)** – Select 'Yes, as one value.' If you had information of individual transactions that make up the opening balance, it is recommended that each transaction is entered individually. Enter the amount of the opening balance by selecting Invoice, which represents a credit balance in the supplier's account.

Click on **Create** and the suppliers record is created with the opening balance.

Example task

To consolidate these steps, create new supplier records for the suppliers, Pentech Office Ltd and Tech Supplies Ltd as above, using the Nominal code Purchases 4000 and the Tax (VAT) code T1 23% Resale, with their respective opening balances. Create a new supplier record for Eircom, using the Nominal code Telephone and the Tax (VAT) code T5 23% Non-Resale and enter the opening balance. Use the first three characters of the name as the A/C reference for each supplier.

You will notice that Pentech Office Ltd and Tech Supplies Ltd appear in red in the Suppliers window, as the credit limit has been exceeded in their account. Change the credit limit to a higher amount, if desired.

When all opening balances have been entered, you can print an Aged Creditors Report to view your entries. The total of the creditors' balances equals the creditors balance in the Trial Balance.

7. Enter Customers opening balance

When entering the opening balance for each of your customers it is recommended, similar to suppliers, that you itemise each transaction. Although it is initially more time consuming, this will give you an accurate picture of the history of each customer account. It will also make it easier to select the correct invoices when entering and allocating your customer receipts in the future. The opening balances must be entered through the Customers module and individually to each customer account.

As new customer accounts need to be created, you can enter the opening balance at the same time as you are creating a new customer record. Set up new customers by opening the Customers module and selecting New Customer from the toolbar. The New Customer window is opened. Enter the following for O'Sullivan's Office Centre:

- **Customer Details (1)** – Enter the name O'Sullivan's Office Centre. Use A/C Ref: 'OSUL' as the code. Enter the address.
- **Contact Details (2)** – No entry is required here.
- **Customer Defaults (3)** – Select the nominal code for Sales: 1000, where the nominal postings will be entered for all customers. Select the default Tax (VAT) Code: T1, as 23% Resale.
- **Credit Details (4)** – Accept the credit terms as set up in the Customer Default settings.
- **Bank Address (5) and Bank Account (6)** – No entry is required here.
- **Opening Balance (7)** – Select 'Yes, as one value.' If you had information of individual transactions that make up the opening balance, it is recommended that each transaction is entered individually. Enter the amount of the opening balance as 'Invoice', which represents a debit balance in the customer's account.

Click on **Create** and the customer record is created with the opening balance.

Example task

Create new customer records for Cal Computing, Earls Office Centre and Mr Joe Malone as shown previously, using the Nominal code Sales: 1000, and the Tax (VAT) code: T1 23% Resale, with their respective opening balances. Use the first three characters of the name as the A/C reference for each customer.

You will notice that the customers appear in red in the Customer window, as the credit limit has been exceeded in their account. Change the credit limit to a higher amount, if desired.

When all opening balances have been entered, you can print an Aged Debtors Report to view your entries. The total of the debtors' balances equals the debtors balance in the Trial Balance.

Method 2: Set up opening balances using the Opening Balances window

This method is displayed in the Opening Balances window as shown (s6). Here you can see at a glance how far on you are with entering balances, marking tasks as complete and creating customer and supplier records as you complete the process. To use this method select **Tools > Opening Balances**. *Note:* This is an *alternative* method for entering opening balances

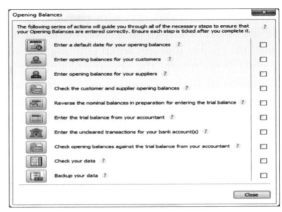

s6

and should *not* be used to enter balances if they have already been entered.

In the Opening Balances window, complete each listed task. As you do so, a tick is added to the task's checkbox.

Select each icon on the left and enter the appropriate opening balances.

 'Enter a default date for your opening balance' – Enter '30/11/2014' as the default date.

 'Enter the opening balances for your customers' – The customers need to be set up before using this option (s7).

s7

 'Enter the opening balances for your suppliers' – Again, they need to be already set up (s8).

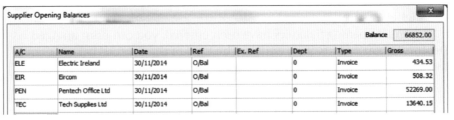

s8

'Check the customer and supplier opening balances' – This will report on the Aged Debtors Analysis (detailed) report to check your customers' opening balances and an Aged Creditors Analysis (detailed) to check your suppliers' opening balances.

 'Reverse the opening balance in preparation for entering the Trial Balance' – If discrepancies are found, correct them before proceeding.

 'Enter the trial balance from your accountant' – The Trial Balance Entry window is displayed. Enter your trial balance into the table until the Balance box is zero and both the Debit and Credit totals display equal amounts. Click **Save**.

 'Enter the uncleared transactions for your bank account(s)' – If you want to reconcile transactions that have not yet cleared your bank account, you need to enter these separately so that they are added as individual items to the bank account record. As with customer and supplier opening balances, the double-entry bookkeeping also affects the Suspense account.

When you complete this task, a reversing journal is generated between bank accounts and the Suspense account. This journal uses the default opening balance date. Select 'Enter the uncleared transactions for your bank account.' The Bank Opening Balances window opens. Enter each uncleared bank transaction into the table. Click **Save**.

 'Check opening balances against the trial balance from your accountant' – Select this to generate the Period Trial Balance report and confirm the recorded opening balances are correct. The Criteria for the Period Trial Balance window appears. Click **OK** to generate the report. Check that the values in the report match those you expect for your opening balances. Check the Suspense account has a zero balance.

 'Check your data' – This is an optional task, but it is a good idea to check your data to ensure everything is working as it should. If there are no problems, the File Maintenance window appears, informing you of this. To continue, click **OK**.

 'Backup your data' – Select this to take a copy of your data in case your computer fails or if you encounter data corruption. If you have a recent copy of your data it can then be restored. The Backup window opens. Enter the backup details and then click **OK**.

Period Trial Balance

You have now entered all the opening balances as at 30 November 2014 for
Equipment Supplies Ltd, either by method 1 *or* method 2 as explained above.
The Suspense account is now cleared and the Trial Balance should display as
shown (s9).

	Period Trial Balance		
To Period:	Month 12, December 2014		

N/C	Name	Debit	Credit
0010	Furniture	34,500.00	
0011	Office Equipment	29,000.00	
1100	Debtors Control Account	102,630.00	
1200	Bank Current Account	27,450.00	
1201	Petty Cash	1,600.00	
2100	Creditors Control Account		66,852.00
2200	VAT on Sales		5,448.00
2201	VAT on Purchases	2,792.00	
3000	Capital		22,491.00
4000	Sales of Goods		337,148.00
4001	Repair Income		13,033.00
4951	Opening Stock	16,448.00	
5000	Purchases	164,300.00	
7000	Salaries	36,960.00	
7001	Printing, Postage & Stationery	9,600.00	
7002	Delivery Costs	690.00	
7003	Telephone	1,842.00	
7004	Light & Heat	1,790.00	
7005	Rent	15,000.00	
7006	Miscellaneous Expenses	123.00	
7007	Bank Charges	247.00	
	Totals:	444,972.00	444,972.00

s9

Trial Balance

To view the Trial Balance, select **Modules > Financials**. Select
Trial Balance from the toolbar. Click on Run to preview the Trial
Balance. The criteria window is opened. Click **OK** to preview the
Trial Balance.

The company has now been set up with the opening balances, where
transactions for the month following (December) can now be entered in the
ledgers.

6.9 Nominal Ledger and VAT Reporting in *Sage 50* Accounts

Learning outcomes (Accounting Manual and Computerised 5N1348): 9 (part) and 10 (part)
Learning outcomes (Bookkeeping Manual and Computerised 5N1354): 10 (part)

The nominal ledger, also called the general ledger, is the main accounting record of a business. It is home to the nominal accounts your business uses to monitor where your money is, where it comes from and where it is going. These nominal accounts make up your company's assets, liabilities, income and expenses. As a whole, they are referred to as your Chart of Accounts (COA). These have already been set up for Daly's Pharmacy Ltd. As you record transactions, *Sage 50* Accounts uses double-entry bookkeeping, so that one of the nominal accounts is debited and another account is credited. For example, when you enter a Sales invoice, the entry is entered in the Sales Ledger. The double-entry is:

Debit: Customer with the total of the invoice.
Credit: VAT with the VAT amount.
Credit: Sales with the net amount.

You do not see the double-entry when you enter most transactions in *Sage 50* Accounts, but all nominal ledger accounts are updated automatically, including the Trial Balance, Profit and Loss account and Balance Sheet.

The nominal ledger is used to enter transactions that do not fit into the normal operations of the Customers, Suppliers Ledger or the Bank modules. These are transactions that are not related to Purchases, Sales or the Bank accounts, for example, adjustments to the accounts, where you need to debit one nominal ledger account and credit another. Typical entries posted to the Nominal ledger are:

- Depreciation
- Provision for bad debts
- Accruals and prepayments
- Accounting for stock.

The nominal ledger is used to set up all the nominal ledger accounts that are needed to enter transactions for a company.

The nominal ledger may also be used to make other adjustments at the end of the financial year, for example, transfer amounts from one nominal ledger account to another where the amount was incorrectly posted to the incorrect nominal ledger account.

Open the company Daly's Pharmacy Ltd in the *Sage 50* Accounts window.

S1

To open the nominal Ledger, select **Modules > Nominal Ledger** or you can select Company from the link at the left-hand side of your screen (s1). When opened, you can see the nominal ledger accounts used by Daly's Pharmacy Ltd listed with the running debit and credit balances. You can double-click on any of these accounts to view the transactions entered in the Activity tab.

Print Trial Balance

The Trial Balance gives a summary of the balances on all the nominal ledger accounts for a particular period end. Since all the entries have debits equal to credits as they were entered through the Customers, Suppliers and Bank modules, the Trial Balance will always balance. This does not mean that all the entries in the system are correct: entries could be omitted, incorrect amounts could be entered or the incorrect menu could be used.

Links

- Nominal Ledger
- Department
- Activity
- Chart of Accounts
- Financials
- Financial Reports
- Budgets

S2

To print the Trial Balance of Daly's Pharmacy Ltd, select **Modules > Financials**. Alternatively, open the Company or Nominal module and select Financials from the Links pane (s2). From the Financials window select Trial Balance from the toolbar. Choose the print output by selecting Preview and click on **Run**.

Trial Balance

The criteria window opens to display the date end of the Trial Balance. It displays the year end date. Click **OK**.

The Period Trial Balance is produced for Daly's Pharmacy Ltd, as displayed (s3). It shows the summary of the account balances for the month-end November only, as there are no transactions entered for December. You will notice that the VAT is displayed in two sections: VAT on Sales and VAT on Purchases, to give an overall VAT refund due of €1,112.07.

You can also view the Trial Balance by selecting Reports from the Financials window. The Finance Reports browser appears, listing all

Reports

Period Trial Balance

N/C	Name	Debit	Credit
To Period:	Month 12, December 2013		
1100	Debtors Control Account	2,132.84	
1200	Bank Current Account	2,739.83	
1201	Petty Cash	145.00	
2100	Creditors Control Account		9,024.61
2200	VAT on Sales		917.06
2201	VAT on Purchases	2,029.13	
3000	Capital		5,000.00
4000	Sales		4,805.84
5000	Purchases	9,939.50	
7000	Wages	1,780.00	
7001	Light & Heat	274.28	
7002	Insurance	520.00	
7003	Motor Expenses	81.30	
7004	Printing & Postage	55.00	
7005	Bank Charges	50.63	
	Totals:	**19,747.51**	**19,747.51**

S3

available financial report folders, and their respective reports. Open the Trial Balance Reports folder. Highlight the Transactional Trial Balance report from the list of reports and select the output option you require. From the Report Browser toolbar, select the action you want to take. Depending on which report you selected, the Criteria window may appear. This includes only those criteria that are appropriate to the report selected. Set the criteria options as required. When you have set the criteria you want to apply, click **OK**.

Nominal Ledger Account Enquiry

You can view details of any nominal ledger account to see all the transactions that are posted to it. Return to the Nominal Ledger

s4

module and you will see the list of nominal accounts that have transactions recorded. Select Nominal Record from the toolbar or double-click on the nominal account you wish to report and select the Activity tab. The activity on the Bank Charges account is displayed as shown (s4). Alternatively, highlight the Bank Charges account and click on Reports. The Nominal Report browser window appears, listing all the available nominal reports for the Bank Charges account. Select Nominal Activity report from the list of reports and from the report browser window, select the action you want to take. The criteria window may appear and select the criteria options as required. When you have set the criteria, click **OK**.

Another faster method of reporting on a nominal account is to select the nominal account from the Nominal window and click on Activity in the toolbar.

Audit Trial by Nominal Accounts

The Audit Trial by Nominal Accounts reports on all transactions sorted by nominal accounts. Regardless of what the source was (Suppliers, Customers, Bank or Nominal modules) this will print all transactions that were entered within the reporting period. From the Nominal Ledger module, select all the nominal accounts on your screen. To do this, make sure that none are selected by clicking Clear at the bottom of the window. Then click Swap and all the nominal accounts will be selected. Select Reports from the toolbar and the Nominal Report browser window opens, listing all the available nominal reports.

Select Nominal Activity report from the list of reports on the left-hand side. From the report browser window, select Nominal Activity report and the criteria window is displayed. Select the criteria options as required. When you have set the criteria, click **OK**. (This report is not displayed here due to the large number of accounts in the report.)

Financial reports

Financial reports such as the Profit and Loss and the Balance Sheet reports are accessed from the Financials window.

Profit and Loss report

The Profit and Loss report shows whether or not the company is trading profitably. To generate the Profit and Loss report, in the Financials Module, select Profit & Loss from the toolbar. The Print Output window is displayed. Select Preview to preview the report and click on Run. The criteria window opens where you can select the period transactions for the report. This is defaulted to the start and end of the financial year, which is normally the selected period for the report. Here, you can run a Profit and Loss report for the current month, a range of consecutive months or for any financial year by selecting the date criteria. The Chart of Accounts (COA) is displayed as that set up for the company in the COA configuration. Click **OK** to generate the report.

Profit and Loss

From:	Month 1, January 2013			
To:	Month 12, December 2013			

Chart of Accounts: Daly's Pharmacy Ltd Chart of Accounts

	Period		Year to Date	
Sales				
Sales	4,805.84		4,805.84	
		4,805.84		4,805.84
Cost of Sales				
Purchases	9,939.50		9,939.50	
		9,939.50		9,939.50
Gross Profit/(Loss):		(5,133.66)		(5,133.66)
Overheads				
Overheads	2,761.21		2,761.21	
		2,761.21		2,761.21
Net Profit/(Loss):		(7,894.87)		(7,894.87)

s5

The Profit and Loss account is displayed as shown (s5). Note that it shows a net loss, as closing stock has not yet been entered in the accounts. The layout is displayed as set up in the COA of Daly's Pharmacy Ltd. You can click on the blue links to see a category breakdown. For example, click on the link Overheads to view the overheads category breakdown.

Balance Sheet

The Balance Sheet shows the assets and liabilities of the business. The profit (or loss) from the Profit and Loss report is transferred to the Balance Sheet and added to (subtracted from) the retained profit of the business. In the Financials module, select Balance Sheet from the toolbar. The Print Output window is displayed. Select Preview to preview the report and click on Run.

The criteria window opens, where you can select the period transactions for the report. This is defaulted to the start and end of the financial year, which is normally the selected period for the report. Here, you can run a

Balance Sheet report for the current month, for a range of consecutive months or for any financial year by selecting the date criteria. The COA is displayed as that set up for the company in the Chart of Accounts configuration. Click **OK** to generate the report. The Balance Sheet is displayed as shown (s6).

Balance Sheet				
From: Month 1, January 2013				
To: Month 12, December 2013				
Chart of Accounts:	Daly's Pharmacy Ltd Chart of Accounts			
	Period		Year to Date	
Current Assets				
Debtors	2,132.84		2,132.84	
Bank Accounts	2,884.83		2,884.83	
VAT Account	1,112.07		1,112.07	
		6,129.74		6,129.74
Current Liabilities				
Creditors	9,024.61		9,024.61	
		9,024.61		9,024.61
Current Assets less Current Liabilities:		(2,894.87)		(2,894.87)
Total Assets less Current Liabilities:		(2,894.87)		(2,894.87)
Capital & Reserves				
Capital & Reserves	5,000.00		5,000.00	
P & L Account	(7,894.87)		(7,894.87)	
		(2,894.87)		(2,894.87)

s6

The layout is displayed as set up in the COA of Daly's Pharmacy Ltd in your Student Resources. You can click on the blue links to see a category breakdown. For example, click on the Bank Accounts link to view the breakdown of the bank current account and the petty cash account balances. If you want to display these bank balances separately, you can change the COA layout.

Adjustments to final accounts – entering nominal journals

Nominal, or general, journals are ledger transactions that do not fit into the normal operations of the Customers, Suppliers or the Bank modules, e.g. accruals, prepayments, depreciation. Everything related to VAT is entered through the Customers, Suppliers or the Bank modules. Remember that if you journal from within the nominal ledger, *Sage 50* Accounts has no means of finding out whether the transaction has a VAT element.

To enter a nominal journal

A journal entry moves money from one nominal account to another. Every journal consists of credit and debit values so that every credit must have a debit and vice versa. This does not mean that for every single debit item you must post a single credit item. You can post several debits, but one balancing credit, and vice versa. As long as the net difference between your postings is always zero, that is, the total value of credits equals the total value of debits, you can post the journal. It is important to adhere to strict double-entry bookkeeping principles, when recording journals. We will now enter the closing stock figure for Daly's Pharmacy Ltd. We will also assume that 30 November is the end of the Daly's Pharmacy accounting year, as final accounts are normally prepared at that time. We will also assume that the business has no opening stock and that closing stock at 30 November is valued at €8,000.

Note: Two new nominal accounts will need to be set up in the nominal ledger, but these can be created while entering the journal entry. It may be easier to set up these accounts before you enter the journal entry. If you wish to do so, the two accounts are:

1. Stock – Use the Type: Current Assets, and the Category: Stock. This represents the stock figure in the Balance Sheet. The number 1000 will be automatically assigned to this account.
2. Closing Stock – Use the Type: Cost of Sales, and the Category: Closing Stock. This represents the closing stock for the Trading Account. The number 5005 will be automatically assigned to this account.

To enter the nominal journal, return to the Nominal module or open the Company module. Select Journal Entry from the toolbar. The Journal Entry window is displayed (s7). Enter the following details:

- **Reference** – Enter a reference such as Closing Stock.
- **Posting Date** – Check the Posting Date. Your current program date is entered for you automatically, which should read 30/11/2013. You can use the Calendar to choose the date.
- **N/C** – This represents the first nominal account, where we debit the stock figure in the Balance Sheet. If this account has not yet been set up, use the down-arrow and click on New to create a new nominal account. Otherwise choose the account from the drop-down list.
- **Name** – The name of the account you selected appears automatically.
- **Ex. Ref** – You can enter an extended reference to identify the journal. There is no need to enter any here.
- **Dept** – There is no need to enter anything here.
- **Details** – Enter a description for the journal, i.e. 'Closing Stock'.
- **T/C** – The VAT code is defaulted to T9, non-VAT, for this transaction. Whatever code you use, *Sage 50* Accounts does not calculate the VAT for you; neither does it post VAT to the VAT Control Account, as all VAT transactions should only be entered in the Customers, Suppliers or Bank modules. Remember that no VAT details should be entered through the Nominal ledger.
- **Debit** – Enter the value of €8,000 in the Debit column.

S7

On the second line of this journal, record the credit entry, which is to credit the Closing Stock in the Trading Account. You will need to add a new nominal account for Closing Stock in the Trading Account, if not already added. Use the nominal account number 5005, which will be displayed as Type: Cost of Sales, under the Category: Closing Stock, in the Trading account. Enter €8,000 in the Credit column. The Balance box displays the difference between the debit and credit values for the journal. Before you can save the journal the balance must be zero. Click on **Save**.

The double-entry to record the closing stock of a business is:

Debit: Closing Stock (Current Asset in Balance Sheet)
Credit: Closing Stock (Trading account).

If you now run a Profit and Loss report for Daly's Pharmacy Ltd, the closing stock is entered in the Trading Account as part of Cost of Sales, showing a revised Net Profit of €105.13 (s8).

If you run a Balance Sheet report, the Stock figure is entered as part of the Current Assets (s9). Note the effect the closing stock has on the Profit and Loss account and Balance Sheet.

Time: 22:16:42		Profit and Loss			
From:	Month 1, January 2013				
To:	Month 12, December 2013				
Chart of Accounts:		Daly's Pharmacy Ltd Chart of Accounts			
		Period		**Year to Date**	
Sales					
Sales		4,805.84		4,805.84	
			4,805.84		4,805.84
Cost of Sales					
Purchases		9,939.50		9,939.50	
Closing Stock		(8,000.00)		(8,000.00)	
			1,939.50		1,939.50
Gross Profit/(Loss):			2,866.34		2,866.34
Overheads					
Overheads		2,761.21		2,761.21	
			2,761.21		2,761.21
Net Profit/(Loss):			105.13		105.13

s8

Time: 22:32:28		Balance Sheet			
From:	Month 1, January 2013				
To:	Month 12, December 2013				
Chart of Accounts:		Daly's Pharmacy Ltd Chart of Accounts			
		Period		**Year to Date**	
Current Assets					
Stock		8,000.00		8,000.00	
Debtors		2,132.84		2,132.84	
Bank Accounts		2,884.83		2,884.83	
VAT Account		1,112.07		1,112.07	
			14,129.74		14,129.74
Current Liabilities					
Creditors		9,024.61		9,024.61	
			9,024.61		9,024.61
Current Assets less Current Liabilities:			5,105.13		5,105.13
Total Assets less Current Liabilities:			5,105.13		5,105.13
Capital & Reserves					
Capital & Reserves		5,000.00		5,000.00	
P & L Account		105.13		105.13	
			5,105.13		5,105.13

s9

Other nominal ledger adjustments

Other adjustments to final accounts include:

- Depreciation
- Provision for bad debts
- Accruals and prepayments.

Journal Entry

To enter these adjustments in *Sage 50* Accounts, choose Journal Entry from the toolbar in the Nominal ledger module. Note that nominal accounts would need to be set up to enter these adjustments.

The Journal Entry window is displayed *as examples* of the above adjustments (s10). They do not form part of the accounts of Daly's

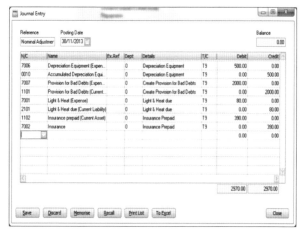

N/C	Name	Ex.Ref	Dept	Details	T/C	Debit	Credit
7006	Depreciation Equipment (Expen.		0	Depreciation Equipment	T9	500.00	0.00
0010	Accumulated Depreciation Equi.		0	Depreciation Equipment	T9	0.00	500.00
7007	Provision for Bad Debts (Expen.		0	Create Provision for Bad Debts	T9	2000.00	0.00
1101	Provision for Bad Debts (Current.		0	Create Provision for Bad Debts	T9	0.00	2000.00
7001	Light & Heat (Expense)		0	Light & Heat due	T9	80.00	0.00
2101	Light & Heat due (Current Liability)		0	Light & Heat due	T9	0.00	80.00
1102	Insurance prepaid (Current Asset)		0	Insurance Prepaid	T9	390.00	0.00
7002	Insurance		0	Insurance Prepaid	T9	0.00	390.00
						0.00	0.00
						2970.00	**2970.00**

Reference: Nominal Adjustmer Posting Date: 30/11/2013 Balance: 0.00

Save Discard Memorise Recall Print List To Excel Close

s10

Pharmacy Ltd. The account description has been edited below to demonstrate clearly the accounts that require the double-entry. Also note that a range of double-entries can be entered in the same menu as long as the Balance displays 0.00.

Depreciation of fixed assets

Nominal accounts need to be present for Depreciation Expense (Profit and Loss account) and Accumulated Depreciation of fixed assets (Balance Sheet). Set up these nominal accounts with the following Type and Category:

- Depreciation Equipment (Expense) – Type: Overheads; Category: Overheads
- Accumulated Depreciation of Equipment – Type: Fixed Assets; Category: Fixed Assets.

The double-entry is:

Debit: Depreciation expense account (Profit and Loss account), increasing the expenses and reducing the net profit in the Profit and Loss account
Credit: Accumulated Depreciation of fixed assets (Balance Sheet), reducing the net book value of fixed assets in the Balance Sheet.

Provision for bad debts

Nominal accounts need to be present for Provision for Bad Debts Expense (Profit and Loss account) and Provision for Bad Debts (Current Asset in Balance Sheet), which will reduce the debtors figure in the Balance Sheet. Set up these nominal accounts with the following Type and Category:

- Provision for Bad Debts (Expense) – Type: Overheads; Category: Overheads
- Provision for Bad Debts (Current Asset) – Type: Current Assets; Category: Debtors.

The double-entry is:

Debit: Provision for Bad Debts Expense (Profit and Loss account), increasing the expenses and reducing the net profit in the Profit and Loss account
Credit: Provision for Bad Debts (Current Asset in Balance Sheet), reducing the debtors figure in the Balance Sheet.

Accruals

If there are expenses accrued at the end of the year, you will need to set up a nominal account for accruals (Current Liability in Balance Sheet). Set up these nominal accounts with the following Type and Category:

- Light & Heat (Expense) – Type: Overheads; Category: Overheads
- Light & Heat due (Current Liability): Type: Current Liabilities; Category: Creditors.

The double-entry is:

Debit: Expense account (Profit and Loss account), increasing the expenses and reducing the net profit in the Profit and Loss account
Credit: Accruals account (Current Liability in Balance Sheet).

Prepayments

If expenses are paid in advance at the end of the year, a prepayments account (Current Asset in Balance Sheet) would need to be set up. Set up these nominal accounts with the following Type and Category:

- Insurance Prepaid (Current Asset) – Type: Current Assets; Category: Debtors
- Insurance (Expense) – Type: Overheads; Category: Overheads.

The double-entry is:

Debit: Prepayments account (Current Asset in Balance Sheet)
Credit: Expense account (Profit and Loss account), reducing expenses and increasing net profit in the Profit and Loss account.

The categories that you use in setting up nominal accounts are dependent on the structure of your COA set-up. All of the nominal adjustments that you perform in the Nominal ledger will automatically have an effect on the Profit and Loss account and the Balance Sheet of the company.

VAT Returns

Load the company Daly's Pharmacy Ltd. To view the VAT Return, select **Modules > Financials**. Click on VAT Return on the toolbar. The VAT Return – NEW window is displayed (s11). Check the dates for the return in the beginning 01/11/2013 to 30/11/3013 are correct. There are only entries in the accounts for November 2013, but VAT would normally

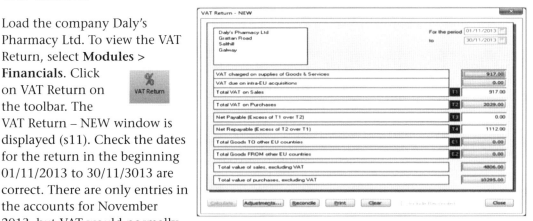

be returned on a two month basis, that is, November/December 2013.

Click on Calculate at the bottom of the VAT Return and the entries will be displayed as shown. A message box will display the amount of transactions found for the VAT return. Click **OK**.

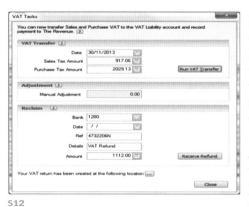

If you are satisfied with the return, click Reconcile. Otherwise, click Adjustments to enter adjustments in the return. After clicking Reconcile, a message box will display 'Flag transactions for VAT?' Click **Yes**. A VAT Tasks window will display, where the VAT on Sales and the VAT on Purchases are transferred to the VAT Liability account (s12). When you click on Run VAT Transfer, *Sage 50* Accounts will make an entry to clear the VAT on Sales and VAT on Purchases, and post to the VAT Liability account. The double-entry will be:

S12

Debit: VAT on Sales and *Credit:* VAT Liability account with €917.06, transferring the balance on the VAT on Sales to the VAT Liability account. *Credit:* VAT on Purchases and *Debit:* VAT Liability account with €2,029.13, transferring the balance on the VAT on Purchases to the VAT Liability account.

You can also record a payment or receive a refund from the Revenue using this method. Do not record a refund until it is actually received.

Click on Run VAT Transfer and the VAT will be transferred to the VAT Liability account.

If you return to **Modules > Nominal Ledger**, you will notice that the VAT on Sales and the VAT on Purchases are showing a nil balance, where the balances were transferred to the VAT Liability account.

In the VAT window, the VAT Return is displayed, where you can select at any time to print the report. If you wish to print the VAT Return in order to complete a VAT3 Form or to file online, select the VAT Return from the VAT window. Click on Print and Run the report.

Review assignments

Assignment 1

Open *Sage 50* Accounts and load the company Equipment Supplies Ltd. The opening Trial Balance at 30 November should already be entered. Use the source documents contained in your Student Resources and enter the transactions for December 2014. Remember to set the program date to 31 December 2014. You may need to set up additional supplier, customer and nominal ledger accounts.

Assignment 2

Open *Sage 50* Accounts and load the company Equipment Supplies Ltd. Perform the following tasks.

Task 1

The customer, O'Sullivan's Office Centre, has gone into liquidation and the balance outstanding in the account is to be written off as a bad debt. Enter this transaction in the appropriate ledger. *Note:* The company is entitled to claim a VAT refund for a specific bad-debt write off, which for this customer is 23%.

Task 2

1. Enter the following nominal ledger adjustments (for which you may need to set up appropriate nominal ledger accounts):
   a. Closing stock at 31 December 2014 is valued at €5,640.
   b. There is stock of stationery on hand, valued at €672.
   c. There are salaries outstanding of €410 at the end of the year.
   d. The company wishes to create a provision for bad debts, equal to 2% of the debtors balance at the end of the year.
   e. Depreciation is to be provided on the furniture at 20% per annum straight-line, and on the Office Equipment at 10% per annum straight-line.
   f. Rent of €15,000 in the accounts is for the period 1 January 2014 to 31 March 2015.
2. Print the Trial Balance, Profit and Loss account and Balance Sheet for the year ending 31 December 2014.
3. Print a nominal ledger account enquiry for Printing, Postage & Stationery.
4. Prepare a VAT Return for November/December 2014. *A sample copy of a VAT3 Return is in your Student Resources.*

Assignment 3

Load the company, Watchworld Ltd, and run a VAT Return for March 2014. Complete the VAT3 Return for March 2014 only. *A sample copy of a VAT3 Return is in your Student Resources.*